Dr Susan Mitchell is an Adjunct Professor of Creative Writing at Flinders University, a radio and television broadcaster, columnist and public speaker. She has published fifteen books documenting, narrating and analysing all aspects of Australian society, particularly the role of women, starting with her bestselling *Tall Poppies*. She has presented radio programs on the ABC and commercial networks and her own television program, *Susan Mitchell: In Conversation*.

susanmitchell.com.au

Also by Susan Mitchell

The love story that shaped a nation

MARGARET & GOUGH

SUSAN MITCHELL

hachette
AUSTRALIA

Some chapter titles in this book are lines from Herman Hupfield's beautiful song 'As Time Goes By', immortalised in 1942 (also the year Margaret and Gough were married) when it was sung by the character Sam in the classic Hollywood movie *Casablanca*.

hachette
AUSTRALIA

Published in Australia and New Zealand in 2014
by Hachette Australia
(an imprint of Hachette Australia Pty Limited)
Level 17, 207 Kent Street, Sydney NSW 2000
www.hachette.com.au

10 9 8 7 6 5 4 3 2 1

National Library of Australia
Cataloguing-in-Publication data

Mitchell, Susan, 1945– author.

Margaret and Gough/Susan Mitchell.

ISBN 978 0 7336 3244 0 (pbk.)

Whitlam, Gough, 1916–
Whitlam, Margaret, 1919–2012.
Whitlam, Gough, 1916– Marriage.
Whitlam, Margaret, 1919–2012 – Marriage.
Australian Labor Party – History – 20th century.
Prime ministers – Australia – Biography.
Prime ministers' spouses – Australia – Biography.
Social change – Law and legislation – Australia.
Social change – Political aspects – Australia.
Australia – Politics and government – 20th century.

320.99406

Cover design by Christabella Designs
Front cover photograph: Newspix
Back cover photographs: (top) Fairfax; (middle and bottom) Newspix
Author photograph: Impressions Photography
Text design by Bookhouse, Sydney
Typeset in 11.75/17.75 Sabon Pro
Printed and bound in Australia by Griffin Press, Adelaide, an Accredited ISO AS/NZS 14001:2009 Environmental Management System printer

FSC
MIX
Paper from
responsible sources
www.fsc.org FSC® C009448

The paper this book is printed on is certified against the Forest Stewardship Council® Standards. Griffin Press holds FSC chain of custody certification SGS-COC-005088. FSC promotes environmentally responsible, socially beneficial and economically viable management of the world's forests.

To Mary, my prima donna

'The two greatest joys earthly life has to offer [are] either a passionate devotion returned, or a lifelong happy marriage.'

W. H. Auden,
foreword to Dag Hammarskjöld's posthumous *Markings*

'I believe in you.'

Robert Browning,
in a love letter to Elizabeth Barrett (1845)

Contents

Author's note

There have been many hundreds of thousands of words written about both Gough and Margaret Whitlam. Gough has written about his political career in numerous volumes and in a vast library of speeches. Having written the biography of Margaret Whitlam, I realised that there was still another story to be told. The story of their partnership and their love for each other is the key to the underlying strength of all they achieved both individually and together.

From the moment they entered the public stage, the media and the Australian public became fascinated with them. They were unlike any other political couple that we had known.

The fact that they were both very tall gave them the appearance of natural leaders. They were both well educated, well spoken, erudite, witty and shared a vision of Australia that no other Prime Minister and his first lady had ever articulated.

Each of them had a very distinct and different personality from the other and yet it was hard to think of one without the other.

I wanted to tell the story of that extraordinary near seventy-year relationship, both personal and political, both private and public.

He had no small talk, she had the gift of easy conversation.

He was often ill-at-ease in company and preferred his books. She was warm, inclusive and jollied him along.

He had a vicious tongue and a volatile temper. She always tried to see the best in people but was a great sulker when hurt.

He was easily flattered. She never burst into flames on a first meeting.

He knew everything about the ideology, history and heroes of every civilisation since the Greeks. She trusted her instincts.

They always saw each other as equals and never hesitated to express their different viewpoints.

Theirs is a story of respect, struggle, success, failure, disappointment, growth and resilience.

It is a story of how these two extraordinary people led the Australian nation into an exciting and turbulent new era and how their legacy lasted long beyond it. Gough and Margaret Whitlam were to Australia what Franklin and Eleanor Roosevelt were to America.

It is a story of how a culture was changed politically, culturally and socially. It was the strength and endurance of their dynamic relationship that enabled these changes to be enacted and the values that they engendered to endure.

Why, long after they were no longer residents of the Lodge, did their mere arrival at Opera in the Domain cause a seated crowd of many thousands to stand up and applaud them?

This book will explore why they have been so loved and admired (and at times reviled) by the nation. Never before or since has there been a Prime Minister and his wife who have been the catalyst for such passionate feelings.

All of their married life they spent together, standing tall and strong. Neither one would have developed into what he or she became without the other.

He may have written and passed the laws that changed the nation but she made it possible for him to do it. Through every major political change, every election campaign, every triumph and every loss, they were always together. Side by side.

It is impossible to think of one, without the other.

Prologue

SYDNEY, *December 1939*

It was love at first sight. The members of the Sydney University Dramatic Society had gathered for a Christmas cocktail party at the house of the daughter of Alice Jackson, the editor of the *Australian Women's Weekly*. It was a stylish gathering, with all the guests in their best finery despite the December humidity.

Margaret Dovey had arrived on time, dressed in a sophisticated light green ensemble which matched her eyes. The house overlooked the harbour, which was shimmering and sparkling like the chatter from the university students who milled about with cocktail glasses in their hands, their heads full of the latest Noël Coward play.

Friends of Margaret Dovey and Gough Whitlam had told each one about the other, Margaret's friends emphasising the fact that she would be able to dance cheek to cheek with him, Gough's friends telling him she was great fun, a good conversationalist and had swum for Australia in the Empire games.

Margaret's long, dark brown hair was still damp from swimming earlier in the afternoon. It wound elegantly around the top of her head in two perfectly formed plaits. She stood straight-backed and confident; people were drawn to her because she made them feel at ease and listened to what they had to say. She laughed often and was always quick with a witty response.

The evening was sultry and the room was soon crowded with damp bodies and high-pitched laughter. As Margaret moved out towards the verandah to see if she could catch a small breeze, she glimpsed a tall, dark-haired, handsome young man towering above the crush. Their eyes met, literally across a crowded room.

For Margaret, 'He was quite the most delicious thing I'd ever seen.' For Gough, it was an 'instant chemical reaction'.

Apart from the attribute of his height, he was very well dressed, elegant almost, which was one of her top requirements. She immediately noted he had exactly the same widow's peak in his slicked dark hair as her favourite film star. When she was a schoolgirl her one and only fan letter had been sent to Robert Taylor. In return, she had received a signed photograph. And here he was, the Australian version, in the flesh, introducing himself to her.

They danced and talked and flirted with each other all evening. It was as if no one else existed. Their friends looked on, smiling and passing knowing glances to each other.

The most popular swoon song in 1939 was Oscar Hammerstein's 'All the Things You Are'.

As they danced and he mostly talked, Margaret could not get the words of that song out of her head.

She was twenty. He was twenty-three.

She was 6 foot 2, he was 6 foot 4.

This night was the beginning of a love story that was to last almost seventy years. It would change each of them. It would change a nation.

1

As the twigs were bent

Gough's father, Fred Whitlam, who named his son after his father Henry Hugh Gough Whitlam, was a quiet, unassuming man with a very high intellect. Having attended his local state primary school in Armadale, Victoria, he won a much coveted scholarship to Wesley College, one of Melbourne's most prestigious and academically successful private schools. Its educational objectives were 'to provide a classical and general education of the highest order, such as to fit a young gentleman for mercantile life, for the public service, and for matriculation to the University'.

Fred proved himself a brilliant student; he was a champion debater and placed great emphasis on the use and power of words, their nuances and their grammatical accuracy. Even though he possessed a deep personal religious belief he was best known for his broad tolerance of views different from his own.

His parents did not have the social position or the money to send him to university but in December 1900, at the end of his final year at Wesley College, he topped the state in the Victorian Public Service examination. This was excellent timing because in January 1901, Australia became a federated nation and an entirely new Commonwealth Public Service was needed. Fred had found his lifelong career. It was a perfect fit.

By 1913 he was in the Commonwealth Crown Solicitor's office. He had studied hard at night school qualifying as an accountant and then graduated in Law in 1914. A frugal and unpretentious man, Fred's only indulgence was to buy himself a new book every pay day. This was to become the only real indulgence that he or his future family ever really allowed themselves. They were not mean. They were Baptists who did not believe in spending money on unnecessary acquisitions; they were not interested in the trappings of wealth or its pretentious displays. Books were pathways to knowledge, not ostentatious forms of intellectual superiority.

Margaret's father, Wilfred Dovey, came from a family of corn and chaff merchants in Kelso, now a suburb in Bathurst in New South Wales. The sign on what was once their shop is still visible. Wilfred was the firstborn of Thomas and Mardi Dovey in 1894. Eventually his parents separated and his mother became a trained midwife, much in demand in country areas. Wilfred was a bright student who, after attending local schools in regional Bathurst, won an academic scholarship to Sydney Grammar, the prestigious private boys' school still situated in the centre of Sydney. He boarded with a family in Stanmore and went on to win a bursary to Sydney University, where he completed an Arts degree and then started Law. The outbreak of World War I ended his studies. Photographs show him to be tall (6 feet 3 inches) with thick brown hair, brown eyes, aquiline features and olive skin. He was a lively, gregarious man with a wonderful singing voice which he loved to demonstrate and a warm, rich speaking voice.

When Fred Whitlam was twenty-four he fell in love with sixteen-year-old Martha Maddocks in the Collins Street Baptist Church. She too was tall. Quite deaf as the result of a childhood injury, she had taught herself to lip-read and could hear, but only when spoken to clearly, loudly and directly. This would influence the manner in which her son would address people. She was known for her wit, her sharp tongue and her strong will. When they married in 1914, after Fred had finished paying for his legal studies, Martha coughed during the wedding service rather than promise to 'obey'. Not that Fred cared that she was strong-minded. He simply adored her.

A framed photo in a prominent place in Margaret and Gough's apartment of a very beautiful young woman, peach-skinned, dark-eyed and dark-haired, was that of Mary Duncan, Margaret's mother. Margaret believed she was 'one of the unsung beauties of her period'. Always elegantly dressed and well presented, appearance was very important to her, perhaps because she had not had a mother to fuss over her after she was nine years old. Her mother had died of meningitis as a result of an ear infection. Her father's family was from Portlethen, outside Aberdeen in Scotland, and Margaret's mother was always very proud of her Scottish heritage. Her father was a carpenter who had arrived in Australia in 1884 when he was twenty. After the death of her mother, Mary Duncan and her two siblings, then aged seven and two, were looked after by relatives, especially when her father had to work outside of Sydney. Normally he returned home on weekends to be with his children, but one weekend in 1907 when it was very hot and he had work to finish, he jumped into a river to cool off. Almost immediately he had a heart attack and drowned. Mary was now an orphan but determined not to wallow in self-pity.

As the eldest child, she was expected to take charge and be responsible for the other children, even though she had aunts and uncles who cared for them all. She had won a coveted scholarship to the selective school for bright girls, Sydney Girls High, and was awarded academic prizes. Sydney University and an Arts degree followed, complete with a bursary for her tuition for the first year.

She was, however, forced to leave her university studies in the second year because her uncle, who had taken over the financial control, refused to pay for their continuation. This was very much in accordance with accepted attitudes in that period, which considered advanced education for women a waste of money as they were destined for marriage and motherhood.

Mary Duncan had loved university. Not only was she good at her studies, but she had thrown herself into the many social activities of the clubs. The Glee Club was the Sydney University Musical Society and one of her favourites. It was there that she met Wilfred Dovey, a tall, imposing young man who, like her, loved to sing, dance and perform on stage.

They were married in August 1914, and four days later, at only twenty years of age, Wilfred was called up to fight in 'the war to end all wars'.

Margaret's parents were a well-matched, gregarious, handsome couple. Having been forced to leave university and with a husband away at the war, Mary Dovey did not sit around bemoaning her fate. That was not her way. She simply accepted the situation and got on with it by taking on teaching jobs, in both academic subjects and sports, in small private primary schools.

After only fifteen months, Wilfred returned from the battle-front with dengue fever and was judged no longer fit for active service.

As an Arts graduate, he took a teaching job at Brisbane Grammar and completed his Law degree by correspondence. Mary was extremely helpful with his studies, spending hours summarising law books from the library. Meanwhile, she continued her own war work, making quilts and sewing on crosses for the army hospitals. Charity work with the Red Cross was to continue her entire life, during which she held various leadership positions. Making a contribution to the community was very important to her.

On 11 July 1916, Fred and Martha's first child, Edward Gough Whitlam, was born. He was always known as Gough to avoid confusion with his maternal grandfather, Edward Maddocks. In 1918, his father Fred was promoted to the Sydney office of the Commonwealth Crown Solicitor and the family moved from suburban Melbourne to Mosman, then Chatswood, both suburbs situated on Sydney's upwardly mobile North Shore. Martha was delighted to be able to run her own house, away from her in-laws and family pressures. She had very firm views on the best methods to bring up children and was determined to practise them to the letter.

In 1920, their second child, Freda, was born. Martha brought each of her children up as individuals, catering to what she saw as their particular strengths. Gough was slow to speak but once he did, it was in complete sentences. No baby talk for him. The family first heard him speak when, after listening attentively to his father telling a joke, he said, 'That was a good one, Father.' Humour, the ability to use it and respond to it, continued to play a large role in his life.

Books were central to his and his family's world. The Whitlam home had no radio as it was viewed as a distraction from what children could learn from books. Martha had decided that Greek and Roman myths were less cruel than the traditional English nursery rhymes and fairytales and so ancient myths and stories filled their early lives. None of the traditional Grimm's fairytales filled their dreams – young Gough's imaginary world was peopled with characters such as Prometheus, Orpheus, Oedipus and Odysseus. He was a sensitive little boy, easily moved to tears. His mother once found him weeping while looking at a picture of Persephone. When she asked him what was wrong, he sobbed, explaining that Persephone had been taken away from her mother by the evil Hades. Gough's emotional bond with his own mother was very strong. But it was his father to whom he looked for advice and instruction.

Both his parents took their roles very seriously and were determined that their children would be nurtured and disciplined to the strict plan they had both devised, which they believed would prepare the path towards the fulfilment of their individual talents. It was a very unusual method for bringing up children, especially in that period where children were to be seen rather than heard and they had a great deal of freedom to roam around with their friends outside the home. Gough's parents focused their life on their children's needs and the protective bubble of the home in which they were raised. They were a close and loving family and Gough was always safe in the knowledge that he was central to their world.

Born on the nineteenth day of the eleventh month in 1919, Margaret Elaine Dovey was a much wanted and much adored first child. Her parents had waited five years for her mother to become pregnant. Even then, the initial diagnosis had been that Mary Dovey had 'a growth'. Fortunately, the doctor finally admitted that she was, in fact, seven months pregnant. Margaret's father was so furious he threatened not to pay the full fee. When his daughter was born he was so overjoyed with her that he forgot his threat entirely. The front page of the family Christmas card for 1920 displays a bonny one year old; a long-legged, chubby-cheeked baby in a long crocheted dress with a matching bonnet. She is sitting up, unafraid, looking straight at the camera. From her first Christmas photo, Margaret's confident interest in life and what was around her is apparent in her steady gaze.

In her nineties, when Margaret dug out the photo and stared hard at it, she said, 'I looked like a proper baby, didn't I? Well cared for. Loved and wanted.'

That simple statement encapsulates how she began her life and continued to live it. In any relationship in which she became involved, she behaved according to the rules by which she had been nurtured. As a wife, a lover, a mother and a friend she did her best never to let you down, never to betray you and always to let you know you were loved and appreciated.

In 1921, when Fred Whitlam was promoted to Deputy Crown Solicitor, the family moved again, this time to the leafy Sydney suburb of Turramurra, where they were delighted to be able to build their first house. After attending several primary schools, Gough was finally enrolled at the recently opened

Knox Grammar in 1925, chosen because of its short walking distance from his home. He studied French and Latin with great success and his school reports noted 'his very lucid mind'. From his earliest days he was praised for his intellect and his factual knowledge, which became his abiding obsession, apart from his delight in his mother's cooking. Sport did not interest him. His only form of exercise was the long walks he took with his father while they engaged in serious, intellectual conversation.

Life for young Gough was structured around an ordered routine, and the seasons rolled by with regular familiarity. Summer holidays were always spent in Melbourne, where the children stayed for several weeks alone with both sets of grandparents. Christmas Day was divided into roast turkey for lunch at the Maddocks's and supper with the Whitlams. Being the first grandchild, Gough was adored and cosseted by both families.

In 1924, Margaret's brother Will, or William Griffith Dovey, arrived. Margaret wasn't overjoyed to see him, particularly when she noticed that her mother and her grandmother Mardi were giving him all their attention. When her mother gave Willie bigger helpings of Margaret's favourite coffee ice-cream, Margaret challenged her. Her mother's reply was, 'Because he's little and he likes it.' It made Margaret very cross. She declared, 'When I'm grown-up I'm going to buy a whole block and eat it all myself.'

In order to compensate for what Margaret clearly thought was her mother's preference for her little brother, her father made a special point of taking her to the beach with him every Sunday morning. Side by side, they strode along the beach, dumped their towels and belongings and jumped into the surf.

Her father was a competent swimmer but not as good as her mother, who had swum competitively at school. After their swim Margaret and her father would lie together on their towels, both of them slathered in oil, getting a tan. It was young Margaret's special time of the week.

Willie was an outgoing, funny boy, and very tall, like Margaret. When he was one, grandmother Mardi brought Alice, a country girl, to live in with the family as a babysitter and a maid. It was quite common for middle-class families in those days to have live-in maids. When Margaret's parents were out, Alice read them stories from Arthur Mee's *Children's Encyclopaedia*. These were very different from the stories Gough was read from *The Myths of Greece and Rome* by H.A. Guerber. She also told Margaret stories from the films she had seen, but left out the sexy bits. She was jolly and cheerful and very much a part of the Dovey family for the next twenty years.

When Margaret was five, she trotted off very happily with her mother to attend the local Bondi Infants' School, a lovely old red-brick building which is still standing. In fact, in August 2005 Margaret Whitlam returned to her original classroom to open it as an 'artist-in-residence' studio, named after her.

The Dovey home was a rented, semi-detached house in Bondi (in the cosmopolitan eastern suburbs of Sydney). It had an upstairs and downstairs and a neat little garden. Her parents had a special nameplate made for it. Kabakaul was the first town her father had been sent to in 1914 when serving in the first expeditionary force to New Guinea. 'Kabakaul' was Margaret's first home and she was the jewel in the crown of her parents' lives.

Her earliest memory is of standing on the front lawn, dressed as a fairy. Her mother took a photo of her in a dress she had made, with tiered layers of white organdie, threaded with satin ribbons and a pair of matching white organdie wings. A sparkling star had been placed in the middle of her headband.

Margaret, long-legged and skinny, was acting up for the camera, arms outstretched, a cheeky smile on her face. She displayed an early love of performance and her mother indulged her wish to be a fairy because she did not want her to miss out on anything because she was already so tall. Margaret's early life can be marked by the different uniforms she wore for her chosen activities.

When she was five her mother enrolled her in ballet classes. Off they would go, hand in hand, to the basement of the old Maccabean Hall in Darlinghurst. So confident was she of her skills as a ballet dancer that when she was seven and her mother took her to see the great ballerina, Anna Pavlova, young Margaret stood up during the 'dying swan' scene, announcing loudly, 'I can do that!' Her mother hissed, 'Margaret, sit back on your seat,' but Margaret refused and kept shouting out, 'I can do that!' Eventually her mother had to restrain her from demonstrating her skills in the theatre.

And then there were her music lessons, organised by her mother for 7.30 am. Miss McGarrity walked up the hill from her home nearby and climbed the steep steps to the Doveys' house twice a week. Margaret threw herself into her lessons, practised hard, passed all her exams but, honest to the core, said her skills as a pianist were 'merely adequate'.

Swimming, however, was her real talent. Having taught her to swim, her mother encouraged her to join the Bondi Swimming

Club; Mary would eventually become its president. Not only was it a sport that Margaret's parents loved, it was a sport where being precociously tall was an advantage. By the time she was seven, Margaret was swimming in competitions. By the age of nine she had made the club finals.

On Saturday nights district swimming carnivals were held at the Coogee Aquarium, which was used as a swimming pool during the summer. Having no car, Margaret and her mother caught a tram from Bondi Beach to Bondi Junction and changed trams for Coogee. Unlike her mother, who sat through the twenty-five heats that led to the final, her father only attended the major heats. Even when Margaret travelled with the team, she would look up from the pool and see her mother's smart little red or green hat in the crowd. She was always there, clapping and cheering her on.

The only time Margaret found being taller than other children her age uncomfortable or embarrassing was when she and her mother went into the city to buy her clothes. Shop assistants could never resist remarking, 'My, what a big girl you are.' Her mother simply ignored them and would direct Margaret's attention to something else. Mostly, her mother, who sewed beautifully, made Margaret's clothes. Though this resulted in her mother deciding what Margaret wore, it didn't matter, because she had good taste and was obsessed with dressing well. Margaret described her as always looking very 'snappy'. There was only one occasion when she criticised her mother's dress sense. Mary Dovey once came to a parents' night at Margaret's school wearing a linen dress with embroidery on it. Margaret told her, 'Please don't come to school again in a doily.' She still winced with embarrassment every time she remembered it.

Her adoration of Willie not withstanding, Margaret's mother continued to encourage and take part in every aspect of Margaret's life.

Drama was one of Margaret's great joys. She loved being on stage, even if her height dictated that she would always get the leading male roles. She loved to sing at Sunday School, which she attended every Sunday afternoon at 3 pm, after the family's roast lunch. She always wore her best white silk, long-sleeved dress matched with black, patent leather shoes. Upon returning home she had to cover the shoes with Vaseline to stop them cracking and carefully put them away. There was a ritual and a routine to her life.

From the time she was eight her mother took her to regular symphony concerts, in the seats behind the orchestra, which was all they could afford at the time. Margaret loved observing the faces and hands of the musicians and the conductor. Occasionally her father would join them, but his preference was for opera and the latest musicals. Margaret was always included in the music and theatrical events attended by her parents, except for some shows at the Tivoli because her mother thought them a little 'vulgar' for a young girl.

When she was ten, her father invited her to take her mother's ticket to see a show at the Theatre Royal. Her mother had made her a new silk dress and even allowed her to wear a pair of her silk stockings. When her father was proudly escorting her back from drinks for special guests in the manager's office (there were no bars in theatres), she snagged her silk stockings on the side of a seat. Visibly upset, she announced quite loudly, 'Pa, I tore my stocking.' He told her to calm down and not worry about it. 'But they're Mum's, they're Mum's,' she said, even more loudly.

Her mother described these public outbursts as her 'extrovert stage'. Her father continued to adore her, however she behaved.

In early 1927, when Gough was nine, his father was promoted to Assistant Crown Solicitor, a position which was based in the newly emerging national capital of Canberra. Fred spent that year in hostel accommodation in Canberra while waiting for his house to be allocated and his children to finish the school year. Most weekends he commuted to Sydney. He chose to endure a five-hour trip each way rather than disrupt the children's education and their settled home life.

In January 1928, Martha, Gough and Freda left their home at Turramurra for Canberra. Their last night in Sydney was spent at a cinema watching *Ben Hur: A Tale of the Christ*. Martha had chosen it as a treat for the children. It was a silent two and a half hour epic drama which Freda loved. The cruelty inflicted on the Christians, however, was very upsetting to Gough, even though it was during this year that he had stopped going to Sunday School. He had absolutely refused to accept that God could create the world in seven days. When he failed to get satisfactory answers to his many questions on this topic and others from the church leaders, he simply stopped being a believer. Neither of his parents would ever have forced him to attend church. In fact, his father chose which church he attended based solely on the quality of the preaching. His faith was strong, but he refused to be bored.

When they were all finally settled in the train compartment, about to leave, Freda with a new doll and Gough with a new book, they were shocked at their mother's sudden tears. As the train pulled away from the station, she began to sob. She hated leaving Sydney as she had loved her life there; she did not want to have to start all over again in a strange city that seemed not much more than a name, bare paddocks and some public buildings. The children did not begin to understand their mother's tears; for them, the move was just another new chapter in their lives. Martha knew it was where she was destined to spend the rest of her life.

Gough was enrolled in Telopea Park School, which was the only government secondary school in Canberra. It was too early for the private schools to have really established their reputations. He was very tall for a twelve year old and his direct and clearly enunciated manner of speaking – developed because of his mother's hearing problem – often led others to consider him rather snobbish and arrogant. It was clear to his teachers at Telopea Park that he was an excellent student, especially in language studies. They placed him in Year 8 even though he had not yet completed the full first year of mathematics at his previous school. Already a dedicated perfectionist, like his parents, he had come to expect that he would be a high achiever, but this disruption in his education and the lack of a national curriculum meant that he always struggled to maintain good grades in mathematical subjects.

The Whitlam family life in Canberra revolved almost entirely around discussions of politics and the various abilities of the parliamentary performers. Gough's fellow students, mostly the children of public servants, absorbed politics and parliament as a normal part of their lives. It was on a school excursion to parliament that young Gough glimpsed his first Australian Prime Minister. The sight of Stanley Bruce, confidently lounging on the government front bench, his spats in full view, made a lasting impression on the young boy. Here was a man of style, a man of power who luxuriated in it.

Telopea Park extended his reading from Greek and Roman myths to Shakespeare, Dr Johnson, Samuel Pepys, John Dryden and Alexander Pope. He developed a genuine love of literature and immediately began to write poetry in the style of Pope's Augustan satire for the school magazine, which he later edited.

Gough was very fond of his younger sister Freda. She tells the story of how, when she was a little girl, she and a friend wrote a letter to the Fairy Queen, which they placed in the bell of a flower in the front garden. When they returned later, they found an answer written on a scrap of exercise book. It was signed 'Titania'. Flushed with excitement, they rushed inside to tell Freda's mother that they had received a letter from the Fairy Queen. Gough's bedroom overlooked the front garden. When she recollected this story years later, Freda was very moved by the sensitivity and caring of her then twelve-year-old brother.

Both children developed an early and lifelong passion for reading. Freda would read any book she found anywhere. Gough preferred to own brand-new books which, once having read, he kept in meticulous order in his very tidy room. The Whitlams in Canberra were a tight family unit who simply loved being at home, together.

Their Baptist background was reflected in both parents being teetotallers, having no interest in frivolous pursuits and a firm focus on education and self-improvement through knowledge gained from books. They were not, however, joyless Bible-bashers. There was much laughter and banter between them, but their pleasures were simple ones enjoyed within the family.

Often on a Sunday afternoon, Fred Whitlam would play the piano and the family would happily sing along.

Fred's unmarried brother, George, a devout Baptist and also a Canberra public servant, came to live with them. Mealtimes consisted of Martha's fine cooking and Gough testing himself in debate against his father and teasing his more staid and dogmatic Uncle George. His mother adored her son's wit and erudition and he played up to her. His father was more serious and considered in his views than Gough's mother, who voiced strong and sometimes acerbic judgements. While his father, ever the proper public servant, liked to set out each side of an argument in a fair and reasonable manner, Gough was more like his mother, who took a view and stuck to it. He loved practising the art of argument in an attempt to persuade others to his point of view. Everyday life for young Gough was like an endless Oxford seminar. He thrived on it.

Their house was overflowing with newspapers, journals and magazines from all over the world. The walls of their dining room were lined with books and after the meal, each member of the family leant back from the dining table to the bookcase behind them and selected an encyclopaedia to read. They would continue to sit there in quiet companionship.

Whenever Gough asked a factual question of one of the adults he was told, 'Look it up.' All he had to do was select one of the many encyclopaedias or history books from the overflowing book shelves that occupied every room but the bathroom. Philosophical and political questions were always directed at his father. Mr Kurshed K. Lalkaka, a Parsee, was a regular visitor for dinner at the Whitlam house. One evening young Gough asked his father, 'Is Mr Lalkaka's God the same as our God?'

His father replied, 'Of course.' Fred Whitlam had ensured that both of his children understood the injustice of racial or religious prejudice. This was not common among Australian families at this time, who tended towards bouts of xenophobia.

As a student at Telopea Park Gough found himself teased by some students for being different, an oddity. These days he would have been labelled a nerd. He still refused to play sport, preferring to swim or walk. This was because his height made him feel ungainly and conspicuous. He avoided anything that might result in him being mocked. His reaction to their teasing him because he was different was to withdraw from the group and read alone rather than mix with other students. His father's interest in correct language and grammar had rubbed off on his son, who became an early convert to linguistic pedantry. The tendency to correct mistakes in other people's use of language never left him. It also didn't endear him to those he corrected, as they took it as a personal affront. Gough never quite understood this reaction, as he thought he was adding to their education. He also – it must be admitted – liked to show off. He was a performer as well as an aesthete.

The love of knowledge developed in him a lifelong tendency to give long, detailed answers to any question. It never occurred to him that others might not want a PhD answer to a simple question. He always tried to give the most erudite and complete answer, believing it was absolutely necessary to take all questions seriously.

He never learnt the art of small talk. Casual conversation bored him. It was, for him, a complete waste of time. Why bother conversing with someone unless it was about something in which you were interested or you had a contribution to make? Family was no exception to this rule.

His meticulous obsession with detail also extended to his personal appearance. If they were going to stare at him, he was determined it wasn't going to be because of his clothes or his grooming. During his first months in Canberra he learnt to use his tongue like a whip to deal with those who continued to tease or criticise him. They thought twice before they did it again. He had a lethal tongue and a quick temper. He always went in for the kill; there were no half-measures with young Gough. Not that he ever discussed the teasing from other students with his parents. There was no such concept as 'emotional intelligence' in that era, or in that house. As Baptists, his parents were good people but outpouring of personal slights or emotion was discouraged and considered rather indulgent. As Gough no longer believed in God, he did not have the outlet of church or prayer through which to express his personal doubts or conflicts, and so he repressed them.

Students from Telopea Park were given free rein to browse among the books in the Library of Old Parliament House. For Gough it was heaven and he spent much of his free time there, purely out of interest and wonder at the range and depth of the books. Even though he was studying French and Latin, after school he learnt German, adding Greek in his spare time. It was as if he couldn't cram enough knowledge into his head, such was his intellectual thirst.

By the time they had to choose a secondary school for their daughter, Margaret's father was a successful barrister. They chose SCEGGS (Sydney Church of England Girls' Grammar School), a private girls' school nearby in Darlinghurst.

It was the middle of 1930 when she and her father boarded the tram and he walked with her to her new school on the first day. As they walked together down the hill of Forbes Street in Darlinghurst, famous for its brothels, her father said, 'There's no need to look to the left or right, Margaret. Just stare straight ahead, as you are going to walk past dens of iniquity.'

Margaret had no idea what he was talking about and didn't think about it because she was so keen to get to school early. Her aim was to get on the swing under the biggest tree in the schoolyard. Later on, she joined in sessions in the prefects' study where they discussed their next dramatic performances. She needed no encouragement to dress up and play the clown. She and her best friend, Sonya Johnston, used to do the minuet together, with Margaret's tunic tucked up into her knickers so she could play the male lead.

At fourteen, as was expected of all good Anglicans, Margaret was confirmed as a member of the Church of England. Her mother was Presbyterian, her father baptised C of E, but they seldom went to church. Margaret wasn't really sure what she believed, but she loved the colour and ritual of the daily chapel services at school and was a most enthusiastic singer in the choir.

Her teenage years were her most self-conscious. By the age of fourteen she had reached her full height of 6 feet 2 inches. School dances were agony. Boys rarely asked her to dance and if one did muster up the courage he would find himself staring at Margaret's navel. Margaret made fun of it instead of letting it get her down.

Her mother instructed her in how to overcome her social shyness in group situations. 'Just stand by the door, Margaret, look around and if you know anybody, go up to them. If you don't know anybody, then introduce yourself and find out who they are. You know full well that you look just as good as anyone in the room. So off you go.' Margaret did as she was told and, as her mother had promised, it worked.

Margaret filled her life with activities that gave her pleasure and was convinced that, 'Everything will improve when you reach university.'

Her father encouraged her speaking talents. Those were the days of elocution and school eisteddfods and Margaret competed in what was called 'reading at sight'. When she was fifteen she came third, at sixteen she came second and in her final year at school she won the top prize. She received her award standing proudly on the stage of the Sydney Conservatorium, her parents smiling and clapping loudly in the audience.

She had also decided she would become a famous stage actress. The school, however, didn't have drama classes so she had to content herself with the annual school plays directed by the English teachers.

Addicted to reading, she won *The Collected Works of Shakespeare* as a school prize for 'home reading'. When students returned from the summer holidays they had to write an account of what books they had read. Margaret loved nothing better than curling up with a book in a large comfy armchair, her long legs hanging over one of the armrests. When her mother told her to go outside in the sun and get some fresh air, she'd take her book and continue reading it on the swing outside the back door.

Her father always gave her books for her birthday and Christmas presents. She had read most of Kipling and Dickens but also comics like *Schoolgirls' Own*. In fact, she read anything she could get her hands on.

The school took their pupils to concerts in the Sydney Town Hall, where Sir Bernard Heinze would take them through all the instruments of the orchestra. She continued to learn music as an extra subject at secondary school, becoming totally besotted with the romantic composers, particularly the Russians. It took her thirty years to extend her passion to Mozart and Wagner.

Her best friend, Sonya, was very musical, played the piano beautifully and they sang in the choir together. They were inseparable and always went on organised school trips together. Once when they were on a ski trip to Mt Kosciuszko a boy called Margaret 'a big Jew with a big nose'. It was her first experience of overt discrimination. She was shocked that anyone would attack her for no reason. She also had no sense that she led a privileged life and simply took all her trips and treats for granted, assuming that was how everyone lived. She was shielded from the deprivations suffered by others during the Depression. She was oblivious to anything outside her immediate world of home and school and swimming.

She remembered her time at SCEGGS as good fun, but the fact that neither she nor Sonya nor Pip Street (daughter of the famous feminist and agitator Jessie Street) were ever made prefects angered her. Sonya couldn't care less, but Pip and Margaret were furious that they never got to wear the coloured badge of a prefect on their blazer pockets.

Margaret blamed her failure on the fact that she was caught running a school sweep for the Melbourne Cup. Her father was a keen racing man and Margaret saw nothing wrong in what she had done. When she was given a Saturday morning detention (the worst sort), her mother was so furious she marched down to the school to confront the headmistress on Margaret's behalf. The word 'ridiculous' was used a lot by her mother. Margaret was given a Wednesday detention instead, but clearly there was a black mark against her name. Treating people with fairness became one of the touchstones of her life.

While she was happy at SCEGGS, she was not devastated to be leaving it. She could not believe the number of girls who, on the last day, were sobbing uncontrollably with their arms around each other. She was far too excited by what the next chapter in her life held. She was always looking forward to new possibilities and new adventures. And – let's not forget – new kinds of fun.

The onset of the 1930s Great Depression meant that Gough was well aware that some members of his class had parents who were unemployed. His family was insulated from it because of his father's senior position in the fast-growing bureaucracy of the nation's new capital. His father, however, took the time to explain the causes of this economic decline to him, emphasising that some of his fellow students were less privileged, through no fault of their own. Kindness and generosity were to be extended to those less fortunate than yourself. Gough's mother was always the first to bake cakes and biscuits for newcomers to their neighbourhood and during the Depression she gave food generously to the stream of unemployed men who knocked on her door. Every day, she prepared a great pile of cut lunches not only for her own family but for the increasingly needy who came seeking help.

Their house in Canberra was a big mock Tudor whose bare backyard Gough's father transformed into a productive vegetable garden, the produce of which Gough's mother used in her delicious meals. Gough developed a lifelong passion for fresh, healthy produce. Unable to fully contribute to the increasingly fast-flowing conversation at the dining room table because of her deafness, his mother enveloped her family, especially her son, in the warmth of her fine home cooking. He became an enthusiastic trencherman at the family table and a lifelong gourmand. The pursuit of ideas and the sharing of good food were synonymous for the young man. When he was a student at the University of Sydney he visited the new continental food section in David Jones city department store for the first time. He spread his arms wide as if to embrace it all, sighed, and declared to his companions, 'Isn't civilisation wonderful?'

The early teenage years that formed Gough's development marched hand in hand with the development of the new national capital. As he grew into early maturity, so too did Canberra. He saw, first-hand, every day, how a federal government, through centralised planning, could construct the best possible urban environment for all its citizens. Equal opportunity meant that every new suburb was supplied with a school, sporting facilities, roads and sewerage.

Gough's long walks with his father were wonderful opportunities for father to explain to son how the public service mechanisms were necessary to making it all happen. Gough learnt from an early age how good government could directly improve the life of its citizens.

His mother's pride in him instilled a firm belief that he would grow up to be a force for good in the world, and the desire to help those who were less fortunate.

His father also engendered, in both his son and his daughter, a fierce pride in being Australian. Freda remembers being brought up to 'be proud that we were helping to build the national capital'. Young Gough never lost his strong sense of pride in belonging to this nation. One of his poems written at this time, while lauding the glories of the arts in European cities, emphasised that:

We have the verdant vista of the New,
New skies to scale, new paths to pioneer.

In these two lines we can sense the bubbling ambition inside this young man who was looking forward to scaling new heights and pioneering new paths. At this stage he had no clear idea how and where he would make his own contribution to the nation, but the urge to do so was strong. His somewhat aloof manner hid the excitement and passion that lurked within. He was far too shy to expose himself to possible rejection from those who did not share his vision or his commitment.

The most dramatic political event to occur at this time was the decision by the New South Wales Premier, Jack Lang, to refuse to repay interest due on British war loans, in order to maintain social welfare payments to those hardest hit by the Depression. The *Sydney Morning Herald* took a hard line against Lang's proposals for greater public spending and pressured the New South Wales Governor, Sir Philip Game, to sack Lang. It split the federal Labor Party, resulting in the end of the Scullin Labor government. In May 1932 the Governor of New South Wales sacked Lang.

Meanwhile fifteen-year-old Gough had starred in the Telopea Park School Dramatic Society's end-of-year performance at

Canberra's Capitol Theatre. The Governor-General, Sir Isaac Isaacs, also presented him with the special magazine prize for his contribution to the school magazine, *Telopea*.

Despite these public accolades, Gough's father was called to the school by the headmaster to discuss his son's behaviour. Fred was appalled to hear that his son constantly reminded the teachers that he knew more than they did on certain subjects. He was far too quick to display his knowledge and give his opinion, especially when it wasn't called for. His habit of talking back when he considered his argument was the right one was particularly annoying to his teachers and yet he clearly had no conception of how this affected his teachers or his fellow students. He was genuinely shocked when his father informed him that he was leaving Telopea Park and going to Canberra Grammar the next year. No doubt his father thought that Canberra Grammar's insistence on certain standards of behaviour and strict discipline, mimicking those of an English public school, were exactly what Gough needed. He did not take umbrage at his father's decision, believing that his father knew best. Arriving at his new school in 1932, he studied English, Classics, Languages, History and excelled in Latin. He immediately joined the committee of the school magazine, *The Canberran*, and continued to contribute prose poems and meticulous translations of the Classics. He never viewed these interests as esoteric, or even eccentric. They were the products of his parents' upbringing and wishes for his future success. He was, above all else, a loving and dutiful son.

At the end of Gough's first year at Canberra Grammar, the Governor-General handed him the Fifth Year prize for Languages. What really angered him, and still does to this day, is the fact that even though he had gained the highest marks in Divinity, he was not awarded the prize. The headmaster told him the reason was that he didn't believe in what he had written. For Gough, this was a clear act of injustice: the prize should go to the student with the highest marks, regardless of their personal beliefs. It was his first experience of being the victim of irrational and unfair treatment and being powerless to change it.

Knowing the importance of being able to mix socially, his parents encouraged him to take formal dancing lessons and to attend social occasions with students of his own age. They instructed him in the proper way to address his elders and the correct rules of social behaviour. As long as he knew the accepted guidelines, he would be secure in his ability to mix socially outside his family circle.

At the end of 1932, even though Gough had completed his Leaving Certificate, his father, ever vigilant regarding his son's development, decided he was too young, at sixteen, to go to university. He returned to Canberra Grammar where, at the end of 1933, he was awarded a Canberra Scholarship 'to read for a Classics Degree at the University of Sydney'.

However, his mother's uncle, James Steele, who was head-master at Carey Baptist Grammar School and himself a classical scholar, recommended to Gough's father that Gough study Ancient Greek in order to include it as part of his university Classics degree.

And so the education of young Gough required that he return to Canberra Grammar to study Ancient Greek and sit for his Leaving Certificate for the third time. He succeeded in being Dux of the Fifth Year, gaining the school prize for Languages and Classics, coming fifth in the state for English and third for

Latin. When he finally left Canberra Grammar to take up his scholarship at the University of Sydney, the school magazine opined that Gough Whitlam 'by some strange caprice of fate happened to be attending school as a pupil instead of as a master'.

Margaret had been so busy with all her various activities and interests that she had not really spent much time on academic study. Even though she had matriculated, she had not passed well enough in Latin or Maths to fulfil the set requirements to do an Arts degree at Sydney University. In those days you had to have matriculated in a language and a science subject in order to be accepted into Arts. Margaret was shattered. It was the first time in her life that she had been prevented from doing something she wanted to do. And her parents couldn't fix it. They never once expressed their disappointment with her results, but encouraged her to set her sights on other goals. When she showed some interest in doing nursing like her grandmother, her father said, 'Why not do medicine?' He even took her to the medical school. Seeing all the dead babies in bottles and specimens of body parts soon killed that idea.

When she suggested journalism, her father took her to meet Frank Packer, for whom he did legal work. Nothing but the best for his girl. Packer was the owner of the largest number of newspapers and magazines in Australia at that time and when he asked her 'So, girlie, what do you want to do – the social notes?' she replied that while she liked socialising, she preferred court reporting.

'Oh no, girlie. Our girls only do social rounds.'

That was the end of journalism for her. While she liked engaging in the social rounds, she didn't want to make a career out of it. If she was to do journalism, it was to be serious, not trivial. Despite the fact that she couldn't do the degree she wanted at university, Margaret was not dejected. 'I always feel when something ends, something new is going to begin and it's going to be just as exciting.'

Besides, there was her swimming. All her years of training at Bondi Swimming Club and competing in carnivals had finally paid off. In 1937, she had the strong feeling that she was hitting her top form in the breaststroke. Her father was so excited at the thought of his daughter competing in the Australian Championships, she overheard him telling a neighbour, 'If Margaret wins the national championships, I won't call Bob my uncle.'

He was not disappointed. Miss Margaret Dovey became the 1937 Australian Breaststroke Champion. Winning this award meant that she qualified to be part of the team to compete in the Empire Games, the forerunner of the Commonwealth Games, the following year.

At seventeen her body was long, lean and powerful. Her face had an openness, an innocence. Her warm smile broke often into laughter. Her long brown hair hung in a perfectly braided plait down her back. She was everything her parents had hoped she would become. They had given her all the gifts that good parents can bestow on their children – unconditional love, a safe and secure home, a strong family life and the confidence to approach the world, and her future, without fear. Now she was rewarding them.

In January 1938, swimming well in the Empire Games was Margaret's only preoccupation. She was training hard and totally focused on winning a medal for her country. Then fate struck her a cruel blow.

Just before the opening of the games in February, she contracted a debilitating streptococcal infection in her throat. There were no such drugs as sulphur or penicillin available then to cure her. Every day that took her closer to the big race, she could feel the infection getting a stronger grip. Her strength was draining away from her. As a child she had regularly contracted bronchitis and experienced bouts of pleurisy and pneumonia, but she simply would not and could not give in to this infection.

Her father was totally distraught. He fed her oysters and asparagus in the hope that they would build up her strength. Nothing worked.

A week before the big competition their doctor advised her that she was not well enough to compete. She simply refused to believe him. And continued to train. The day before the opening, her father was still searching for medication that could give her some relief. To no avail. She was not allowed to march in the opening ceremony because she had to swim the next day and it was necessary to conserve whatever strength she had left.

On the night of the big race her mother, father, brother and friends were sitting side by side in the stands, fingers crossed. Margaret stood on the blocks, the lights sparkling on the blue lanes of the pool. She felt so achingly sick she was afraid she might just fall in. When she eventually dived into the water for the 220-yard (200-metre) breaststroke, she was sure she would sink like a stone. Every stroke seemed to drag her backwards, not forwards. Her arms and legs were dead weights as she struggled to push them through the water.

She didn't sink, however it took every last ounce of energy in her tortured body just to finish the race. This is not a Hollywood story: not only did she not get a place for her country, she came last.

Shaking with exhaustion, she dragged herself out of the pool. She was consumed with mixed emotions of shame, embarrassment and disappointment. Rationally, in retrospect, she admitted that she should have withdrawn from the race. But emotionally, Margaret was not a quitter. No one, not even her parents, could have convinced her to quit that race.

It takes a great amount of courage and determination to face the possibility of public failure but it takes even more to force yourself, against all the odds, to 'give it a go'. 'At least I gave it my best shot,' she said, seventy years later, a firm believer that there is nothing shameful about trying and failing in life. She took responsibility for her decision and never regretted it. When the result is not what you would have wanted, you just 'take it on the chin and get on with it'. Nevertheless, the first taste of public failure leaves its mark.

* * *

At the beginning of 1935, having been thoroughly and rigorously prepared for the next phase in his life, Gough Whitlam, now eighteen and a half, a year older than most first-year university students, was finally allowed to leave the protective bosom of his family.

His new home was St Paul's College, the oldest residential university college in Australia, and the most conservative. Then and now, it insists that its all-male residents attend dinner five nights a week dressed in jacket, tie and academic gown. His father had chosen it because it had the necessary discipline and rigid adherence to ritual and structure that he believed his son needed. He also hoped (a forlorn hope) that Gough's religious faith would be restored. It never was.

Still much taller than most of his fellow students, Gough was now good-looking, more self-confident and often described as resembling the film star Robert Taylor. His innate shyness was still there at his core, but his manner and bearing were such that no one would ever have suspected it. Obsessed with correctness of dress, social protocols and proper behaviour, he often appeared more mature than he actually was.

He settled in easily by simply replacing the strict routines and expectations of his home and his parents with that of the institution of St Paul's. Rigorous and regimented, St Paul's social calendar became his social calendar and along with all the other residents he attended the College's annual dances, debates and revues. He edited St Paul's magazine, *The Pauline*, and worked in the college library, taking pleasure in redressing its conservative political bias.

In the first year of his Arts degree he studied English, Latin, Greek and Psychology. As a student of Classics, he would major in Latin and Greek, eventually becoming a Classics scholar. His only form of rebellion was his determination to make people laugh in college debates. At this, he was very successful. He dutifully wrote weekly letters home to his parents where the only jarring note was a request for more money. Fred was by nature and lifelong habit a frugal man. He kept his son on a minimal budget to ensure that he didn't succumb to wasteful spending and frivolous pursuits. It worked. Gough had no money to explore anything outside of college activities. He patched the elbows of his jacket and washed his own socks. Before asking for a replacement for his well-worn brown Harris tweed jacket he sent his parents detailed calculations to prove that when amortised, the jacket had cost them a mere twopence a day. Having argued a rational case for a new jacket, he was duly sent the money to purchase one.

It was important for Gough to look smart and 'blend in' with the crowd, particularly when he still towered above most of them. One aspect of his personality that did stand out, however, was his inability to resist showing off the depth and breadth of his knowledge. He visibly enjoyed proving people wrong and seemed incapable of not scoring points off those less intelligent or learned. He was, like many shy people, thoughtless and insensitive to the hurt and embarrassment he caused in others. He never seemed to realise that this behaviour was a fast track to making a lifelong enemy. He had then, and still has, a total intolerance for boredom, trivia and banality. His humour was, however, often directed at himself. He loved to assume a tone of self-mockery which many people misunderstood. For example, when he was asked what he would do when he eventually met his maker he replied, 'I would treat him like an equal.'

He rarely drank, the result partly of his Baptist upbringing, but mostly due to his lack of money. He spent what little extra he had on films and cheap seats at classical concerts.

His full schedule of classes did not leave him much time for study and his marks gradually declined after his distinction in first-year Latin. His twenty-first birthday was a non-event. Telegrams arrived from his mother, father, sister and relatives. His parents sent him a cigarette case engraved with his initials and the *Oxford Book of English Verse*. Nothing extravagant or over-the-top. He had no money for big celebrations and as the actual day was a Sunday, reaching what was then known as 'your majority' was, for him, a total fizzer.

By the time he finished his Arts degree in 1937 his marks were not high enough to secure him a future career as an academic. Nor had he met any lecturer who had inspired in him a desire to pursue such a career. He graduated with second-class honours, majoring in Classics, and immediately enrolled in a Law degree. Why Law? His father's influence. However, by the end of his second year he found himself 'somehow involved with it'.

In 1938, Gough became smitten with a young Italian violinist, Guila Bustabo, who was not only considered brilliant but was very beautiful. With her long black hair and classically Roman features she took Australian audiences and music critics by storm. Her first concert was in Canberra; Gough Whitlam, home for the term break, attended with his parents. At the reception afterwards given by the Canberra Musical Society, Guila asked to meet the young man who looked like Robert Taylor. He even saw her off at the station on her way to her next concert in Newcastle. Gough attended all her Sydney concerts and they saw each other several times, though her mother was always present as chaperone. He held an afternoon tea for her at St Paul's and after her last concert at the Sydney Town Hall he and a friend accompanied Guila and her mother to Romano's, a top-class Sydney restaurant. The *Sun* newspaper noted their descent together down the steps of the Town Hall, in their social column. Mr Whitlam was described as 'a law student who has unusual literary tastes and abilities as a poet'.

Gough received a necktie from her from Paris, but their paths never crossed again.

In truth, he was much more excited by his new edition of *The Pauline*, which, as editor, he had revamped. It was, in his opinion, an outstanding success. So delighted was he with his talent for editing and publication that he became editor of the undergraduate Sydney University magazine, *Hermes*, and co-editor of the Sydney University Law Society Journal, *Blackacre*.

Margaret had finally decided to enrol in Economics at Sydney University. It was a poor substitute for Arts, but she added German and English as extra subjects. It soon became very clear to her that she was bored to death with her Economics subjects. In any case, studying was not high on her list. University offered so many other exciting possibilities. The only problem was how to fit them into her days and nights. There were so many places to go, people to meet, books to read, plays and ballets and concerts to attend. And, more importantly, the decision regarding what to wear on every occasion.

Her mother had been right. All her self-consciousness and shyness had disappeared the moment she walked through the gates of the university. She had blossomed into a fun-loving, socially confident young woman. She had also discovered she was very skilled at flirting 'with good-looking sorts'.

Like her mother and father before her, she immediately joined the Sydney University Dramatic Society (SUDS). She knew her height would prevent her from gaining leading female roles but she didn't care. She happily took on minor roles and voice-overs. So in love with the theatre was she that she started wearing pancake make-up and eyeshadow in the evening to create a dramatic presence.

Her father's success at the Sydney Bar had enabled them to move from Bondi to the more exclusive eastern suburb of Vaucluse. Their semi-detached house had been replaced by a bay-windowed villa which they first rented and then purchased. It was set in a beautiful leafy garden that overlooked Sydney Harbour. Margaret's brother, Willie, was still living at home, studying at Sydney Grammar, his father's old school. Like Margaret, he was very much involved with sporting activities.

Margaret still joined her parents at the theatre and the latest musicals. She loved to spend time with them and their friends, singing the songs from the latest shows – the theatre programs always included the words in the back. Whenever her parents' friends came over for bridge, at the break for tea and cakes they would all stand round the piano, which her mother played, and sing heartily. Their home was a place of fun and pleasure where they shared their enjoyments with family and their many friends. Margaret's friends loved to visit because they were always made to feel so welcome.

Margaret was now taking private singing lessons with a woman she had previously met at one of her mother's musical societies. Not only did her teacher have the exotic name of Lu Drummond, she lived as an independent single woman in a flat on top of a building in Bridge Street in the city, where she taught her students. Margaret thought she was fascinating and bohemian. Miss Drummond also taught them Italian, in case they chose to sing opera. Some of the students – such as Joan Hammond and Kenneth Neate – became big names, which made it all the more meaningful when another student told Margaret that Miss Drummond thought she had real talent. She compared

Margaret's voice to that of young Kirsten Flagstad, who was very highly thought of at that time.

Secretly, Margaret still dreamt of a career on the stage or in the concert hall. She kept up her lessons until her second year at university when war was declared and Miss Drummond gave up her teaching for war work.

Even though the spectre of war loomed over Margaret's head she had so many activities on the go that she didn't have time to think about it. Often not home in time for dinner, she would find a sandwich and a small thermos of warm milk left on her dressing table by her thoughtful mother.

Margaret was mostly a dutiful daughter, except for the time when her parents were away and, having invited her friends home for a party, she took down her mother's collection of precious plates from the high shelves in the living room and dumped them in her father's billiard room. Of course she forgot to put them back. When her mother returned home and discovered her precious plates discarded in the billiard room, she was so hurt that she didn't even speak of it. This only made Margaret feel worse.

Not that Mary Dovey was averse to speaking her own mind or standing up to her husband in an argument. Whenever they were having a serious row they shut the bedroom door. That didn't stop Margaret from putting her ear to it. Her mother was usually complaining about her husband coming home so late from the Lodge. He would often call her a bitch in the heat of the argument and she would intone in a prim and proper voice, 'I am not a female dog.'

Wilfred Dovey was a well-known barrister, raconteur and man about town. When he died, Margaret's aunt told her in a conspiratorial tone, 'He was a wonderful man but there were times when he was very naughty.' Margaret assumed that by 'naughty' she was referring to dalliances, which she knew he would have undertaken in a discreet fashion. He would never have done anything to hurt or embarrass his family.

He was a handsome, charming, dapper man who often wore a monocle – and there was always a twinkle in those eyes. Margaret inherited that same twinkle. She loved to flirt and make witty and wicked conversation. When she was a child and often asked what she planned to do when she grew up she would always reply, 'I'm going to be a social butterfly and go on moonlight exertions.' (There were trams at that time advertising moonlight excursions.) She admits that she was a social butterfly and very intent on experiencing moonlight exertions at university. Not that either of her parents had ever spoken to her about sex. It was just assumed that good girls didn't go 'all the way'. She had indulged in the usual showing of private parts with other kids behind the Presbyterian Church and the rest she worked out for herself from reading books and looking up words she thought might be naughty in the dictionary.

Always prepared to discuss any subject honestly and straightforwardly – she could never stand people who were coy about sex – she admitted to indulging in a bit of experimental masturbation and liking it.

When she was at university she said there was a lot of 'foreplay but no real play'. The spectre of an unwanted pregnancy was ever-present. Nevertheless, Margaret said she liked it so much she would have been game to give it a go. One of her suitors actually said, 'I can't do this to you. You're too nice. We're too young.' She was thinking, 'Go ahead, I'd love it.'

She knew there were women who preferred other women, but it was never spoken about. The only lesbian she can remember from that time was a top sportswoman at school – a tall, handsome, blonde fencer. Her sexuality was never discussed; she and her friends just considered her to be 'different'. Only long after they had all left school, when this woman had still not married, did they discuss it.

Gay men, or men who were suspected of being homosexual, were called 'the brown suede shoe brigade' because those who wore such shoes were considered a bit 'suss'. She also remembers them being called 'pansies', but the name 'poofter' came later. Such men were charming, good fun and great dancing partners at balls. Margaret and her friends didn't care what their sexual orientation was, as long as they were good dancers. If someone was really keen on someone they might say 'You're wasting your time there,' but Margaret said even that didn't happen very often. Ironically, it was the era of Noël Coward, whose homosexuality was also never discussed. Margaret and her friends simply adored his songs, his plays and, most of all, his wit and sophistication.

Even though she had read Christopher Isherwood's *Goodbye to Berlin* and the poetry of W. H. Auden and was well aware that they were homosexual it didn't really mean anything to her, because no one ever spoke about it openly.

Sex and romance and sophistication were always on Margaret's mind. She was very keen to find herself a man with whom she could fall romantically, hopelessly, in love. She yearned to be totally swept away with romantic passion.

When she was eighteen she would announce publicly that if she wasn't married by the time she was thirty she intended to 'take lots of lovers'. Looking back on it, she realised that the only men who would have been available at that time if you were thirty were 'closet homosexuals or left-overs'. Most people married young.

Her other aim that year was to play a part in a SUDS production. Her height was still a limitation, but she was cast as a handmaiden in *Lucrece*, a play adapted by Thornton Wilder. It didn't matter that Margaret was very tall because the leading lady spent most of the play seated or prone. It was only a small part, but she was personally named by the theatre critic for playing it well. However frustrated she might have been with the fact that, despite all her training and love of acting, singing and dancing, her height would always be a barrier, she didn't let it depress her. There was no point in dwelling on it or bemoaning it because there was nothing she could do about it. Hers was always a 'glass half full' attitude. It was an approach to life based on pragmatism and choice, not a knowledge of psychology or philosophy. Quite simply, for Margaret, life was there to be lived and if you approached it positively, it was more enjoyable. She was always a disciple of the principle of 'seize the day' or, if necessary, 'seize the hour'.

In March 1938, she entered the world of Sydney society by making her debut, as did many of her friends. She was presented to the Governor of New South Wales and then to the Administrator of the Commonwealth. She was delighted with her partner, who was a young army chap, tall and handsome. Once having 'come out', as it was called, she threw herself even more energetically into the social whirl.

It took a toll on her end-of-year results. Even though she was bored with Economics, when the new term began in 1939 she decided to repeat the subjects she had failed. She also, at her mother's practical suggestion, attended a business college to learn shorthand and typing.

Nothing could stop her throwing herself back into all her sporting, artistic and social activities. She had begun to feel that 'the world was my oyster'.

In September 1939, Australia joined Britain in declaring war on Germany. In October 1939, Gough joined the Sydney University Regiment. He had also become articled to a Sydney law firm, Sly & Russell, thanks to a recommendation from a colleague of his father. Still involved with the St Paul's revues, he also joined SUDS.

Margaret did not remember very much discussion about politics or the war at home during this time. She was not sure whether, once again, it was because her parents wanted to protect her from their worst fears about the future. Perhaps she was just so preoccupied with her dreams of a stage or singing career or falling madly in love with a handsome, sophisticated man that the announcement simply didn't impinge on her life. She seemed to glide effortlessly along, with nothing and no one interrupting her passage.

* * *

And so it was that in December 1939, in the middle of all this frenetic activity, Gough Whitlam attended the SUDS Christmas party. And there, for the first time, he saw Margaret Dovey. Standing tall, like him, head and shoulders above the others, she was slim, elegantly dressed and exuded style and confidence. Her eyes – clear and mischievous – stared directly into his. She smiled as if to say, 'You'll do. I'll have you.' He moved immediately through the crush on the verandah, towards her.

2

The world will always welcome lovers

The morning after their first meeting, Margaret was sitting at the Dovey breakfast table in Vaucluse, sipping her tea, thinking to herself, 'He is the most gorgeous thing I have ever seen in my life.'

Her father looked up at her from his eggs and bacon and asked, 'Was there anybody nice at your party last night?'

She replied, 'Oh. Yes. I met Gough Whitlam.'

'Would he be related to Fred Whitlam?'

'Yes, he's his son.'

At this stage, Gough's father was the respected Commonwealth Crown Solicitor and Margaret's father was impressed. The patriarchs of each family knew of each other. Always a good beginning.

Gough wasted no time in getting himself invited to Sunday lunch at the Doveys'. He had complained that the food at

St Paul's left a lot to be desired when compared with his mother's home cooking. Margaret was not slow in bringing him home to enjoy what she knew would be a delicious lunch cooked by her mother.

As she expected, her parents were immediately impressed with him. Her father approved of his background and his intelligent, witty conversation. Her mother was very taken with his handsome looks, his good manners and his impeccable clothes.

Margaret was just smitten. He had taken to calling her 'Dovey' – his special nickname.

For Christmas that year, Gough gave Margaret a copy of James Joyce's *Ulysses*, which was not only a great novel but considered a prize because there was talk of banning its sale in Australia. Margaret was absolutely delighted, even though he didn't write an inscription to her in it. Not only was her new beau gorgeous-looking and thoroughly acceptable to her parents, but his choice of present showed that he took her interest in books seriously.

Gough would not have signed it because early familiarity in the expression of emotions was not in his upbringing or his make-up. All he ever received as gifts from his parents were books and so it was a natural, but a thoughtful, choice. It also demonstrated to Margaret that he was up to speed with the latest in the literary world.

However, no sooner had he met Margaret and been to her house for Sunday lunch than he was away from Sydney at a training camp with the Sydney University Regiment, a formal unit of the Army Reserve. War having been declared, he was one of thirteen students given leave by the Law faculty to attend camps. Uniforms were distributed alphabetically and by the time they reached Whitlam the few pants and jackets that would fit him had been taken. He was even forced to wear a chef's hat on parade as all the slouch hats had gone.

Having been assigned to 'A' Company, a rifle company equipped with Lewis machine guns, he wrote home to his parents that he was 'not much use ... I'm not mechanically minded, and I'm not physically too well suited to the work. I'm too tall to wrap myself around the gun or bend down to take difficult sights when sitting behind it.'

Once again, his height made him feel conspicuous and ill-equipped. For a perfectionist this was very unsettling. He was moved from Company A and ended up doing office work.

In May 1940, Gough became Prime Minister – in the St Paul's College Revue. Resplendent in top hat, tails and striped pants he satirised Neville Chamberlain using reams of toilet paper to represent the document that Hitler had signed confirming there would be 'peace in our time'. He was an outstanding success. The audience hooted and cheered and he loved every minute that he was centre stage.

That same year his performance was matched by that of Margaret Dovey in the Sydney University Revue. Titled 'The Girl with the Pigtails in Her Hair' her role was a send-up of the film star Deanna Durbin and was written specifically for her by the poet James McAuley.

'Who's the prettiest child, drives the little boys wild. It's the girl, it's the girl with the pigtails in her hair' sang Miss Dovey. It drove the audience wild. At last Margaret had proved that, despite her height, she could be centre stage and steal the show. Both she and Gough were natural performers and each one revelled in the limelight it afforded them.

Their relationship evolved slowly, in fits and starts, for various reasons. Its development is best revealed by a Nancy Mitford–style personal journal kept by Margaret during this period of her life.

Despite her strong attraction to Gough at that first meeting, while he was away at regimental training camps she became easily captivated by other men. The Russian dancers belonging to the Ballets Russes, whom she met at a post-performance stage party after the opening night of the ballet *Paganini*, fulfilled all her romantic and sophisticated longings.

These journal excerpts, in her own words, tell the story and reveal the real young woman beneath the confident sophisticated façade.

2nd Jan 1940

Champagne was flowing — indeed in my view I was so excited I think I drank a little too much. Somehow men — foreign men especially — make me behave in a most peculiar manner and when Lichine offered me his seat I nearly died of embarrassment.

Margaret longed to be courted in the best romantic tradition. Champagne bubbles were nothing compared to the excitement that was bubbling up inside of her when those 'foreign' men paid her special attention.

The heady, sensual power of music only added to her ecstasy.

7th Jan 1940

Music has become a necessary part of me. Whether it's combined with ballet or just comes over the radio I find I am happiest when sensing music. Listened to a recording of Rachmaninov's 'Rhapsody on a Theme of Paganini' this afternoon. Conducted by Stokowski with the piano played by R. himself. Have seen the ballet Paganini three times already and am seeing it again Wednesday.

She also expressed some misgivings about going to the ballet with her mother, who never appeared to become as carried away with the music or the performance as she did. 'Something is missing with her.' This lack of such a total response from her mother detracted from her own enjoyment and she wondered if she would be better going alone.

In that same journal entry she expressed her constant yearning to discover what she really wanted to do with her life.

My mind is very mobile. One minute I'm positive I only want to write and then it's act on the radio. The only part I'm sure about is that it will have to be something artistic or even just 'arty'.

But always lurking was the overwhelming desire to become one of the heroines in one of Noël Coward's plays.

I want to be smooth and witty, elegant and attractive to men with an easy approach to life. At twenty I thought these things would have come but I can see that all my life I'll be waiting for them to come to me, if I don't make the first move.

Margaret was no shrinking violet content to sit and wait for fate to deliver her what she so yearned to be and to become. She was very prepared to take action to make it happen.

This showed a pragmatic approach to a romantic need. It also showed an awareness that you have to take control of your life by taking the necessary initiatives yourself. She recognised that there was no point in sitting around bemoaning the fact that life wasn't delivering what you desired. What was needed was a positive approach, followed by action.

Despite the nonchalance with which she announced to the world that if she wasn't married by the time she was thirty she would be an independent woman who took lovers, like most young women of her generation Margaret was very keen not to end up 'an old maid'. On the other hand, she was not willing to settle for just anyone. She wanted the full box and dice – a good match as well as an all-consuming, mutually satisfying, romantic, blissful love affair. In her mind, it was imperative.

Soon, a rather heavy love affair, one that means something on both sides regardless of the eventual outcome, would be a good thing. While not actually thinking of being an old maid, there seems to be the need for some soul satisfying episode.

However, she was limited in her choice of men by her height, a fact no amount of romantic fantasy could hide.

If ballet men weren't so small they'd be ideal. But even if I did actually fall in love with one, were I to get the chance, I would probably start thinking, 'Isn't this silly, when he's so small'.

It must not be forgotten that being a 6 foot 2 inch woman also means having big hands and big feet. Short men have small hands and small feet and even Margaret would be forced to find the difference between the size of their shoes ridiculous.

Listed in her journal, as in the diary of most young women before and after her time, is a list of 'possibles'. Gough gets a mention – although at this stage in their relationship she doesn't even know how to spell his name. Nor does she know that he was in fact named after Field Marshal Hugh Gough because his great-grandfather had served in the British Army in India under him from 1843 to 1849. Later to become Viscount Gough, he was known for being courageous and charismatic but bull-headed. Many of these same characteristics were to become synonymous with the man whose name she couldn't yet spell.

Why can't John Murray ask me out, or Goff Whitlam?

And then she wonders if her extreme height, like his, is the only reason he is interested in her.

I wonder if Goff really likes me or just thinks he does because I am tall.

By 13 January her journal is preoccupied with what clothes she will pack for her trip to Adelaide and Perth, sponsored by the university swimming club for intervarsity races. She had decided it was to be her last season of competitive swimming. Women were judged very harshly at this time by the clothes they wore – they denoted not only style, but class. Margaret loved classy clothes.

People stared at Margaret because of her height and, as with Gough, it was important to her that what they saw impressed them. She may have been tall, but she wanted to be elegant and smart with it.

13th Jan 1940
Have decided to wear on the train the grey suit and yellow blouse with new glass buttons and my yellow coat – with black shoes and bag and God knows

*what gloves. As yet I haven't any that are both whole and clean — other than
the two pair I washed at lunch-time. Seem to have thousands of blazers — my
pet aversion.*

What books to take with her was also a major consideration.

'I am taking Romain Rolland's Jean Christophe; *Thomas Wood's* Cobbers;
Noël Coward's [Collected] Sketches and Lyrics *and a cheap edition
of Igor Schwezoff's* Borzoi. *A propos — this morning's Penn [a social
column in the* Herald*] had me in the same paragraph as Igor Schwezoff.
I was so thrilled because I saw him at the ballet last night and I think he
recognised me — any hopes in that direction must be shattered, however, as
we will probably not get back until just before the last night of the company
in Sydney.*

On 15 January, Patricia Penn's aforementioned social column
in the *Sydney Morning Herald*, 'Round the Town', reported the
following item. It was titled 'Confusion in the Dovey Household
on Saturday Night'. It seemed that the clocks at the Dovey
home were an hour slow and Margaret missed the Melbourne
Express which was taking her and the university swimming
team to Adelaide. The family had hurled themselves into the car
and sped to Strathfield, but the train didn't stop so they were
forced to return home. The last sentence states, 'No doubt they
[her team mates] are hoping her times in the events will be a
bit faster than the family clocks.'

These constant references to Margaret in the social columns
may give the impression that she was a bit of a snobbish
socialite. However, there was never then, nor at any time in
her life, any hint of the social snob about her. She simply found

these comments amusing and 'diverting', which was one of her favourite words. She thought it fun to be part of Sydney's social scene. Amid all her description of outings, drives, dinners and lunches she revealed her interest in a chap called Nugent in Adelaide.

7ᵗʰ Feb

Feel very excited and don't know whether or not I want this feeling to go away – it's marvellous to live this way. Nugent was at the station and drove Mother and me to the hotel. We were received by the Lord Mayor and his lady yesterday in an infinitely more pleasant atmosphere than Perth or Kalgoorlie. The rooms were attractive and there was decent sherry as well as the usual beer. Nugent has been wearing a super smooth suit since we've been here.

The next few entries are devoted solely to her times with Nugent, which were 'progressing' because of 'an ecstatic experience' which she doesn't dare write down. It's all very 'hush and gush', but ultimately innocent. Nugent is a 'divine dancer' and she notes, 'We even trucked for a time – I can still feel it.'

(Just in case you think there was a typing error – 'trucking' was a form of dancing where you rocked back and forth in rhythm with each other.)

Once again she notes that Nugent 'had on a marvellous suit – double-breasted, lounge-grey with a pale blue tie – really smooth'.

Determined to pursue him, she manages to get herself down to Moana (an Adelaide coastal beach) in Nugent's car. They surfed and drank wine and beer. Nugent had too much and was not allowed to drive the car home. Always the actress, she placed herself up on top of the seat with a fishing net on her head and large black sunglasses over her eyes for dramatic effect in order to be photographed.

By 12 February she is visiting Chateau Tanunda and lunching with John Seppelt, a son of the great Seppelts wine family – which made Nugent jealous.

Despite all her consumption of delicious food and wine she gave an outstanding swimming exhibition at the University Carnival on 14 February. Finally, at long last, Nugent kissed her.

First casually, then very firmly. He knows something is in the air.

All this courting and flirting was going on behind her mother's back.

Even though she was twenty, naïve in many ways, and eager for adventure and experience, she always knew where to draw the line. No matter how much she was tempted, she remained in control.

She loved having a good time, but never lost her sense of decorum. You would never have found her drunk and dishevelled. Manners were always important to her, because they indicated a civilised style of behaviour. Throughout her life she insisted on addressing other people in a respectful manner; setting a table properly; and expected waiters to serve food from the left and take the plates away from the right. These were the standards of civilised living inculcated by her mother. Her father never banned her from smoking (she thought it very fashionable), but would not allow her to smoke in the living room because it wasn't dignified behaviour for a young woman at that time. She was never openly a rebel against these social niceties, but nor was she one for unnecessary pomp and ceremony.

The 8 March entry in her journal refers to her father giving her money to fund all her activities, thus releasing her from her mother's power.

Finally there is a reference, on 24 March, when she is back in Sydney, to 'Gough' – she has at last found out how to spell his name.

Gough Whitlam took me to a dance at the Australia last night. Vodka was the highlight of the night. I had two glasses. We also drank a 1930 hock at 7 shillings a bottle – none of the other women did and I felt most depraved. Gough insisted that I looked imperial and regal. Funny that he should suddenly turn up like this – but after all he's only out of camp a week. My new brocade impressed him.

Meanwhile, Gough had written to his parents, 'Dovey looks rather well in red things.' The fact that he even mentioned her in this manner would have alerted them to his special interest.

By 23 April her mother had convinced her to return to university, enrolling in Economics II, Economic History, German I and Psychology. Her mother had also struck a compromise with her by agreeing that she should enjoy herself and not worry about exams. Margaret's real interests were still literary and her journal revealed that she was trying to work on a radio program and had some ideas for 'a couple of novels and plays'.

On 20 May, having been in Gough's company again, her journal states:

This is not the usual elated feeling. I think it goes deeper. I don't 'tremble at his touch' but I feel a certain concern and interest in everything he does. We shall see.

How Gough was feeling about their relationship is not recorded, nor is he open to discussion of such emotional introspection. When Margaret asked him why no one ever called him by his first name, 'Edward', his reply was, 'I'll let you call me Edward.' This kind of gesture was all she had to reassure her that she was somehow special to him.

All their friends thought they were a very handsome couple and that her charm and natural ease with people was a perfect fit with his clever, sometimes biting wit. By the end of May she was prepared to admit to her journal that when Gough came to dinner he 'both impressed and was impressed by the family. I never feel at all embarrassed or uncomfortable when I'm with him.'

They had already invented special names for each other. One day she rang him up at work and said to the solicitor who answered, 'Hello, goon. It's Dovey.' They both thought this was hilarious.

June entries in her journal contained her first references to the war. She had been elected secretary of the university's war effort.

By now, she and Gough had been out together to dinner, supper and dancing at Romano's, shared Sydney Symphony Orchestra concerts, films and many dinners at the Doveys'. They often went out in a group of friends and, depending on how much money the men had, they ate pies at Harry's Cafe de Wheels or dined at Romano's.

It was clear that they were both interested in the same things and enjoyed each other's company. On 10 June Margaret learnt that Gough had asked someone else out, which led her to believe that he was cooling off because he was scared of the consequences – 'How could any children of two tall people be anything but taller?' Once again, it was her height that weighed heavily on her.

This conclusion also reflected her underlying fear about their future offspring. Gough, however, said he had no such fears; his only worry was his lack of an income to support a wife and then a family. As far as he was concerned, it was always Margaret.

All her fears and insecurities dissolved, however, on 9 July when they shared their first kiss. At last! He kissed her. Again and again.

I got quite a shock last night when it happened that I intended to ask for an explanation tonight – but the same thing occurred. It's almost as though everyone were decided.

She even contemplated the possibility of them being the first couple in their group of friends to get engaged.

In the meantime she was very busy with her training courses at the VAD (Voluntary Aid Detachment) at Sydney Hospital, her performance in *Twelfth Night* and her knitting enough balaclavas for those friends who were about to leave for the war.

She was, by now, getting to know Gough very well.

He is being very difficult – at times so marvellous and others a beast.

No details are given, particularly about his being a beast, but nothing he said or did put her off him. He was definitely 'the one'.

On 19 November 1940, Margaret turned twenty-one. Her parents took her and Gough and some of her friends to a special dinner at Romano's, where Noël Coward was performing and the Bollinger flowed. It was the exact opposite of the non-event of Gough's twenty-first birthday.

Georgie Swift was a year behind Margaret at university, but she soon became one of her closest friends. They were both members of SUDS and had performed together in *The School for Scandal*. Margaret played the male lead in performing the minuet, with Georgie (5 foot 2) playing her female partner.

Georgie was gorgeous-looking and the only girl Margaret knew who wore a Lamotte suit to university. They used to speak only French to each other on the tram to and from university because they thought it made them sound sophisticated. One afternoon on the tram, they were discussing their friend Barbara Glasgow, who, unlike them, had read Marie Stopes's guide to sexuality and contraception, a publication considered very risqué at that time. Barbara was having an affair with Guy Marton, a lecturer in Greek at the university. Margaret and Georgie confessed to each other that they hadn't done 'it' yet.

Georgie was one of the friends invited to Margaret's twenty-first birthday celebration. Barbara wore a blue lamé dress which looked very sexy. Margaret's father picked them all up in a hire car and Georgie said it was clear to everyone that he totally adored his daughter. It was a special evening. Noël Coward sang 'The Last Time I Saw Paris' and they all cried.

Everyone knew Bill Dovey as a colourful personality in Sydney and also a distinguished judge. He and Margaret's mother were wonderful entertainers. Georgie said she loved going over to the Dovey house because it was such good fun. 'No one stood on ceremony and it was always very jolly.' This was almost the total opposite to Gough's family, who were rather reserved and quiet.

They always welcomed Gough's friends, but the conversation was serious and a long way from the pursuit of fun.

After a post-Christmas trip to New Guinea where she stayed with a former school friend Jeanette Best and her husband, Nick Leahy, and having found the morals of the tropics rather shocking, Margaret returned home early in the new year of 1941, confirmed in her chastity.

Her journal confirmed her conclusion 'that anyone can do it – simply anyone – and I'm so glad I did not succumb'.

Her next journal entry recorded that:

Darling Edward [Gough] will be out on Sunday. I am so excited – his sweater will be finished and I have a new photo in which I achieve a certain degree of intensity. I do hope he will ask for one.

She added, 'And I think I want to become engaged too.'

Once again Margaret showed her awareness that if you want something you have to decide to get it and then act on it.

Nugent had just announced his engagement to Joy Minnett and Pip Street had confessed to her that she was secretly engaged to Jack Fingleton. The Streets wouldn't let her announce it, but she was determined to be married before Christmas. Margaret's best friend, Sonya, was to marry Cedric on New Year's Eve 1941. Barbara Glasgow intended to have Johnny marry her when he came back from the war. There really were only Georgie and Margaret who were not engaged out of their close group of friends.

Margaret hated to be left out of the swing of things, but Gough did not initially commit to her wishes. This was not because he wasn't thinking about it, but because he still wasn't earning enough money to support a wife, which in those days was expected of a married man. He did not, however, discuss these issues with her. Or anyone. It was not his habit to engage in personal exchanges or confessions.

Margaret spent that year doing a social work course which she liked, having transferred from Economics, which she loathed.

Her journal ended in July 1941. Margaret suspected she stopped because she was too busy doing other things. On her father's recommendation, Gough had started work with the New South Wales Supreme Court judge Victor Maxwell. Very much a part of the Dovey family by now, and a regular guest for lunches and dinners, Gough made this decision without discussing it with his father. He neverthless made it clear to his family that it had all come about through the Doveys. They couldn't help being a little hurt that he was now more influenced by the Doveys than his own family, but in their Baptist way, never expressed this to him.

Margaret's father, knowing how keen his daughter was on this chap, probably guessed the reason was lack of money and took action to do something to help the engagement along. He would have done anything for Margaret, but there was also a genuine respect and affection for Gough from both her father and her mother. He was clearly a very suitable match, who came from a respectable and respected family. And if Margaret had decided he was what she wanted, then the Doveys would do all they could to help it happen.

In August 1941, Robert Menzies resigned as Prime Minister after losing his party's confidence in the House of Representatives. Menzies confided in one of his top public servants, namely Fred Whitlam, that he feared his political career was over. Eventually a new Labor government was formed, under the leadership of John Curtin.

On 7 December the Japanese attacked Pearl Harbor. Gough still had one year left to complete his legal studies, but on 8 December, the day after the Japanese attack, he signed up for service with the RAAF. He was told it would be several months before he was called up, but during that time he would learn Morse code and undergo preliminary training. He trained three nights a week while continuing to study law. And see Margaret.

She was by now a commissioned officer in the VADs. She had been to several training camps, where they seemed to do not much more than a lot of marching. She also learnt first aid and Morse code. Their uniforms were khaki trousers and shirts. She also wore a cotton hat known as a giggle hat. It was hardly designer smart but, with the perspective of her new profession, namely social work, she appreciated that it was very practical.

Gough had registered for the air force rather than the army because he remembered the limbless survivors of World War I who on their return were forced to become lift operators. He said, 'While they killed you off in the air force, you were more likely to survive in one piece.'

Over Christmas 1941 and January 1942, Margaret's mother rented a holiday house on the Central Coast. Many of Margaret's friends were invited to stay a few days with them. Among them was, of course, Gough Whitlam. Whether this was a clever ploy to get them together before he went off to war, only Mary Dovey and her husband knew. Whatever her motives, it worked.

One day when they were on the beach a friend of Margaret's with the nickname Tiddles asked Gough, 'When are you going to hang the rock?'

'What do you mean, hang the rock?' he asked.

She pointed to the third finger of her left hand and said, 'On Margaret's finger.'

Gough laughed, but he took the hint and realised that with a bit of help from his parents and hers, together with his weekly air force salary, he could in fact support a wife.

Margaret said that his actual proposal to her was, 'I wouldn't mind if we got hitched.' Beneath the Greek and Latin quotations, the learned epithets from the great poets, Gough was still that shy Australian boy who, when it came down to it, proposed marriage in a manner bashful and unromantic. She, of course, accepted immediately, having already decided that it was time for her to be engaged.

The onset of war engendered an immediacy and an urgency to marry, no doubt because both parties wanted to experience romantic love and love-making before the man went off overseas to fight in the war. All of Margaret's friends were getting married. On New Year's Eve 1941 she was bridesmaid to her best friend, Sonya. It was the traditional task of the bridesmaid to pack the bride's going-away case. Margaret filled Sonya's case mostly with nightdresses which, as Sonya laughingly told her when she returned, was the last thing she needed on her honeymoon. Margaret hooted at her own obvious lack of sophistication.

Sonya's wedding was small and held at her home, but Margaret still had to give the bridesmaid's response to the best man's speech. She stood up and said, 'This wedding is all very new and exciting because I am the one who usually sleeps with Sonya and shares her room.' This was followed by an explosion of mirth from the guests. Margaret was at first shocked until she realised what she had said and joined in the gales of laughter.

Having achieved her engagement goal she noticed that the family appeared to be more excited about it all than she did. Margaret's attitude was her usual 'Let's get on with it.'

Gough's version of events is factual and bears no trace of the deep emotional and sexual attraction he felt for Margaret. His highly intellectual and emotionally frugal upbringing in what was essentially a Baptist tradition did not encourage romantic or florid outpourings of feelings. Except towards God. And he didn't believe in him.

This is how he described his decision to marry Margaret.

In those days one used to think of getting married, but of course one could never afford it. When I joined the air force I had, by the standards of those times, sufficient income to support a wife. During '40 and '41 I used to go for lunch on Sundays at the Dovey home in Hopetoun Ave, Vaucluse. I saw a lot of Margaret over Christmas 1941 and New Year 1942 at Terrigal. I had become an associate to Justice Maxwell in the Supreme Court through Margaret's father, Bill Dovey. He'd recommended me. He was a good bloke. I liked her parents and we all got along very well. After they came back from Terrigal I was there for dinner on the Sunday and it had been arranged for me to meet Bill Dovey in the dining room while the rest of them were out on the verandah. Except the aunt was hovering when I sought permission. There was nothing pre-nuptial – that was usual. Certainly, proper girls didn't.

The fact that he didn't mention his own previous sexual experience was probably because he had been much too busy to woo anyone but Margaret. There may, of course, have been a stray dalliance, but no doubt he had read extensively on the topic before he entered the marriage bed.

The Doveys had already accepted Gough as part of their family. Fred Whitlam and Bill Dovey had become acquainted through the political and legal circles of Sydney and Canberra. Margaret's father had been briefed by Gough's father at the Royal Commission on National Insurance. Bill Dovey was a member of the war-time Aliens Classification and Advisory Committee that met in Canberra, and Mary Dovey met the Whitlams formally during one of these visits.

When Margaret and her mother were invited for dinner at the Whitlams' in Canberra, Margaret's first impression was that they were rather 'prim and proper' compared to her parents. She didn't see much of Gough's mother, who spent most of her time in the kitchen. Freda Whitlam revealed that her mother didn't at first quite approve of the pipe-smoking, monocle-wearing Judge Dovey, who was well known as someone who loved punting, the races and a Scotch. Or two.

To Martha and Fred, the Doveys were rather risqué and bohemian. In fact, the two families had almost nothing in common apart from the relationship between Gough and Margaret.

When Gough wrote a letter to his parents telling them of his engagement to Margaret, there was no response except congratulations from his sister Freda. He was hurt by their silence and wrote again to assure them that both of Margaret's parents thoroughly approved of the union and that was that. Letters of warm congratulations soon followed. Martha adored her son and was probably a little upset at the ease with which he had slipped so happily into the world of the Dovey family. The Whitlams' main fear was financial, as they had formed the view that since he had left home he had become rather extravagant in his tastes. Gough refuted this with the explanation that his only indulgence was clothes, 'which is due to over-compensation in view of my physical make up'. He did concede that Margaret had been 'used to everything', but she had not, he assured them, 'lost all sense of proportion'.

Freda thought Margaret was relaxed, warm and completely at ease. She noticed that she was very skilled at conversation and socialising, which she thought would make her an excellent wife for her brother, who had always lacked these skills.

Even though Margaret had developed all the social graces, she was not as worldly as she appeared. All her life she had lived in a protected bubble of, if not wealth, then financial comfort. Both her parents had done everything they possibly could to give her the best education and a wide range of skills and experience. She was very much 'in love' with Gough, very sexually attracted to him, as he was to her. With Noël Coward's songs swirling in her head and war on their doorstep, she didn't really stop to think much about how well she really knew this Robert Taylor look-alike to whom she was pledging her lifelong devotion.

Gough had also grown up in a protected home environment. Nurtured like a hot-house plant, everything in his life had been planned around his upbringing. His mother doted on him, cooked him special dishes; his father did his best to teach him all the necessary qualities that he believed he would need to fulfil his talents and make his mark in the world. Both his parents had extremely high expectations regarding what he would eventually do with his life.

All Margaret really knew about him was that he was very intelligent, extremely well read, had excellent manners, was impeccably attired and her parents thought highly of him. And, of course, that he was taller than she was and the best-looking of all the men she had fancied. All her friends were marrying in the frenzy of pre-war excitement – so why shouldn't she? Her dreams of becoming an actress or a singer or a novelist had melted into the background. She didn't think about what the future held, but focused on the present and the fulfilment of her romantic and sexual dreams.

Gough was no womaniser and most of the time had more important things on his mind, like food and books. He and Margaret shared many things in common, including a good education, a middle-class background, professional fathers, adoring parents, a love of theatre and music and reading, a love of good food and, most importantly, a belief in the importance of humour. Their coining of joking names for each other was to become a lifelong habit.

Gough felt at ease with Margaret and her parents. She was sophisticated in her dress and her tastes, and very skilled in the art of small talk and witty conversation. He fancied her as she clearly did him, but he knew that with girls of her class there would be no sex unless they were married. He was off to war – who knew what lay ahead? He wanted to make passionate love with her and know the joy of sexual pleasure before he was called up. Now that he could support a wife, what was the point in waiting?

3

All the things you are

On 22 April 1942 Edward Gough Whitlam and Margaret Elaine Dovey were married in St Michael's Anglican Church in Vaucluse, a fashionable eastern suburbs church.

At 4 pm on this warm, sunshine-filled day Gough, very handsome in his air force uniform, his best man 'Rag' Homes and Dick Harris in regular suits, waited patiently inside the church for the bridal party to arrive. Canon Arthur Garnsey, whom Gough knew from St Paul's, was officiating.

The matron of honour, Margaret's best friend Sonya (now Mrs Cedric Ashton), and bridesmaid Freda Whitlam wore sapphire-blue velvet dresses. Their bouquets of yellow roses shaped like tulips with red tips had been chosen by Margaret's mother.

To the fulsome chords of the wedding march, and on the arm of her beloved father, glided the smiling bride. Her off-white satin gown, heavy and elegant, had been made by her mother.

French lovers' bows embellished the heart-shaped neckline and each sleeve. She carried a scented bouquet of camellias and gardenias. Her aunt, a milliner, had made the generous veil, which was adorned with carefully placed gardenias. Her only jewellery was a single strand of pearls, a birthday gift from her parents on her twenty-first birthday. Her father was positively beaming with pride as he led his daughter down the aisle. Gough, ever the romantic aesthete, had chosen the love music from *Tristan and Isolde*, but the organist could not oblige. The service included the traditional music and religious rituals. They took the traditional vows. Margaret even promised to obey, although she said she never took that part seriously.

There were 120 guests, which was considered a big wedding for war-time. The time of 4 pm had been chosen in order to accommodate those from the legal fraternity, who would have finished their work by then and felt free to enjoy themselves. Sonya's husband Cedric, whom she had barely seen since their wedding, surprised and delighted her with his late arrival at the end of the ceremony, due to some unexpected leave.

The guests moved from the church to the Doveys' home in Vaucluse, where they had drinks in the living room, moved along the back verandah, placed their presents on a long table and proceeded downstairs to the large marquee in the back garden, which overlooked a sparkling blue harbour. A special table had been set up for the bride and groom, but Margaret did not want to sit there like a bride doll. As always, she wanted to be where the action was. While she was mingling and chatting with the guests in a trance of sheer pleasure, Gough was withdrawn and aloof, pacing the back lawn. Margaret thought his behaviour 'a bit quaint', but didn't let it worry her. Nothing was going to spoil her day.

It was only after he had delivered his groom's speech that she noticed he really relaxed and began to enjoy himself. Like an actor before a performance, he had been intent on going through his lines in his head and perfecting the wording and timing of his jokes. He received a big laugh when he began by expressing his pleasure at being able to address a 'full' bench. This not only referred to the large number of judges and KCs present but to the fact that large amounts of Johnnie Walker whisky were being consumed, courtesy of one of Bill Dovey's friends.

Margaret's mother was overjoyed at the success of the event and swirled from one group of guests to another, giggling with the women and flirting with the men.

For her going-away outfit Margaret wore a mid-blue dress and jacket in a wool fabric called 'tissus michel'. Her dark hair was braided with one plait wound across and another behind her head. She had been growing it since she was ten. Gough had told her he liked it long.

Eventually they left for their honeymoon in a taxi to Central Station, where they caught a train to Glenbrook in the Blue Mountains and another taxi to the fashionable Lapstone Hotel. It was midnight by the time they arrived. Margaret had packed two huge suitcases with clothes and by the time they were deposited in their room, they both collapsed on the bed, exhausted.

Margaret, although she'd had no real sexual experience, was bursting, in her own words, 'to have a bit of a go'. There were no nerves on her part. She had been waiting for this for a long time and she was determined to make the most of it. In her eighties, she described her honeymoon as 'good fun' and Gough chose the word 'rapturous'.

As for contraception, her mother had 'fixed her up' with some pessaries, which Margaret thought were very messy and like Rice Bubbles: 'Everything was snap, crackle and pop.' It made her giggle.

Free at last to express his true feelings, Gough read Margaret romantic poems from Keats, Shelley and Byron in bed. She couldn't have been more delighted and freely admits that having fully expected to experience an orgasm, she got it. Simple as that.

She did insist, however, that they drag themselves out of bed to dress and have dinner every night. She was determined to show off her gorgeous husband and to wear as many as she could of the outfits she had packed. They saw several young couples they knew who didn't wish to recognise them as they were having what was then known as 'a dirty weekend'.

After four days of wedded bliss they returned, very excited, to their little marriage nest, which was a first-floor flat they had rented in Roslyn Street, Elizabeth Bay, just near Rushcutters Bay Park. It was in a red-brick building called Woodlands and consisted of a bedroom and a sitting room with a kitchenette. The bathroom came off the bedroom, and harbour glimpses were possible from the loo. They had furnished it with whatever they could find. Gough's desk from St Paul's was the dining room table; their dining chairs were a mismatched pair.

Gough wouldn't have a double bed because he knew he had to go away and said they would both be too lonely. The truth was the young sensitive boy still in him would have been too lonely. So they had twin beds pushed together. Margaret's side was right under the window. She loved to tease him by saying, 'You've got me under the eaves.'

Because their flat was on the side overlooking the harbour all the windows had to be covered at night, and they each had a ration card and an identity card. His parents paid the £4.50 for the rent and as she was still at university her father gave Margaret her usual £1 a week for fares and pocket money. As a judge's associate Gough earned £6, half of which he gave to Margaret for 'house-keeping'. She learnt to be a good manager of money and they lived quite well. Breakfast was just tea and toast; Gough had lunch in town, Margaret had hers at university. Dinner was taken together at home, where Mrs Beeton's cookbook was Margaret's bible. Gough loved to read the recipes out aloud for their amusement. He did, however, learn how to boil an egg properly. Recipes from the *Australian Women's Weekly* were very trendy – like rolled veal with stuffing from a Tandaco packet, secured with toothpicks. Sherry parties were very popular and the smart young married couple always had a sherry before dinner. Margaret took on the role of a traditional wife of the time, which was an unspoken contract that the woman did the cooking, the housework, looked after the children and minded her 'p's and q's'.

Although she obliged with the cooking and the housework, as for minding her 'p's and 'q's', she always spoke her own mind and voiced her own opinions. There was never any doubt about that. It never bothered Gough, because his mother had always been equally outspoken. They were both deliriously happy with each other and delighted with their choice of partner. Margaret also liked the fact that she didn't have to compete with anybody when she went to a party. There were also no more worries about being left on the shelf. Best of all, when they danced, his head was on the same level as hers. Besotted though she was with her handsome, clever, witty husband, she was very resolute that he was never to take her for granted. At one party they attended early in their marriage he spent more time talking and dancing with another woman than with her. She immediately called him aside and in firm terms made it very clear what her expectations were of him as a husband. They didn't argue. She simply accused him of being a lazy lover. It never happened again.

Her father had always made her feel important and special. She would never have accepted anything less than first place with her husband. She had also overheard her mother letting her father know in very clear language if she disapproved of his behaviour. While he undoubtedly had achieved higher educational qualifications and had read more books of substance than Margaret, Gough was in no doubt that he had met his equal in his lifelong partner.

Beneath her easy laughter and witty conversation and in spite of her romantic dreams of a Noël Coward existence, Margaret was confident, self-assured and resilient. She would never allow herself to be treated as an appendage to any man, no matter how much in love with him she was. Gough's upbringing ensured that he had the greatest respect for women as equals.

Only six weeks after they were married, he received his call-up from the RAAF to begin his training as an aircrew navigator. While he was away Margaret continued with completing her social work diploma and became commandant of the VAD university detachment. It was not in her nature to sit around bemoaning her husband's absence.

Gough travelled to a succession of training schools in Victoria, New South Wales and Canberra. When he was at Fairbairn Air Base in Canberra he would regularly bring home members of his bomber crew and his squadron for one of his mother's splendid home-cooked meals. After dinner, during which there had been no wine or beer, Gough reverted to his family's habit of sitting at the table and reading. When he passed out encyclopaedias to his RAAF mates he totally failed to register their stunned expressions. He had no idea how eccentric this after-dinner habit appeared to them. If it was normal behaviour for his family, then for him it was entirely natural.

When he was on leave from the camp in Sale, Victoria, Margaret travelled to Melbourne just to be with him. On the long journey back to Sydney in the train she sat next to a soldier who was very feverish. Twenty-four hours later she was diagnosed with scarlet fever. She immediately returned home to her parents in Vaucluse to be looked after and recuperate.

Having never liked mathematical subjects at school, Gough found himself actually enjoying subjects like trigonometry because now they had a direct, practical application. He gained good grades. Flight Lieutenant Lex Goudie, who was Gough's pilot during the war, is on record praising the pinpoint accuracy of his navigation skills.

Margaret appeared to be optimistic about their future together, even though Gough's squadron was patrolling the Arafura and Timor seas and engaging in strikes on Japanese ships, barges and ports.

Not long after they were married, when he was home on leave, they went to the Wintergarden Cinema complex at Rose Bay to see the latest film, *Waterloo Bridge*. It starred her favourite actor, Robert Taylor, who played a British army colonel in love with a ballerina, played by Vivien Leigh. He is called away to the front, and does not know that she has been fired from the ballet troupe and forced to survive by working as a prostitute on the streets. It is renowned as a romantic but classic MGM tearjerker.

When the film finished, it was all too much for Margaret. Here she was, sitting next to her man in his air force uniform, the country was at war and she was so in love with him. Thoughts that she had never allowed to penetrate her customary optimism swamped her. The sudden reality of her situation, combined with the sadness she felt for the two main characters in the film, was overwhelming. She began to sob. Uncontrollably. Such was her distress and overflowing emotion that she was unable to get up from her seat. Gough neither needed nor asked for an explanation. He simply put his arms around her, held her close and in a gentle and caring voice said, 'We'll just sit here until you're calm.' It was some time before Margaret could feel calm. They just sat there, her head on his shoulder.

For the rest of their lives whenever they saw or experienced anything really sad, Gough would take her hand and say 'Waterloo Bridge'. Those two words triggered for them a vivid picture of a young married couple in the dress circle of the Wintergarden in the middle of the war, the young man quietly and gently comforting his sobbing wife. Nothing else needed to be said.

Margaret was very committed to the probationary nursing duties at Sydney Hospital, where the Red Cross conducted its training courses. The long, all-male wards consisted of forty beds with no partitions between them. Margaret's main duties were to watch over the men and assist with dressings, all of which she coped with efficiently. But when one of the patients asked her to get him a bottle, she returned with a bottle of lemonade. His response – 'I need a bloody bottle, I want to have a piss' – revealed her previously sheltered life. But all new experiences were for her part of her discovery of a different life. This even included the institutional lunches of steak and kidney pie followed by bread and butter pudding.

Margaret had moved on from the young woman who wrote her romantic yearnings in a secret journal. The war was now a harsh and present reality to her. Those four days of honeymoon passion with a naked man reading poetry to her in bed had flashed past like a wonderful romantic idyll.

Gough was posted interstate for his training with the RAAF Bombing and Gunnery School in Victoria, where he completed the Navigators' Course, graduating with a commission, ranked as a pilot officer. He was assigned to the RAAF's Squadron 13, which was being re-equipped with Navy Venturas. With Flight Lieutenant Lex Goudie as the pilot and Gough as the navigator, they flew 844 hours together, shared a tent and remained lifelong friends. This war-time experience created a very different Gough from the university intellectual and lawyer in training who Margaret had married. His first brush with death was in Queensland, when the brakes on their Ventura, loaded with depth charges, failed as they were coming in to land. The plane skidded off the end of the runway and up a small hill, where the crew leapt out unhurt. Suddenly the Ventura started rolling back towards them, 'its torn bomb doors open and a depth charge dangling from a single hook'. They all scattered, with

Goudie recalling Gough as 'a most awkward complex of long arms and legs'.

Having graduated in social studies, Margaret's first paid position was with the Family Welfare Bureau in Martin Place in the city. She shared an office with another social worker, Margaret McNamara, which meant that her clients were sometimes embarrassed about having to state their personal reasons for needing assistance. Well aware that the general image of social workers was that of do-gooders, she was determined to give her clients the best practical knowledge and help. She didn't have money to give them, but could help them with advice on how they could earn money or find shelter or gain legal and medical advice. She could help them organise what they needed through government and non-government organisations.

For the first time in her privileged life she came in contact with many of the same people that her father, as a criminal lawyer, represented. Some of them were petty criminals or victims of crime, but most of them were servicemen and their dependants. She put them in touch with Legacy or the Red Cross which, during the war, were virtually government-funded. The NGOs were generally run and funded by various church organisations.

Getting to know the intimate details of the lives of the broader community was an eye-opener for her. She found the work rewarding because she was helping people in need learn how to help themselves. For the first time in her life she was focused on work that was useful to others, especially those less privileged than herself. She witnessed first-hand how a government agency and those who worked for it could make a real difference to the lives of people in need.

Her empathy for those outside her family and social circle became an important part of her maturity. She realised that no matter how desperate their circumstances people needed to maintain their sense of pride and self-worth. She always made an appointment with them before a professional visit in order that they might feel prepared, and was moved by the fact that no matter how poor they were – and some of them had only threepence to spare – they would spend it on biscuits to go with the cup of tea they would offer her. At first she wanted to protest that they shouldn't spend their money on tea and biscuits, but soon realised that it was important to them that they have something to offer her when she visited.

She witnessed first-hand people enduring lives that she could never in her worst nightmares have imagined. In one home a handicapped child had lived his entire life in a pram because his parents had nowhere else to keep him. She gave them the knowledge they needed to get help.

A woman who needed to be hospitalised for an operation and had nowhere and no one to leave her children with came to ask for her help and advice. When Margaret recommended a church home, the woman looked her in the eyes and asked, 'Miss, would you send your baby there?' For the first time in her life Margaret was asked to put herself in the shoes of a woman who, unlike her, had no family or friends to rely on. From then on, that was the first question that Margaret asked herself. She always inspected every place she recommended and thought, 'Would I leave my baby here?'

Even though the working hours were long and the remuneration low, Margaret was very happy with her choice of profession. For the first time in her life she was focused on people other than herself. She liked the fact that she could make a positive change in their lives. It also was important for her to be totally involved in her work while she waited for Gough to join her on leave in their little flat.

Babies were very much on her mind. Many of their friends were pregnant and once Margaret settled into the reality of being married she thought, 'What are we waiting for – let's do it.' When she announced her desire to become a mother to her husband, it was couched in the private jokey word code that they both loved. She said, 'Let's forget about the Rice Bubbles and declare "open season".' Gough roared with laughter and readily agreed.

Five months after she had started her first job, she was informed by the doctor that she was pregnant. She rushed out of his office to ring her mother on the nearest public phone at the G.P.O. 'Guess what, darling – you're going to be a grandmother before you're fifty.'

There was silence at the other end of the phone. (It was years before she discovered that her mother had lied about her age because she was, in fact, two years older than her husband.)

Having recovered from the shock and her lying, her mother was effusive in her congratulations. Her father was 'over the moon' with the news.

Margaret, however, was soon afflicted with morning sickness, except in her case she renamed it 'morning, noon and night sickness'. She had never felt so ghastly in all her life and it didn't stop. Five months into her pregnancy the chief social worker called her into her office.

'Margaret, you are coming into work later and later.'

Margaret replied, 'The way I'm feeling I won't be coming in at all.'

Her nausea never lessened and it wasn't too long before she found it just too much. 'I stayed home and threw up a lot.'

She collected what was called 'the wife's allotment' from Gough's air force salary from the post office every fortnight and his parents continued to pay the rent, which enabled her to get by without working. She certainly wasn't going out a lot. She had always been taught the importance of frugality by her mother. Now she really had to practise it. She was careful with money, but never mean. She genuinely could not bear to waste anything. The only distinction she gained in her academic life was for a social work course called 'Nutrition and Family Budgeting'. Whenever Gough questioned her about her house-keeping expenditure, it gave her great pleasure to remind him of that.

Eventually she found it too lonely in the flat when she wasn't working. Apart from Gough's periods of leave, she preferred to live at her parents' house in Vaucluse. Her mother was on hand for dressmaking and advice and Alice, their live-in maid, was there to help with the baby when it arrived.

During the war Prime Minister Curtin was granted expanded Commonwealth powers. Always the student of what governments could actually achieve with the proper goals, Gough became very concerned that these powers would not be available once the war had ended. The Australian Constitution allowed no such expansion into peacetime when the great tasks of rebuilding and reconstruction would, he could see, make them imperative.

He was a great admirer of the Curtin government and when it was re-elected in both Houses in August 1943, Gough was determined to publicly lobby for a positive response in the proposed referendum to enable the extension of Commonwealth powers for the purposes of post-war reconstruction. When he was on leave awaiting the birth of his first child, he and his father attended the Australian Institute of Political Science summer school in Canberra on 'Post-War Reconstruction in Australia'.

Fred Whitlam, as Crown Solicitor, was the leading draftsman for the 1944 referendum and sent the official documents to his son, who was then stationed in Cooktown. Its aim was to ensure the building of a better Australia after the war – the essentials being full employment, development of national resources, adequate social services and playing a part in the new world order.

Gough campaigned passionately inside his squadron for a 'Yes' vote, holding meetings at night when they weren't flying. Even Margaret received a lecture in the form of a love letter. Clearly she had not shown nearly enough passion for the cause. It began:

> *Darling,*
> *I now approach a moral which I feel I must point out with as little show of impatience as I can when I consider your own general attitude at times.*

He went on to outline, in detail, his argument, ending with:

> *I urge you and for you to urge all our friends to vote 'Yes'.*
> *And so to bed*
> *All,*
> *G (Authorised by E. G. Whitlam)*

Margaret did as she was instructed. But the 1944 referendum failed. For Gough, this result was a disaster for the nation. This was also a forerunner to the major political issues that he would pursue throughout his political life.

Antony Philip Whitlam was born on 7 January 1944, 9 pounds 10 ounces, a bonny, healthy child.

'Mary, have you ever seen a more beautiful child?' pronounced Gough to his mother-in-law when he saw his son a few hours after his birth. This was not hyperbole. He meant it. His face was flushed with excitement and real joy.

Margaret had arrived at the hospital at midnight with her mother and brother, Will, who was home on leave from his service in the navy. The labour took eight hours. Every time the nurse or the doctor said 'push', Margaret replied, 'Push what?' She said she could not really understand what was happening to her, other than the pain.

When mother and baby returned to the Dovey home in Vaucluse, her life revolved entirely around her son and writing letters to her absent husband, mostly about the baby's progress.

Every week Margaret bundled up her son, caught the bus to Rose Bay, had him weighed at the Baby Health Centre and the results recorded in her little book. She was chastised if the baby had not put on the correct amount of weight. If he had put on too much weight she would have to do a test feed to see if he was 'a gobbler'.

She much preferred to take baby Tony to the beach, which she did as often as possible. When he was old enough she would sit him up on the sand while she went for a quick swim. Always, of course, with one eye on the child. The days were full of sunshine, water and playing with her baby boy.

One of her favourite spots was Parsley Bay. When he was about eighteen months old she would let him climb onto her back and, with his little arms fixed around her neck, she breaststroked elegantly through the water. It didn't go unnoticed. One morning a popular radio announcer told his audience about an amazing sight he had witnessed in Parsley Bay while taking his morning swim. Only Margaret knew who the unknown mother and baby were when other people told her the story.

Every two days, without fail, Gough wrote a letter to his wife, addressing her only as 'Darling'. He described to her his daily routines and occurrences, detailed articles or books he was reading and made various requests for clothing, toothpaste and, of course, special foods. In order to avoid war-time censorship he made cryptic references to where he had been. He usually signed off with one word – 'All' – their code for 'All my love'. Sometimes he would quote Noël Coward's message to Gertrude Lawrence on the occasion of her wedding: 'On this, as on every other day, I love you.'

Letters gave him the freedom to express his love and adoration of Margaret, which he usually found so difficult, as an essentially shy man. There was no question that he considered their marriage and Margaret to be the best that human beings could attain. When noting the end of the marriage of a couple who were their friends, he wrote, 'Pity the poor souls didn't and don't know such continuous and constant bliss, such unmitigated and unperturbed romance as has been ours.'

Margaret kept his letters as treasures. This was a love affair and a marriage they both intended to last a lifetime.

On the eve of his last Christmas away from her he wrote, 'I hope you have a very happy one, the last without me for up to half a century at least.' He kept that promise, and more.

That year had been spent by Lex Goudie and Gough Whitlam in Navy Venturas conducting extensive raids on the Japanese. They attacked shipping, supply dumps and installations around

Dobo in the Aroe Islands. From there they were sent to Gove airfield at Yirrkala, on the remote tip of Arnhem Land in the Northern Territory, where they carried out anti-submarine controls and bombing raids on Japanese targets in Timor and the Netherlands East Indies. During one of these raids their Ventura was hit. They were forced to fly back to base on one engine, with Gough safely navigating the plane across the coral reefs 'so that if we had to ditch . . . they could pick us out from the air'. Two weeks later their squadron lost two Venturas in heavy weather on a single day, killing all on board.

His third tour of duty, in the South-West Pacific, coincided with the end of the war. He was able to observe the fading of the empire and the new era of post-colonial national independence. He saw Australia as a nation able to make independent foreign policy decisions; a nation with a new sense of its place in the world and of its power to contribute. This was an international perspective that excited him.

Margaret had no time for such lofty thoughts. She was pregnant again, which meant weeks and weeks of throwing up.

4

You'd be so nice to come home to

After five years of active war service, Gough was finally a free citizen in October 1945. He was twenty-nine, still had a law degree to finish and was on a not very large salary as a judge's associate. Margaret was very pregnant with her second child. The flat was too small for their requirements and they moved into the Doveys' house in Vaucluse, taking over the billiard room downstairs as their private space. Gough had joined the Labor Party in August of that year and within two months had been appointed Minute Secretary of the Darlinghurst Branch. Despite rumours to the contrary, he never even flirted with the notion of joining the Liberal Party. His upbringing, his father's principles, his war experience and his admiration for Curtin made any other choice impossible.

Margaret had never really taken much interest in politics. Her father, as a leading KC, had many contacts on both sides of the political spectrum. Earlier in his career he had contested and failed at winning pre-selection for the conservative United Australia Party. Her mother had always voted Labor because her own father had been pre-selected as a Labor candidate just prior to his tragic drowning.

Margaret had cast her first vote for the New South Wales Labor candidate Jessie Street, because she knew her well as the mother of her school chum Pip. Margaret also knew that Jessie Street was a fighter for better pay for women and remembered that some of the children she had attended Bondi Primary School with had had mothers who were forced to work in low-paid jobs. Gough never pressured her to join the Labor Party and she took her own time to make her own decision.

The loss of the 1944 referendum and the debates that had preceded it made Gough even more determined to pursue three major issues – the extent of Commonwealth power, the role of the Upper House and the position of Indigenous Australians.

Before he served in the RAAF, Gough had met no Aboriginal people. When he was stationed at Cooktown and Gove he witnessed first-hand rampant discrimination and the impact of mission settlements on the Aborigines and their cultural beliefs. It disturbed him deeply. 'Missionaries taught Aborigines that they were Godless, they were heathens and therefore inferior. This attitude applied to all denominations and they destroyed the Aborigines' self-respect.' He also met the Yunupingu family, whose members would agitate for recognition and land rights for the next twenty-five years. He was greeted at the Gove airstrip by Munggurrawuy Yunupingu, holding in his arms his young son, who was the same age as Antony Whitlam. Gough took the young baby in his arms and 'he pissed on me'. In an aside much later he said, 'A lot of people would have liked to have done that since.'

Their second son, Nicholas Richard Whitlam, was born on St Nicholas Day, 6 December 1945. He weighed 8 pounds 6 ounces and was a very strong and healthy baby. Gough once again declared to Margaret's mother, 'Mary, have you ever seen a more beautiful child?'

Alice had finally left the Dovey household to get married, leaving the two Doveys, the two Whitlams and their two young boys.

While living with her parents removed some of the child-rearing burdens for Margaret, it is never easy living with your in-laws. Margaret felt free to speak out but Gough held his tongue as a sign of respect for living in someone else's home. He did, however, enjoy dinner-table competitions over the meanings and correct pronunciations of words. He was always going on about the correct way to pronounce 'kilometre'. Margaret's father would disagree with him and they would have to get out the dictionary. Gough didn't always win but that didn't stop him being a dedicated pedant.

Margaret and Gough, like most young couples with a new family, couldn't wait to have their own home. Fred and Martha Whitlam had never sold their house in Turramurra in Sydney and they offered it to them. Margaret, having been born and bred in the eastern suburbs, had no desire to live on the North Shore, saying, 'It was always another country to me.'

It was also another way of looking at the world. The eastern suburbs and the North Shore are home to two very different

Sydney tribes. (The Whitlams are very much a part of the eastern suburbs tribe; the Howards belong to the North Shore.) Even though it would have solved their housing problems, Margaret was determined that the North Shore was not for her.

Gough's priorities, having grown up in Canberra, were simply to have plenty of space, facilities for the children and a home within walking distance to a city commute. Margaret wanted something near the water. It was, however, impossible for them to find a suitable house in the eastern suburbs of Sydney. Just as Chifley had predicted would happen if the Commonwealth was not given the necessary powers, rising birth rates and increased migration had led to a post-war housing shortage.

The young Whitlams joined thousands of others like them, forced to search on the south-eastern fringes of the city.

Eventually, after a long and desperate series of weekend expeditions, they found what they considered to be the perfect block in Cronulla. Number 2 Wangi Avenue overlooked Gunnamatta Bay and was surrounded by bush. They took out a war-service loan to purchase the block of land and the Rural Bank lent them three-quarters of the cost of building the house (£650) at 4.75 per cent interest over thirty years, guaranteed by Fred Whitlam. Gough used the money his grandfather had left him to study at Oxford (£200) to pay for expenses and all that was necessary to set up a family home.

It was a mile walk or a bus trip to the station and a 55-minute journey into St James Station. It was also half a mile from a rock swimming pool that both Margaret and the children would use regularly over the years.

Cronulla was a far cry from the cosmopolitan eastern suburbs of Sydney where Margaret had previously lived. Still an emerging but rapidly expanding suburb, it was filled with young couples and young families. Unlike the meticulously planned and very well serviced suburbs of Canberra, Cronulla had no sealed roads and no underground sewerage. Margaret's mother had never even visited the suburb and considered it to be at the end of the earth.

'But darling, is there a doctor there?' was her first question.

Margaret and Gough were far too excited at the prospect of building their own home to care what their parents thought. They hired fashionable architect John Mansfield to design the house, which Margaret described as a charming, pretty white cottage with a blue-tiled roof.

Unfortunately, they had to wait a year longer than they had planned to move in because the builder went bankrupt. Nothing, however, interfered with Margaret's enthusiasm. She packed a picnic lunch and the whole family took the train down to the coast on the weekends to inspect the progress. When both boys contracted chickenpox, she left Gough behind to look after the infectious children while she caught the train to Cronulla.

By late 1947 Margaret was prepared to wait no longer. She was determined they would move in before Christmas and the builders could work around them, which they did. They both absolutely adored living in their brand-new home. Margaret took great delight in choosing the furniture. The living room had a beige carpet over polished boards. The three-piece lounge suite was covered in Sanderson's linen that had soft pink and green flowers. The kitchen had blue lino, white cupboards and yellow-and-white checked curtains.

Margaret knew she was very lucky to have a new house when many families nearby were living in garages while they saved enough money to build. Very few of them, apart from the doctors, had cars. The women stayed at home to look after the household chores and the children while the husbands, like Gough, caught the 7.30 am train to the city every day.

Margaret quickly made friends with their neighbours and the women took turns to mind each other's children. They may have had cosseted and privileged childhoods but the married life of the young Whitlams and their two boys was just like that of the ordinary Australians they had chosen to live among.

Having been admitted to the New South Wales Bar, Gough began to slowly build up a practice specialising in the laws of tenancy. Occasionally he took a case for his father-in-law, just to keep up his court profile. However, even though he worked long hours, including Saturday mornings, his earnings were often quite meagre. The days were long and the nights short for the two lovers who had waited so long to be together in their own home. Margaret resented the fact that he worked on Saturday mornings because she thought that, having been alone with the two boys all week, their weekends were a chance for she and Gough to be together and 'play'.

This was certainly not how she had envisaged married life. There was no Alice to help her with the children. And her mother lived too far away. She realised that she had to overcome this resentment because, as Gough explained, they needed the money. This was the reality of her life now. There was no doting Daddy to give her extra money. He did invite her to the occasional lavish lunch though, and always paid for her to go to the Melbourne Cup with them and stay at the best hotel.

The Whitlams of Cronulla were, however, very happy. Her enthusiasm for her house, her endless store of physical energy and her fitness meant that Margaret rose early, organised her chores, stuck to a disciplined routine and soon had an established garden blooming in the bare backyard.

Tony was four by the time they moved to Cronulla. He attended the preschool next to the South Cronulla Primary School. When Margaret delivered Tony there in the morning Nick would cry and plead with her to leave him there too. She always left time in the afternoons to swim with them and play on the beach and the rocks, which were accessible from the end of their street. They were both healthy, turbo-charged little boys who needed to be constantly engaged in activity.

Her only problem was the natural aggression between the young brothers. The closeness of their age meant that they were intensely competitive with each other. They fought hard, one brother against the other. A lot. Even when Nick was a baby, Tony resented the attention his mother gave him. When she was breastfeeding Nick, Tony would try to climb up and sit in her lap. He would say 'I love bubba' and then put his hand over Nick's face as if to suffocate him. By the time they were both at primary school they led rival gangs who fought after school in Darook Park, the reserve below the houses.

In his memoir, Nick confirms this stage in their lives. 'As children [Tony] was the leader of one pack and I was the leader of a younger one. Images of *Lord of the Flies* would not be out of line; fights in Darook Park always finished in tears.'

Nick nevertheless remembers his 1950s childhood as idyllic. He and Tony were free to run and play and swim and have endless adventures at Gunnamatta Bay. Darook Park was a wilderness. With the fathers away at work it was up to the mothers to make decisions and rules about what the children were allowed to do. These were still the days when children were allowed to run up and down the streets, in and out of each other's houses and, in the case of the young Whitlams, into the wild territory of trees and bush and caves below their house. Every house in the street left its back door open for the neighbours and the children to come and go as they pleased.

One Friday night after dinner, all four of them were listening to a radio quiz program called 'Australian National Quiz', which was sponsored by the federal Treasury to encourage people to buy government security loans to be used for post-war reconstruction. Gough answered all the questions correctly and Margaret encouraged him to audition for the quiz. 'Have a go. You'll be brilliant.' In no time, with her words ringing in his ears, he was the New South Wales state quiz champion. The next step was to compete for a position on the team that would compete in the national final.

On the prescribed night, Margaret, their friends from the neighbourhood and all their children gathered around the Whitlam radio, very excited. Margaret ordered them to all be very quiet when the quiz, which was broadcast live, began. Walter Pym was the host.

'Now, Mr Whitlam, who was the king who reigned from about 115 to 63BC, who fortified himself so strongly against poison by the use of antidotes that he could not kill himself and had to get a Gallic mercenary soldier to stab him, as he preferred death to captivity?'

Without a pause, Gough replied confidently, 'Mithridates.'

When Mr Pym responded, 'That's right,' the Whitlam house filled with cheering. Tony and Nick whistled and clapped the loudest and the longest. Margaret gave a bit of a chortle. At last, she thought, all those arcane facts and information that he so loves to demonstrate his knowledge of have come to some use. She was proud of her man – not that she would ever boast about his success. She knew that they were lucky to have the opportunity to make some extra money. Gough became the winner of the Australian National Quiz in 1948, won it again in 1949 and was runner-up in 1950 in the final quiz. His winnings totalled £1000 and he was paid in security bonds.

The initiator and promoter of the quiz, Prime Minister Ben Chifley, had also been listening. The next time he met Fred Whitlam in Canberra he was quick to suggest to him that Gough was exactly the type of man the party needed to take it into the post-war years. When his father passed that information on to him, Gough took it very seriously as he knew Chifley was not prone to flattery. He shared Chifley's view of parliament as the central institution for democratic progress and began to seriously consider his suggestion.

The quiz program was also linked into international contests. One night when the quiz was held in Melbourne, Margaret and the boys joined Gough for a stay in a very nice hotel. It was a treat for all of them. All four were sitting quietly at a table with a white, starched tablecloth in the large dining room, about to have dinner, when the two boys, overcome with excitement, suddenly jumped up from the table and began to demonstrate their skills at somersaulting down the long aisles between the tables. The other diners were thoroughly entertained by their antics, which only encouraged them to perform more wildly. Far from being embarrassed, Margaret and Gough just looked at each other and burst into fits of laughter. Their shared sense of humour was one of their strongest bonds.

Gough met Ben Chifley for the first time when he was selected as a delegate to the New South Wales state conference in 1949. The previous year he had won a tightly contested pre-election ballot for the New South Wales Legislative Assembly seat of Sutherland. His opponent was a prominent Liberal, Mr C. O. Joe Munro, best known as the 'King of Cronulla'.

Gough was far from a natural fit for the Labor Party. The old Labor diehards considered him and his ideas too radical. Not only was he well dressed, intelligent and knowledgeable, they resented the fact that he took every opportunity to lecture them on the correctness of his opinions. He thought he was proving to them he was the right man for the job, and was oblivious to their resentment. In their eyes he was a pompous blowhard who loved to show off his vast knowledge. Others simply dismissed him as a 'silvertail'. According to the unwritten rules, he had the wrong background, came from the wrong class and simply didn't belong. They couldn't work out why he wanted to join them and not the Liberals. It was very hard for him to convince them of his integrity and his sincerity. Finally, he was forced to rely on demonstrating just how hard he was prepared to work to gain a seat.

As he didn't own a car, every spare night he trudged up and down the unsealed streets, door-knocking his electorate. In the winter under the sparse street lighting he was a familiar figure in his raincoat and wellingtons, attempting to make himself known to the voters. He had never acquired the art of small talk but he chatted to them about their families, their children, their dog, drank endless cups of tea and gave out lots of free legal advice.

This was hard slog. He was prepared to do it because he was now confirmed in his goal to enter politics. Margaret had little involvement in these activities as she was pregnant again. Two months before his first election day, on 4 April 1950, she gave birth to another son, Stephen Charles Whitlam, weighing over 8 pounds. But unlike his brothers he was not a hearty baby. Diagnosed with hypertrophic pyloric stenosis, a blockage in the pylorus prevented her milk from entering his stomach, and he was constantly vomiting. Mother and baby Stephen were admitted to the Children's Hospital in Camperdown, where he had an emergency operation to correct the problem. He was nevertheless a very sick baby. Margaret wept the whole time she was expressing the milk which was fed to him with a tube. It was the custom in the hospital to encourage mothers to visit other sick babies in the wards and the sight of little children dying of cancer only added to her fears for Stephen. When Stephen took a dramatic turn for the worse and the nurse found her sobbing, she asked if she wanted to ring her husband to come in and see the baby now, implying 'before it is too late'.

'No' said Margaret, 'that's not necessary, he's bringing the boys in to see him tomorrow.'

Despite her free-flowing tears, she was fiercely determined that her baby would not die. She would simply not allow it to happen. When Gough and the boys came to see him the next day, she told him nothing about her fears. Stephen lived. And grew into another tall, healthy Whitlam.

Chifley's loss at the 1949 election to the resurrected Robert Menzies encouraged Fred Whitlam to decide that he didn't want to endure another change of government. He retired after fifty years of devoted service in the Commonwealth and State Public Services. He continued to play a significant but voluntary role working for the protection of human rights in the United

Nations. In 1950 and 1954, he represented Australia on the United Nations Human Rights Commission.

Meanwhile, his son was door-knocking right up until the very end in order to begin his new career. He had attended as many social functions as he could, with or without Margaret, and was even seen to be sharing a beer with the locals in order to blend in.

On polling day young Tony and Nick were there, proudly helping to hand out leaflets and stick posters on any available space. Gough lost the seat by five hundred votes, but with his usual self-confidence announced that he had at least increased the vote for the ALP. Even more importantly, he had been seen to work hard, do his best and take nothing for granted. Margaret was very impressed with how hard he had worked to prove to the party he was serious. She knew that now he had the bit between his teeth, there would be no stopping him. He was a passionate man and she loved his passion.

Gough was not one for giving in or giving up. His next challenge was to gain pre-selection for the federal seat of Werriwa when the long-serving Mr H. P. 'Bert' Lazzarini retired.

He and Margaret decided to increase their involvement in community activities. And so they began what was to be a lifetime of attending local dances, halls, fêtes and fundraising events. In fact, they accepted every invitation they received. It became a hard habit to break.

For Gough, it was necessary work for his ultimate goal but also an opportunity to listen to what the voters had to tell him. Margaret just loved being out and about, mixing easily with all types of people, having a drink and a laugh. Her professional training as a social worker enhanced her natural ability for getting on famously with everyone. Gough never developed her talent for easy conversation but he greatly admired her skills in communication. It was clear to him that she was more than just an asset to him – she was essential to his future success. He made sure that in the quiet times, late at night when they were in bed together, he whispered those 'sweet nothings' that made her giggle.

Early in 1951, while dashing about doing the piles of laundry that accumulated when you had a working husband, two boys at school and a baby, Margaret slipped on some spilt water and broke her hip. For two weeks she was ordered to stay in bed at home while the doctor did various tests and decided what to do. Her mother came to stay, to run the house and look after the children. This was a huge task for a woman of her age, totally unused to the labour of looking after two energetic boys and a one-year-old baby. Somehow she managed, with Margaret giving advice and directions from her bed. By the end of every day they were both in desperate need of a stiff drink. Or two. This became known – as her family loved to give things their own special name – as 'having a Cronulla'.

Eventually the doctor sent Margaret to the hospital to install a pin in her hip. Her mother stayed on with the help of a babysitter until Margaret returned from hospital, when many a 'Cronulla' was needed.

Late in 1951, Lazzarini announced that due to ill-health he would not be seeking re-election. Gough seized his chance. Reinvigorated, he set his sights and all his energy on winning the Labor nomination for the federal seat of Werriwa.

Nineteen fifty-two began with Gough trudging the streets or catching public transport to visit the constituents. ALP ticket-holders were found among both the working and the middle class of Cronulla, together with miners in the towns towards Wollongong. He had put his name down twelve months before to buy a new Holden but post-war restrictions meant they had to be patient.

Gough's upbringing, although sheltered and academically privileged, did not mean that he ever 'put on side' with people. His Baptist parents had always stressed that everyone was equal in the sight of God. Artifice and snobbery were not to be tolerated. He felt equally at home sitting down with people, having a chat and a cup of tea, whether he was in a well-furnished living room or a temporary shed. His experiences and friendships with his neighbours in Cronulla gave him a clear understanding of many of the problems families were struggling with and he was able to talk about his own life. Politics for him, now, was not something he had researched or studied in a book, it was something he was living. Day by day. Week by week.

Bill Dovey, KC was at that time assisting Justice Victor Maxwell in the Royal Commission on liquor law. He asked Gough to be his junior. The newspapers were making a feast of exposing some of Sydney's notorious underworld figures who were called to give evidence. Gough loved the drama of it all. When Bill Dovey suddenly fell ill and Gough stepped in to his place he made good use of his theatrical skills, earning the delight of the press with his skill of eliciting the most salacious details from those he questioned. He was really enjoying himself.

One of his targets was a well-known Sydney publican, Douglas Barwick, the unlikely brother of the well-regarded Sydney barrister and KC, later to become Sir Garfield Barwick. He never forgave Bill Dovey or Gough Whitlam for the manner in which they caricatured his brother. (Over twenty years later he took his revenge.)

When Gough was written up as 'a prominent barrister', the publicity was a boon to his supporters in the Werriwa ballot for pre-selection. Everyone loves a good headline.

Just prior to the day of the pre-selection, Margaret, who was three months pregnant, had a miscarriage. She found herself floundering in shock and grief. Having already given birth three times with no complications during pregnancy, she could not believe that anything could possibly go wrong. She had to learn how to deal with this inexplicable loss. The doctors all assured her that it was a good thing that whatever had gone wrong had happened sooner rather than later. But she was not consoled. She found herself crying in quiet places, alone. A lot. No matter how hard she tried to 'pull herself together' there was a dull ache inside her that wouldn't go away. She did not cry out of pity for herself, nor did she cry out 'Why me?' to God. She was just very sad for this poor little person who had not made it into the world.

She didn't reveal how she really felt to Gough or the boys but, quietly, she promised herself she would definitely have another child. Knowing she had to go to a local clinic and have a curette, her mother pronounced in her dramatic fashion that 'Margaret will not have any more children.' This only made Margaret more determined. When Gough won the pre-selection, defeating eight rivals by 249 votes to 163, she knew that her life was about to change. She may have married a lawyer but knowing how passionate he had become about politics, she understood that nothing would stop him until he succeeded.

When she discussed with him the possibility of her joining the Labor Party, he made no attempt to persuade her for his own sake. All he said was, 'Just choose the party that has the most things with which you agree. You are never going to be in accordance with everything that a political party puts up.' She thought that was a sane and practical way to approach the question. Not unsurprisingly, she chose the Labor Party. Of course she wanted to support him in whatever he chose to become. Of course she saw such support as part of the commitment she had made when she married him. But, in truth, she would never have joined the Liberal Party because she loathed their sense of superiority, their snobbishness, their belief in their right to rule. But most of all, especially based on her working experience as a social worker, she did not believe they had a genuine commitment to help or care for those less fortunate.

She was not, however, fascinated by the machinations or inner workings of the party machine. With her trademark droll humour and understatement she confessed to finding party meetings 'a bit dreary'. Her solution was to take her knitting. She figured if she was going to be bored she might as well make practical use of the time.

Six months later, in October 1952, Bert Lazzarini died and a by-election was called. The boys were far more excited about the new Holden that suddenly arrived on their front lawn. It was pale blue with the number plate AGK-999, which they pretended stood for Attorney-General.

For their father, it meant an ability to canvass a far greater area than on foot. His driving, however, was atrocious. Nick recalls, 'Father was a terrible driver, always crunching the gears, a danger to himself and others.' Not until they were adults did they find out that one night he had actually flipped the car in the rain outside the Gunnamatta Bay baths.

The children certainly let him know that they preferred to have their mother behind the wheel. One night, a few years later, they were all in the car on their way to the Blue Mountains. Their father was driving. Margaret turned around to check on the three boys in the back seat. Nick and Tony were both asleep. Stephen was sitting up, straight-backed, his eyes wide open.

'Why aren't you asleep like your brothers?' asked Margaret.

'Because I want to be awake when I die,' young Stephen earnestly replied.

Nevertheless, the car was a great asset to Gough as he toured the electorate of Werriwa. So too was the credit squeeze and high employment created by the Menzies–Fadden coalition.

On 29 November 1952 Gough Whitlam more than trebled Lazzarini's previous majority, gaining a 12 per cent swing to Labor. He was thirty-six. Eight-year-old Tony and six-year-old Nick had once again spent the day handing out 'how to vote' cards for their father. Margaret had spent the day in the kitchen, slaving over food for the victory party, with the help of her friendly neighbours. The keg was already gushing in the backyard when the results came through. Party members, polling booth workers, Labor MPs, their wives and children poured into the Whitlam home to celebrate his becoming a member of the House of Representatives. Margaret loved a celebration. Especially a victory.

It was the first of many election nights when Margaret fed the hordes. She was happy to do it with the help of neighbours and party wives eager to cut up the sandwiches and buckets of fruit. Having grown up with her mother's constant celebrations and parties she had developed a talent for organisation and making everyone feel welcome and at home. Her instinct was always to make the most of any occasion. She genuinely enjoyed herself and made other people relaxed enough to join her pleasure. Gough stood around, talking and laughing with a half-full beer in his hand, as people slapped him on the back. There was always a huge cake to cut, together, because he would never know how to slice it correctly without Margaret's expert advice. Amid the cheers and whistles, they smiled at each other above the hundreds of heads crammed together in the backyard. He kissed her and told her how much he loved her.

These nights were a far cry from their elegant dinners together in the plush red velvet booths in Romano's but they enjoyed them just as much. This victory party marked the beginning of a new adventure. They would throw themselves into its challenges, together.

Margaret did not resent the fact that Gough's new political career would determine their future. She was very proud of him. She knew how hard he had worked to get here and was convinced he deserved the success. What she didn't realise was how much the responsibility for bringing up the children, organising their lives and the endless domestic chores would rest entirely on her shoulders. She was now a 'political' wife and had no real idea of just how much more would be expected of her.

Gough was away in Canberra from Monday to Friday. He was a loner, preferring to spend time researching and writing speeches in the parliamentary library than in the bar with the other blokes. He rang Margaret at home every night and always spoke to the boys about their day. He felt guilty about spending so much time away from them but enjoyed his new position in the national parliament. Canberra was his home town. He stayed with his parents, enjoying once more his mother's home cooking. The roads he walked along to get to and from parliament were the same roads his father had walked when he was in the public service. He was buoyed by Canberra's familiarity and its fixed rituals.

His colleagues, however, were still suspicious of him. Even though Chifley had supported his pre-selection because he knew the party needed men like Whitlam, the old guard did not trust him. His background, his education, his pedantry – all set him apart. As a lifelong loner, used to being treated as different, he didn't let it bother him. He did, however, miss his darling Margaret. The children too – but it was Margaret he ached for, just as he had during the war when they were separated. Fridays could never come soon enough for him. Just to see her face smiling at him as he came through the front door lifted the gloom of the loneliness. They each needed the physical and sexual closeness that was such an important part of their happiness.

In Opposition now, due to Chifley's attempts to nationalise the banks, his colleagues were divided on many fronts. What's more, they seemed to enjoy their internal ideological and tactical fights, even if it meant they prevented them from winning the next election. They would rather lose the election than give in to their enemies. Gough couldn't believe how stupid this was for a political party. He kept telling them, 'Only the impotent are pure.' They hugged their hatreds to their chests like life jackets in a storm. This was the beginning of what became the biggest split in the party, which would keep them out of power for the next twenty-three years.

Labor Party members known as the Groupers, a tribe of anti-Communist ideologues, mostly committed Catholics, were based in Melbourne and led by the Catholic layman B. A. Santamaria. Gough noted the large number of Catholics in the parliamentary Labor Party he had joined but was also aware of the anti-Catholic discrimination in the Coalition government, which resulted in no Catholic ever being appointed as the secretary of a government department. The vehemence and discrimination of both political sides surprised and disturbed him. He was against discrimination in any form.

Into this disarray landed Menzies' attempt to pass a bill making the Communist Party an illegal organisation. Garfield Barwick had drafted it and Menzies first introduced it in 1950. Gough despised it. He believed that Communists, like any other party in a democracy, were entitled to run for parliament. He spent his days fighting against the bill and encouraging others to do the same.

Alone in Cronulla, Margaret was involved in her own disputes. The running conflict between her two sons was making her very unhappy. One day, out of sheer desperation, Margaret had locked all the doors and windows in the house with Tony outside. Tony was running from one locked window to another, bashing on them, calling out, 'Mum, let me in. Mum let me in.'

Margaret sat inside the locked house, her jaw fixed in anger, refusing to answer him. They had finally pushed her too far. Both boys were growing taller and stronger every day. She had tried the old line, 'Wait until your father gets home' but they knew that by the weekend she would have cooled down. She also knew that Gough was so pleased to see them on the weekend that the last thing he wanted was to be an ogre. Instead, he tended to spoil them rotten. The week before, in the middle of one of their fights, she had even resorted to ringing up the husband of one of their neighbours to come around and discipline them. He responded to her emergency request but was unwilling to take on the disciplinary role of their father.

So here she was, locked inside her own house with her eldest son bashing on the window. Well, he could wait for her to cool down. He knew she hated fighting, disobedience and rudeness. She knew they were probably missing Gough and were testing her out but she was not going to give in to this behaviour – that way, chaos ruled. Occasionally she would lose her patience and give them a good whack with her hand. The sound was always worse than the sting. Nick would cry. Tony never did.

Gough's solution when he was home on weekends was to set them all chores to be done, like sitting up on the roof to scoop the leaves out of the gutters. Tony loved it but Nick would stand at the bottom of the ladder, pleading, 'No, Father, please, Father.' No amount of pleading would cause Gough to relent.

Recently it had been young Stephen who was in trouble for not completing his chores. Gough was literally chasing him around the garden to make him do it. When they were small he had read to them the same Greek and Roman myths he had been read as a child. Stephen suddenly stopped running away from his father, turned around and shouted, 'Who do you think you are? Apollo?' Gough dissolved into helpless laughter. If you could make him laugh you had won.

Nick and Tony had resorted to cheating. Gough had set them weed quotas. They were ordered to fill so many buckets of weeds from the extra block next door that they had recently purchased and Margaret was attempting to tame into a beautiful garden. When it was time for Gough to inspect the buckets he didn't suspect that beneath the weeds on top, the buckets were filled with soil and rocks. Gough was inclined to trust too easily.

Nevertheless, the boys had all placed their father on a pedestal and were proud of his achievements.

Margaret was still intent on having another child. This time she hoped it would be a girl. The family needed another female presence. When Gough asked, 'Are you sure you're not too old?' she scoffed at him. Who was he to argue?

In June 1951, Ben Chifley died. His authority and the deep affection they all held for him had kept the warring factions at bay. The elevation of Doc Evatt to the leadership only exacerbated the conflict. Evatt's loathing of the party's emerging Catholic right wing, and refusal to submit to the *Communist Party Dissolution Act*, led to his enemies calling him 'The best friend that the Communists in Australia had ever known'. His newly elected deputy, Arthur Calwell, made no secret of his disdain for him or his desire to take over the leadership. It was into this cauldron of poison that Gough Whitlam was plunged when he joined his colleagues at his first Caucus meeting in February 1953.

He finally stood up in the House to deliver his maiden speech on 19 March 1953. It was a speech he had been writing in his head ever since he first made the decision to become a politician. He had deeply researched it, analysed it, dreamt of it, written many drafts of it and practised speaking it, until it was honed to perfection. It was the distillation of all that he had come to believe Australia needed to be achieved to make it the great nation he wished it to become.

A few minutes after he had begun to speak John McEwen from the Country Party interjected. Despite a reprimand from the Speaker, Gough could not resist adding a stinging retort of his own. 'I thought the Minister for Commerce and Agriculture [McEwen] had returned to the more congenial climate of Disraeli's day. I recollect that Disraeli said, on the occasion of his maiden speech, "The time will come when you shall hear me." Perhaps I should say, "The time will come when you may interrupt me".'

And with that first retort, the parliament was aware that Whitlam was not only polished, well educated, intelligent and possessed of a quick wit, he would be someone to be reckoned with. He proceeded to chastise the government for its failure and inefficiencies regarding housing, sewerage, hospitals, schools and unemployment. He backed up his attack with a plethora of detailed research, making it very clear that his own electorate of Werriwa, where he lived with his young family, was a perfect example of what had become national inefficiencies and failures of the Commonwealth to respond to the needs of the post-war generation.

The need for the government to take national responsibility for free education at all levels was a persistent policy goal from the beginning of his political career. 'Everybody in Australia is entitled, without cost to the individual, to the same educational facilities, whether it be in respect of education at the kindergarten or tertiary stage or the post-graduate stage.' Radical words – then and now.

At the conclusion of his maiden speech, Clyde Cameron, the Labor member for Hindmarsh, believed that he had just heard a future Labor Prime Minister. Gough gave the impression he agreed with him. From that day on he became a skilled and powerful parliamentary performer. It was clear that he was perfectly suited to its demands.

Sitting above it all in the gallery, Margaret was not surprised that her husband's performance was of such a high standard. She never doubted that he had all the necessary attributes, knowledge and talent for such a public profession. Always attuned to the overt or hidden reactions of other people, she knew also that political advancement for him would not be easy because his colleagues were suspicious of him, not just because he was so much more erudite and witty than them but because everything about him – from the cut of his suit to the upward thrust of his head – for them spelt 'silvertail'. She knew that he was so absorbed in his work and his parliamentary speeches that he was immune to their snide glances and sneering asides. Even when she pointed it out to him, he dismissed their attitudes. He was at first amused by the hostility of members of the Liberal Party who accused him of being a 'class traitor'.

Just before his political career began, they were both asked out to what they could only assume later was a 'seduction' dinner. One of Menzies' acolytes slipped into the conversation the lure that Menzies was very keen to have him on his side. Their main line of argument was that the Whitlams belonged with the Liberals. They spelt it out. 'How could you possibly mix with "them"? You are both one of "us".' (They were genuinely incredulous that a couple with the background of the Whitlams would actually choose to join the Labor Party, with all its working-class unionists and 'common' people.)

Sick of their failure to even begin to comprehend why he would never join the Liberal Party, Gough retorted, 'You really want to know? It's because the Labor Party cares about the less privileged in our community and the Liberal Party doesn't.' The subject was dropped. Most members at their table settled back to enjoy the dinner and the wine. On the way home Margaret and Gough both snorted at the attitude of the Liberals, who could not possibly accept that class had nothing to do with their decision. For the Whitlams, it was all about the difference in the parties' values.

By the time the baby that Margaret had been so determined to have was due, both of them were desperately hoping for a daughter. On cue, pink-cheeked and curly-haired, Catherine Julia Whitlam, 8 pounds 2 ounces arrived on 2 February 1954. Margaret thought she was very bonny. This time Gough said, with tears in his eyes, 'Now I will have someone who will love me all my life.'

The day after Catherine's birth, the young Queen Elizabeth II was making her Royal Visit to Sydney. Gough's task was to get all the boys ready to take them to the hospital to see their mother and their new little sister and then whip them off to Farm Cove to see the Queen. Tony and Nick wore matching white shirts and shorts, and Stephen, who was only four, looked very cute in his sailor suit as they all lined up outside the window of their mother's hospital room. It was outside of visiting hours so they had to content themselves with waving to their mother, who blew kisses at them while holding up baby Catherine for them to peer at through the glass.

The Queen finally arrived at Farm Cove to be greeted by Prime Minister Menzies on a specially built floating pontoon and then by the Premier of New South Wales, Joe Cahill, when she stepped onto Sydney soil. (The two men had both been determined to greet her first.)

The Whitlam boys were far more excited to spot their grandfather, Bill Dovey, who, having just been appointed to the Supreme Court as Chief Judge in Divorce, was standing head and shoulders above all the other dignitaries on the pontoon, resplendent as ever in his morning suit. All three of them started shouting out, 'Pa! Pa! Hello, Pa! We're over here!' very loudly, waving their arms around wildly while jumping up and down to try and gain his attention. Gough stood by, unable and unwilling to control their loud excitement at seeing their grandfather.

Both the older boys had established very close relationships with their very different grandparents. 'Pa' Dovey smoked and drank and taught them to play snooker and billiards on the full-size table he had in his basement. He also had cases of Coca-Cola which he let them drink at whim. They were aware that he knew a lot of people involved in cricket and football, which he loved, unlike their father, who had no interest in sport.

They also loved to visit the Whitlam grandparents when they were in Canberra. Gough's mother cooked them huge, delicious meals with fresh fruit and vegetables from their Grandpa's garden. Nick particularly liked being taken into Grandpa's book-lined study, filled with the sweet aroma of fresh cigars. Whenever Fred was travelling round the world as Australia's representative at the UN Commission on Human Rights, he always sent them a postcard.

Unlike Stephen, whom both Tony and Nick teased mercilessly, they were very taken with their little sister, Catherine, and loved to pop her in the pram and parade her around to the neighbours.

Margaret's mother was so pleased to finally have a grand-daughter to make pretty dresses for and show off.

After Catherine's birth, the doctor advised Margaret to have her tubes tied. She agreed but was unprepared for how disturbed she felt afterwards. She told one of her friends that it made her feel 'weird' and 'depressed', which was very unusual for someone who was always so positive. The doctor reminded her that she was fit and healthy; so were her four children. Even though she told herself to 'snap out of it, Margaret', it took quite a while for her to come to terms with the fact that she could not have any more children – not that she wanted to, but she hated having the choice taken away from her.

Now that Gough's parliamentary career was in full swing, his absences from home were even longer. As he had no formal electorate office in Cronulla, their home was always open to anyone who knocked on the front door. Margaret welcomed them all with a smile. No one was ever turned away or left without a cup of tea and biscuits. Gough took every one of his constituents' problems seriously and always did his best to solve them. Both of them took their services to the community as a personal responsibility. These were good people who needed their help.

Even if Margaret was in her thongs or her dressing gown, she would invite the visitors in, sit them down and listen to their problems. As the wife of a member of parliament who was also involved in many community meetings and discussion groups like the WEA (Workers' Educational Association), she took herself off to the Penguin Club, where she and others learnt how to properly chair a meeting, be a secretary to a committee, speak off the cuff and the skills of public speaking. She learnt that if you are asked to speak at a gathering or a meeting you don't say, 'Oh no, not me, I'm so inadequate.' You either stand up and say what you have to say or confess that you have nothing to add. Once she knew the rules and had practised the skills, she could contribute, with confidence, to any organisation.

Margaret met every new task with relish. She even enjoyed working out new ways of making the house-keeping money stretch to feed her growing family. Her neighbour and close friend Coralie Glover had three boys almost the same age as hers and they would buy a half side of lamb and share it. One of their neighbours had a contact at the local markets and four of them would buy cases of fruit and share them.

Whenever she managed to get a spare day to have lunch with someone in the city, before she left to go back on the long train journey to Cronulla she would buy two pounds of peas – one for Coralie and one for her – and spend the journey home shelling them. She hated wasting time. It never occurred to her to be embarrassed to be seen shelling peas on the train in her best clothes.

For a young woman who had had a cosseted lifestyle, having to do no domestic chores, never learning to cook and if she needed money only having to ask her devoted Daddy for it, she slipped easily into running a household, bringing up four children alone and enjoying life with her suburban neighbours. When faced with a task, she simply got on with it, devising the most efficient method. For Margaret the analogy of being dealt a hand of cards not of your choice and simply making the most of them was a way of life. What was even more important to her was to enjoy it. She was never bored with being a home-maker.

When parliament was sitting she and the children always listened to Question Time and cheered when they heard Gough's resonant voice. It made them all feel connected to him and his work, despite his absence. Having visited parliament and become familiar with its routines and personalities, she began to picture it like a theatrical play and was soon engrossed in the power games and the impassioned speeches. Question Time was her own personal soap opera. She never missed it.

Balls were very big in the 1950s. Every Friday night there seemed to be a local ball somewhere in the electorate. And they were expected to attend. Sometimes the Whitlams would race to three different social events in one night. These were not the kind of events they had attended in their youth, where you would find them mentioned in the social pages. Margaret couldn't have cared a hoot. She never moaned about having to spend precious weekend time being the wife of a politician because that wasn't how she thought of herself. Her mother was still making her wonderful clothes and she loved to dress up and have a good time with whoever she met.

The truth was, she was very happy. Fun, for her, was always there for the taking. One night she and Gough were at a ball in Cronulla with a group of local doctors and their wives. There was a fair on in the village so they all left the ball, jumped on the Ferris wheel – the women in their long ball gowns, the chaps in their dinner suits – had a couple of rides and went back to the ball. Often on Saturday nights they would share babysitters and have dinner parties where they would all bring a dish, to make it easier on the hostess. Both she and Gough threw themselves into their new political life and responsibilites in Cronulla with gusto.

Running a family practically on her own had given Margaret a new confidence and a sense of her own authority. Richard Glover, now a Sydney lawyer, son of Margaret's best friend and neighbour Coralie, had enjoyed many days running wild in the bushland and the caves with the Whitlam boys, but none of them ever had any doubt that Margaret was the boss. Whatever she said went, or they were in trouble.

She taught them all to swim and would give any one of them a good clip under the ears if they misbehaved according to her rules. Glover's fondest memories are of Margaret's Sunday lunches, famous for her special spaghetti with bolognese sauce. They would all sit together – neighbours, friends and the party faithful at one long table. Margaret sat at one end, Gough at the other. Margaret kept the conversation flowing. Glover was impressed with her manner of treating everyone as equals, no matter who they were. Unlike some of the other mothers, she was never in her husband's shadow; she never deferred to him. Even then, she was confident in being her own person.

When Catherine was one year old, Margaret was very excited about them all going to Coffs Harbour for the summer holidays. After only a week, however, she felt so ill she insisted they pack up. She thought to herself, 'If I'm going to die, it's going to be at home.' She had a raging thirst and on the trip back drank constantly from a bottle of lemonade. Nick grabbed the bottle from her and had a swig, which explained why when Margaret was diagnosed with hepatitis, so was Nick. He was very upset because he missed out on his school's swimming championships, for which he had been practising very hard. Both of them were ordered to stay in bed, drink lots of fluids and take no fats. From her sick bed, feeling as if death might be a welcome relief, Margaret farmed out Catherine, Tony and Stephen to various people while Gough looked after Margaret and Nick until parliament resumed. He was hopeless at cooking, so the neighbours fixed that. He did, however, read to them at length whatever historical book or constitutional treatise he was absorbed in at the time. They were just happy to have his complete attention.

Margaret swam regularly and played tennis with the locals. She and Gough even managed to squeeze in occasional visits to the ballet, the theatre or a concert. If they couldn't go together they would take it in turns to babysit and each would go with a friend. Even though she had established a household rule about the children sleeping in their own beds, whenever Gough was babysitting she would come home and find one or more of them in their double bed. The children knew he was a softie. He spent so little time with them, he couldn't help indulging their every wish.

Apart from Gough, the rest of the family were all keen swimmers and sports lovers. Knowing how much they would enjoy it, even if it wasn't his top priority, he had managed to get them all tickets to the 1956 Olympic Games in Melbourne.

Gough was not the sort of father who kicked a ball around with his sons or had the time to come to their swimming carnivals but their mother was always there. Nick said he never thought of his parents as anything different or special from all the other parents. He was hurt when other children accused his father of being a Communist – he didn't know what it meant but knew it was an insult. Nevertheless, he ignored it and continued to feel proud of him. Because of all the people who came to their home seeking help, the children knew he looked after the immigrants and was on the side of the workers. 'He made us feel good about ourselves and [about] what he was doing.'

Theirs was a simple childhood where there was love, security and good healthy food. Books were plentiful and their only real luxury.

Gough did occasionally take Margaret, Tony, Nick and Stephen to what they considered 'weird' events. One was a visit to the Sydney Showground in Moore Park to experience Billy Graham's Australian Crusade. Another was a visit to the Sydney Stadium for a performace by legendary US entertainer Bob Hope. Even though they could not understand why their father would make these strange choices, it is obvious that Gough wanted to experience one of the most successful persuaders in Billy Graham, and Bob Hope had the best sense of timing of any comic entertainer. These were both skills that Gough knew a successful politician – particularly one who wanted to lead the nation – would need. Who better to teach him the secrets of such skills than these two?

Not that there was much time for either skill, given the current state of his party. The secretive grouping led by Santamaria continued to create deep conflicts and suspicion. Because Gough did not belong to any faction or group, it was assumed that he was an Evatt supporter. Although both of them were essentially loners, Gough's objection against the outside influence of the anti-Communist Catholics – who later split the party by becoming the DLP – 'was that they were neither Democratic, nor Labor, nor a party'. He called it a cult.

Gough often allowed his tongue free rein when attacking his opponents. He enjoyed the theatricality of the parliamentary jousting. As if performing for his wife, who he knew would be listening on the radio at home, he relished his castigation of his enemies' flaws. Later that evening when he rang her, they would share their delight at his barbs. He called Garfield Barwick 'a bumptious bastard', said Wentworth manifested a 'hereditary streak of insanity'. Sometimes, however, he went a step too far in his cruelty. When he called Billy McMahon 'a quean' he returned to apologise, but most members who had been present considered he had damaged not just McMahon but himself. Always lurking behind the confident façade of the learned politician, was the the 'too smart by half' schoolboy, who just couldn't resist a cruel but devastating quip. The problem was that an hour later he had forgotten the incident; he would have moved on. What he failed to recognise was that the victims of his viperish tongue never forgot. Or forgave.

Margaret was well aware of this tendency in her husband to overstep the mark. On occasions she had been the target of his verbal whiplashing. It hurt her. Sometimes it even reduced her to tears. He was always rather shocked when he was forced to realise that he had gone too far and immediately set about trying to apologise to her. She, however, was a sulker, and sometimes it took her several days to forgive him, despite his attempts to make it up to her. He had a quick and blood-rushing-to-the-head temper which was often over as soon as the wounds had been inflicted. Even though he often regretted it when the recipient was someone he loved, he seemed incapable of controlling it. Years of a Baptist upbringing based on the suppression of extreme emotions meant that when the banks of temper burst there was a flood of vituperative words which, once said, were impossible to take back. Margaret's anger was usually based on a rational argument against behaviour which she refused to tolerate. It was designed to correct the behaviour, not to inflict personal hurt. Her method of punishment – silence and coldness – was an effective deterrent where her husband was concerned because he hated to be 'in her bad books'. He also respected her for refusing to tolerate what he knew to be his explosive temper. His political opponents, however, were never given that respect. Adversarial politics suited him and he was an increasingly skilled player of the game.

Despite the occasional bout of domestic jousting, they were both very content with their life in Cronulla. Margaret had worked hard to make her domestic chores less onerous, leaving her more time to read and engage in activities she enjoyed, like concerts and theatre in the city. She had also wrested control over her boisterous boys, who had been forced to accept that her word would always be backed up by their father. She had made some very close friends in the local community and as a couple the Whitlams were popular and respected for the work they did to improve the living conditions in the district.

Life had finally settled into an even and enjoyable routine for all the members of the Whitlam clan. Just when Margaret and Gough thought they could finally settle back and relax, a huge spanner was thrown into the well-oiled machine of their daily lives.

The fundamental things apply

In 1955, Gough arrived home to the open arms of his beloved Margaret with the news that they had to move house. She was not pleased. Just as he had predicted, the post-war housing boom had spread itself long distances from the city of Sydney. The huge wave of young married couples and immigrants desperate to establish a new life for themselves and their families swamped the new suburbs despite their lack of basic facilities. Gough's electorate of Werriwa had become so popular with people choosing to live there that the Electoral Commission had made the decision to divide it into halves and redistribute the boundaries. Gough had to choose which of these two electorates he would represent. Taking the name of Werriwa with him he had made the decision to represent the subdivisions of Liverpool,

Cabramatta and Fairfield, which included 65 per cent of the electors in the western half of his old electorate.

It was necessary to live in his new electorate to prove that it was where his new allegiances lay. This meant the Whitlams had to leave their much loved home at 2 Wangi Avenue and all their friends in Cronulla.

Tony, the eldest, who had been very young when they moved to Cronulla, was furious. He had his long-established friends there and had just started loving to surf with his mates. Nick also had his gang but was more like Margaret in his attitude towards the future: the present was good but the future was a new adventure. Stephen and Catherine were too young to really care.

Margaret was at first devastated at having to leave the house that she had so lovingly planned and decorated. Even more important was the garden surrounding their house and the one she had established on the block next door that Gough's quiz winnings had secured for them. Gough explained to her that his future as a politician depended on this move and, as an additional lure, he added the vision of a bigger house that would more easily incorporate four children.

Ever the pragmatist, she grieved the loss of her first home and then looked forward. When they couldn't find a house large enough to accommodate their large family, they bought a block of land on a former vineyard in Cabramatta and planned a new house.

This one was also designed by an architect and was split-level in the latest fashion, with four bedrooms. Unlike the others on the block, which were mostly small fibro houses, theirs was all brick with a peacock-blue front door and huge blue-and-white awnings to shade the large glass windows. Margaret was very pleased with it, especially as this time the cupboards and shelves were the right height for a very tall family.

Once again Margaret did the hard slog of making a garden from dirt and rubble. She was especially fond of the climbing pink Lorraine Lee rose which she trained over the top of the front door.

The miscarriage had determined that she had two separate groups of children. Tony and Nick were the Cronulla kids. Stephen and Catherine were the Cabramatta kids. Tony persisted in his reluctance to leave Cronulla. Cabramatta was rural. Most weekends would find him with his thumb up, hitch-hiking a ride back to Cronulla to surf with his mates. Margaret and Gough didn't try to stop him; they knew the importance of friends when you were a teenager.

Nick was also reluctant to leave but, being the most gregarious of all the children and the most like his mother in temperament and outlook, he soon decided to join in all the local activities of the athletics club. He revelled most in practising his flirting skills with the Cabramatta girls at the local dances.

Stephen was seven when they moved and, unlike his older brothers, had no interest in sport. Like his father, he preferred to read books and stay at home.

Tony and Nick made a habit of picking on Stephen because they said he didn't have to do chores like they had been forced to at his age. This was probably true because their father was much busier now and had many more people making demands on him. Catherine was three and has no memories of living in Cronulla.

Margaret's mother was very displeased with the move. On their first Christmas in Cabramatta, which was not on the coast like Cronulla, it was so hot that she spent most of it in the bath, trying to cool down. 'From now on Margaret,' she announced, 'all Christmas days will be spent in Vaucluse.'

Margaret was sorry to have been forced to leave their first home but looked forward to a new chapter in their lives. She immediately started another WEA women's group like the one she had joined in Cronulla. Stephen used to sneak into the living room on the nights he called 'Mum's culture evenings'. He told his mother he liked to listen to 'the convos'. Margaret made sure she never lost contact with her Cronulla friends by continuing to invite them to her even bigger Sunday lunches.

Richard Glover remembers going to one lunch where twenty-five people were seated at the long table. Just prior to lunch being served Gough read something in the paper that caused him to go ballistic. He stood up from the table and started shouting, pacing around the room, his temper totally out of control. Margaret, hearing the rumpus, suddenly appeared in the dining room with the spaghetti ladle still in her hand. Glover thought she might be going to hit Gough with it.

Firmly but very calmly she said, 'Gough, we can't have this behaviour in front of all these people. Now settle down, darling, and go back to your seat.' Gough stopped in his tracks, closed his mouth and took himself quietly back to his chair at the head of the table. Not another word was said.

Only Margaret could admonish him in this way. She knew exactly what tone of voice to use, what words to say, in order to calm him down and make him gain control of himself. He responded to her words because he respected her judgement. He also knew that she always had his best interests at heart. When he was in the full fury of the tornado that was his temper, he was either incapable or unwilling to stop himself. Tony, the firstborn, was well aware of his mother's calming influence on his father. He had witnessed his father's tendency to 'spin right out of control' once his temper or his bull-headedness took over. Margaret was the only person who could bring him back to earth. Tony observed how she gave him 'a level grounding in what normal, mainstream life and behaviour was like'. She simply refused to let him indulge himself in an emotional tirade in front of other people. Such behaviour was to her rude and totally unacceptable.

By 1958 both Tony and Nick were attending Sydney Boys High, which was one of the top selective secondary state schools in New South Wales. Entrance to study involves passing a very strict exam. Even the very rich could not buy their sons a place there. Both Tony and Nick were openly proud that they had gained entrance in their own right.

Being a great joiner of clubs, Margaret joined the school's Ladies' Auxiliary, becoming its president in 1959. Most of the students at the school lived in the eastern suburbs. The drive from Cabramatta was over an hour and a big commitment for her, but she was prepared to do it as she saw it as part of being a responsible parent. She fully understood that Gough had other commitments.

Stephen attended the local Cabramatta public school and so did Catherine as soon as she was old enough. They both loved Cabramatta as it was then, particularly the freedom of being able to roam the open spaces and visit the stables with the huge mulberry tree across the road from their house. Their favourite after-school play activity was to swing from the ropes they had tied to the massive gum trees and fly out over the creek.

Gough had grown up in Canberra when it was an unfinished city. Cabramatta's unsealed roads and houses surrounded by paddocks were familiar sights to him. Margaret, on the other hand, having grown up in cosmopolitan Bondi and exclusive Vaucluse, liked the unfamiliar aspects of Cabramatta. She was a woman who embraced difference because it spelt new experiences, new adventures.

Despite the intensity of the summer heat, Cabramatta had no swimming pool. Margaret was forced to drive herself and the children to the pools in Bankstown or Granville. Edna Ryan, the well-known feminist and social reformer on the Fairfield Council, joined forces with Margaret to establish the Cabramatta swimming pool. Margaret was the first president of its swimming club and Catherine has vivid memories of her with a timing watch around her neck, directing the swimming races with great command and enthusiasm.

While Margaret had been overseeing the building of the new house and settling the children into their new schools and new neighbourhood, Gough had been reconsidering the relationship between the Labor Party and the obstacles that the Constitution presented to the possibilities of reform. Membership of the Parliamentary Joint Committee on Constitutional Reform gave him a detailed knowledge of the inner workings of the parliamentary committees and cross-party cooperation and review. This was the true nuts and bolts of government, which to many members meant hours of boring work. Gough realised it was the true pathway to reforming the Constitution. It opened his mind to possibilities that had previously been considered closed to the party.

This was the catalyst, the major leap forward in his intellectual evolution. Chifley had railed against the barriers of the Constitution which he said 'had been erected by conservatives in Australia, been interpreted by conservative High Court judges and so there's really not much future for reformed government'. Gough had finally found a way to change all this.

The Committee's report, which had a distinctive blue cover, became Gough's bible. Section 96, through grants to the states, offered possibilities for public enterprise in Australia. Section 127 excluded 'aboriginal natives' from the census and the Committee's recommendation to repeal this section was the beginning of constitutional changes to grant human rights and land rights to Aboriginal Australians.

Gough talked to Margaret of his despair at the internal brawling, the deep ructions and seemingly insoluble tribal and religious hatreds of his party, which continued to be trapped in the past. He believed that the only way forward was leadership – his leadership. She agreed with him and encouraged him to pursue that goal.

On Remembrance Day in 1959 – a day that would become synonymous with the name Whitlam from 1975 onwards – it was the quiet, calm voice of fellow politician and returned serviceman Lance Barnard who suggested his next political move. 'The Doc will be going. You ought to stand for Deputy.' These words were life-changing for Gough, Margaret and the ALP.

Unlike Gough, Lance Barnard had a Labor pedigree that stretched back for three decades. He was jovial, gentle and unambitious and therefore the perfect numbers man for the leader he hoped Gough would become. They were exact opposites in terms of personality and talents. These two opposites formed a great team.

On 19 November 1959 Margaret also made a life-changing decision. It was her fortieth birthday. She celebrated by having her hair cut; she had been growing it since she was a child. Having rung her mother to tell her of the decision, they met at David Jones in the city. A hairdresser called Antoine cut off her plaits and gave her what was fashionably called 'a long bob'. Margaret was instantly delighted with the result. All traces of grey hair seemed to have disappeared and her hair now appeared glossy and thick.

By sheer chance she bumped into her father in the city after lunch. He kissed her on both cheeks, then looked at her and exclaimed, 'Good God, girl! What have you done?'

Margaret replied smugly, 'I've had my hair cut.'

He responded favourably, unable to take his eyes off her because she looked so different. 'And you've had it dyed too.'

Pleased with this observation she said, 'I have not. Absolutely not.'

Gough, however, when he saw it, was very displeased. He had always loved her long hair. It was the fact that she had just gone ahead and cut it off without discussing it with him that upset him the most. This was not a matter of his being proprietorial. He had simply loved how his wife had looked. The fact that she would make an instant decision, knowing he would care, showed an insensitivity on her part. He was hurt rather than angry. Not that he would ever admit to being vulnerable over such a trivial thing as a hair-cut. Of course he soon became accustomed to her new look and frequently told her how attractive she looked. The young man who had read her romantic poetry on their honeymoon was still there, even if he was preoccupied with section 68 of the Australian Constitution.

In March 1960, when Arthur Calwell was elected leader, replacing Dr H. V. Evatt, who was taking up the position of Chief Justice of the NSW Supreme Court, Calwell was surprised when Whitlam was elected as his deputy. Barnard had worked his magic. At forty-three Gough was the youngest ALP deputy leader since 1920, he was unaligned in terms of factions, he was not a Catholic or even a religious man and he was determined to drag the party out of the past and into the future as a government and not an Opposition. His skills as a parliamentary performer had singled him out as someone who could really take it up to the Menzies government. In fact, Menzies himself treated his questions with respect, answering them promptly. Gough had also shown a mastery of the new medium of television. He seemed to revel in its power, much as Menzies had dominated on the radio. With Lance Barnard working behind the scenes, gathering support, they were a winning combination. Gough had spent six years on the back bench, researching and planning policies, preparing himself for this possibility.

Always the loner, apart from Barnard he had made few friends. His solitary childhood and cloistered family life had not prepared him for the tribal rituals or male bonding that constituted Australian mateship in politics. Nevertheless on 7 March 1960 he was duly elected Deputy Leader of the ALP. His pairing with Arthur Calwell as leader caused an unusual outbreak of optimism in the party. Graham Freudenberg, a talented young journalist, became Calwell's press secretary and Whitlam appointed John Menadue as his private secretary. These two men were to become essential to Gough, both personally and politically, throughout his future career.

The *Canberra Times* was keen to point out Gough's failings as a future leader. 'Mr Whitlam would appear to have difficulty in interpreting the phrase self-discipline and his impetuous remarks and offensive terms directed at some government members in debate have reduced him in stature in the eyes of experienced politicians on both sides of Parliament.'

John Menadue soon became well acquainted with his temper. He knew that ten minutes after his outburst Gough didn't know what he had said or realise what hurt he had inflicted. Tears from some members of his staff were not uncommon. Menadue witnessed how hard he drove himself and knew that he expected the same from those who worked for him. His signature impatience made him ill-equipped to deal with those who could not match his energy or pace.

When Menadue first met Margaret he was immediately impressed with how warm and friendly she was. 'She always asked after my family, remembered the kids' names, where they were and what they were doing.' Gough on the other hand was ill-at-ease, even with his staff and other ALP members. Menadue saw a man who was 'very shy – painfully so at times . . . We all project a public persona to protect our private self. For politicians it is even more important. His confidence on the public platform was often at variance with the diffident private person.'

Margaret, he soon came to realise, was 'an enormous help in stabilising and sustaining him. She was calm and sensible. Her feet always firmly planted on the ground.' Even when Gough was irritated by her good advice, Menadue noted that he always said, 'She is a very good wife to me.'

Gough's weaknesses were openly on display for everyone to observe: his pedantry, his impatience, the way he showed off his erudition. His major strength was his skill with, and deep knowledge of, words, matched with a faultless memory. He could quote *Hansard*, the Classics, Acts of Parliament, the Bible and list the endless details of most major historical events, from ancient Greeks to the present. His childhood, his upbringing, his parents and his education had instilled in him an extraordinary amount of knowledge. He was always aware of the power of words to inform, persuade or defeat those who sought to outwit or contradict him. At official parliamentary dinners and lunches he outperformed every other leader, except Menzies.

Menadue described working with him as like being inside a powerhouse. He found him awe-inspiring, iconoclastic in his ideas and full of energy and excitement when expounding his big-picture ideas for change and reform, not just for the Labor Party but for the nation.

Menadue also enjoyed his droll sense of humour. He appreciated that Gough was aware of his inclination towards self-aggrandisement and was always prepared to send himself up. For example, whenever he set off the security alarms at airports he would proclaim, 'I think you will find that is my aura.' The problem was that many people took him literally and failed to appreciate his particular sense of humour.

Unlike many in his party, Gough knew that their support base needed to be expanded to include the ever-growing post-war sector of white-collar workers and middle-class employees. He worked hard at broadening the party's base because he knew the days when they could just rely on blue-collar trade unionists and the working-class faithful were over.

He was also aware of the misogyny and discrimination against women within the party. As early as 1960 he spoke of his support for feminism and the struggle of women to be treated as equals. At the New South Wales ALP Conference he berated the party for its failure to nominate a woman for the Senate. He was always a vocal supporter for equal pay.

His mother, having died in 1958 before he was Deputy Leader, never heard her son supporting women's causes. She had been a very strong woman, with firm beliefs which she was always confident in expressing, and would have been very proud of him. His father, who had always adored her, lasted only three more years without his beloved Martha. He died the day before the federal election in 1961, with Gough by his bedside.

Margaret described Fred Whitlam as a true gentleman, a pillar of the church, a highly intelligent and modest man. 'I wouldn't say he was self-deprecating – but he was a very modest man. Not like his son in that respect.'

Gough was always much more like his mother in his aggressive and judgemental opinions of people. She had encouraged this in him, together with an ability to argue a case and stick to it, no matter what anyone else said. Gough's father was much more measured in his judgements and solicitous of others' opinions.

His parents, despite their different natures, were always a close and devoted couple. Every day Fred had picked a violet for his wife, as they were her favourite flowers, and she would add it to a vase, next to all the others. Whenever he was gardening she would place two cups of tea on the windowsill for him, in case he was very thirsty from his hard labour. They loved each other deeply for all their lives.

They also both totally adored their only son, who always returned their devotion. Even when he was eighty and the subject of his relationship with his parents was mentioned during a television interview for a documentary, his eyes filled openly with tears as he said, 'My parents meant a great deal to me ... and their memory still does.' His words were choked but viewers had a rare glimpse of an emotional man.

Gough and Margaret each parented the way they had been brought up. Their children all attest to how much they were loved and nurtured.

Margaret had worked hard at perfecting her organisational skills. She had witnessed her mother organising her life in a manner whereby everyone's needs were met. She worked out how to get large amounts of food on the table in a short time, involved herself in all of the children's educational and sporting activities, and kept the house neat and tidy as well as having regular trips to the city to have lunch with friends.

The only area in which she failed was restricting the older boys' enjoyment of picking on their younger brother, Stephen. They called him 'the weed' or 'the puny one' and predicted he would never reach the age of thirteen. They mocked him for not being interested in sport and for imitating their father. Margaret could do nothing to stop this 'bullying and disgraceful behaviour'. She knew that if she took Stephen's side too often, it would only make it worse for him. Like most teenage boys, Tony and Nick took no notice of the fact that it upset their mother. They called Stephen and Catherine 'the brats' because they said they had many more privileges as younger children than they ever had. Margaret admitted that this was probably true because when they were little, she and Gough didn't have much money.

Tony is still of the firm belief that Nick was really his mum's favourite because he was a swimmer and always getting out of chores. He says that none of them are like her in their natures. 'She was a lot more sentimental than us. She wanted everybody to be happy. It was quite genuine. She instinctively wanted to see the best in people and really tried to be nice about them.' Whenever they were all engaged in a heated family discussion, Margaret would interrupt by saying, 'That's enough. Let us speak of fruit and flowers.' They would all send her up for it.

He says the only person he ever heard her really criticise was Janette Howard.

Gough, on the other hand, Tony says, really does hate some people and bears them grudges. 'Somebody could be a most charming host but if they spoke ill of one of his policies, he would never forget or forgive them. Never.'

What impressed Tony most about his mother was that she never panicked or overreacted. When Nick was about fifteen and a bit of a lad with the girls, Margaret answered the phone one night and a young girl said, 'I'm pregnant by your son Nick.' Margaret said, 'Just a second, you'd better talk to Nick about that.' Nick immediately took the phone and asked, 'Who the hell is this?'

It was clear that it was all teenage rubbish but what impressed Tony was how cool his mother was. She seemed to take it all in her stride and know exactly the right response.

Nick said that his mother, whom he took to calling Margaret or Margot, never talked to him about sex. All she would say

Edward Gough Whitlam and Miss Margaret Dovey on their wedding day at St Michael's in Vaucluse, Sydney, 24 April 1942. (SMH Picture by N. Brown/ Fairfax Photos)

July, 1963. Gough and Margaret meet son Nick, then seventeen, for lunch aboard the Italian liner *Galileo* in Brisbane. Nick was aboard the freighter *Port Alfred*, moored nearby, in which he was working his passage to the United States to enter Harvard University.

ABOVE: Gough at a Labor Party picnic at the National Fitness Camp in Sydney, 1972. (Photo by News Ltd / Newspix)

LEFT: 1965, Sydney. Then Deputy Opposition Leader, Gough with Margaret, Stephen and Catherine at Sydney Airport ahead of their tour of New Zealand.

(Photo by News Ltd / Newspix)

1 December 1972. Margaret and Gough share a toast with Bob and Hazel Hawke in the St Kilda Town Hall on the eve of the 1972 federal election. (News Ltd / Newspix)

ABOVE: Gough and Margaret with the Emperor and Empress of Japan, 1973. 'One feels such an ox in the presence of these finely built people,' Margaret commented. (NAA A6134 K16/11/73/68)

RIGHT: With Imelda Marcos of the Philippines at the opening of the Sydney Opera House, 1973. (NAA A6135 K26/10/73/26)

BELOW: Gough, Margaret and the then Deputy Premier of China, Deng Xiaoping, with interpreter Li Zhong (rear) in 1973. Margaret often accompanied Gough on official overseas visits. (NAA A8746 KN15/11/73/70)

ABOVE: The PM and his wife: Gough and Margaret pose for an official photo in the grounds of the Lodge, 1973. (NAA A8746 KN24/9/73/7)

RIGHT: 29 November 1977: now the former Prime Minister. Gough and Margaret dancing together at the Sutherland Civic Centre in Sydney.

(Photo by Guy Wilmott / Newspix)

Gough and Margaret in Sydney in 1983 when Margaret was made an Officer of the Order of Australia in recognition of her work in the community, education and the arts. She was delighted.

(Photo by News Ltd / Newspix)

Margaret and Gough with their grandson Edward Hugo Whitlam (aged eighteen months) at Nick's home, November 1982.

(SMH Photo by Robert Pearce, Fairfax Photos)

1987: Margaret holds up the front page of the *Daily Telegraph* newspaper covering the ALP's landslide victory in the 1972 federal election at the Bicentennial Historical Record launch in Sydney.

(Photo by News Ltd / Newspix)

Gough and Margaret at Sydney's Opera in the Park in 1989. Journalist Kristin Williamson described them as 'political royalty in Australia'. (Photo by Michael Perini / Newspix)

28 May 1996. At the presentation of an honorary doctorate from the University of New South Wales Australian Graduate School of Management to Nick Whitlam. (L–R) Margaret, Nick, his wife Judy and Gough. (Photo by Nick Cubbin / Newspix)

January 2003: Gough and Margaret perform the balcony scene from Shakespeare's *Romeo and Juliet* at the State Library of New South Wales. They offered their acting services for the opening of the library's Nelson Meers Heritage Collection of rare texts. (Photo by Chris Pavlich / Newspix)

Gough and Margaret in September 2006. (Photo by Brianne Makin / Newspix)

just before he went out on a date was, 'Just remember, that girl is somebody's sister.'

By the time they left home to go to university Tony was 6 foot 7 and Nick 6 foot 4. The two younger children were also growing fast. Margaret just kept cooking healthy food and piling it on their plates until they were no longer hungry.

The one ritual that Nick remembered their father insisting on was shoe-cleaning every Sunday night. 'He would clean his shoes to perfection, spitting and buffing on the Kiwi and polishing to a high shine. All of the children were expected to do the same. And they did.'

Stephen took on the role of cooking for himself and Catherine if their parents were at a function. Catherine remembers her mother in short skirts 'above the knees', thongs on her feet, hose in her hand, always trying to revive the garden in the summer heat.

> She would let me and my best friend, Eileen, romp around on the lawn in our bathers while she sprayed us with the hose. She laughed along with us. Dad was always away a lot. I'd get very irritated when he came home because all our routines changed and Mum suddenly had to be available for electoral commitments that involved him. I would always ask her to bring me home something nice. She never forgot.

To a large extent, Margaret and Gough lived an ordinary life: the father worked away from the home, the mother looked after the house and the children. There were family squabbles, rivalries, jealousies, some resolved, others not. Theirs was a pretty normal everyday Australian existence. Except that always present, beneath the surface of their daily existence, was the inexorable movement towards a future that would mark them out as extraordinary.

In 1962, when Arthur Calwell was unable to take advantage of a European trip that Menzies had approved for the Opposition leader to familiarise themself with the entry of the United Kingdom to the European Common Market, Gough, as deputy Opposition leader, took his place. Margaret, of course, accompanied him. Despite his obsession with European history and culture he had never travelled abroad; he had never actually seen the cities or experienced the cultures that had been etched into his mind since he was a child.

Their first city to visit was Athens. Margaret thought Gough would faint, he was so excited to be on the steps of the Parthenon. He became the self-appointed tour guide and history lecturer for both Margaret and John Menadue, who had come as Gough's staff member. Menadue was utterly amazed at the depth and detail of Gough's knowledge about every city they visited. He could not believe how much knowledge this man had crammed inside his head. In galleries, Gough physically leapt from one painting to another, instructing them on every aspect of both the art and its place in the cultural history of the country. This would continue for six or seven hours, by which time Menadue said his legs were aching and his brain was numb. Gough was like a starving man at a banquet who could never seem to get enough sustenance. The more he sucked in, the more he desired. He wore them out. Nothing seemed to tire him.

Margaret was always the one to call a halt. 'John and I have had enough for today, darling. Leave something for tomorrow.' Menadue said that Gough would stare at her defiantly, grind his teeth, mutter something to himself and obey her.

As much as she loved it all too, Margaret knew when it was time to sit down, have a glass or two of wine and savour the experiences of the day. Obsessive and unrelenting as he was, Gough would have continued until midnight, oblivious to the fading energy of his companions.

Menadue described Margaret as 'a wonderful companion, warm and easy to be with, a tower of strength'. Without Margaret's calming presence and patient control of her husband's excessive enthusiasm, it is likely that Menadue would have collapsed from sheer exhaustion.

Gough felt and looked very much at home with the diplomats and leaders of European parliaments. This was his métier. No small talk, just discussions with a purpose. They met an amazing range of famous and powerful people, including Pope Paul VI, President Johnson, Billy Graham and the Black Panthers.

Back on home turf, it was back to hard slog. The ALP had failed to tackle the reform that was desperately needed and the split with the DLP was a running sore. In speech after speech Gough made it clear that his commitment was to equality of opportunity, not the doctrine of socialism to which the left wing of the ALP rigidly adhered.

In all these public meetings Margaret was always there, sitting in the audience, listening. And always knitting. She hated to be idle and found that knitting justified hours and hours of hearing her husband expound the virtues of section 96 of the Constitution – the charter of public enterprise. All the new and radical programs that Gough was proposing could in fact be funded through this section, which enabled the federal government to make grants to the states. He described precedents in overseas countries they had visited where federal funding of programs had achieved amazing reforms. Even though Margaret was therefore fully versed in all his intellectual and political arguments through hearing him espouse them so often, Gough never discussed them in any detail with her. He maintained a clear division between parliament and home, for which, it must be said, Margaret was grateful.

When he was with her or at home, he focused on family issues. If one of the children asked a political question he would, of course, answer it. But that answer could take a long time. A very long time. He was incapable of providing anything less than what he considered the best possible explanation and analysis of any question that interested him. And everything interested him, or could be linked to something that interested him.

One of the biggest policy differences between him and Calwell involved the White Australia policy. The party's continued commitment to this racist policy was to him 'ideologically intolerable and morally indefensible'.

In 1961, Whitlam had joined with Don Dunstan, the charismatic and progressive South Australian state member for Norwood, to prepare a paper advocating the removal of the words 'Maintenance of White Australia' from the party's plat- form. Arthur Calwell was furious with them, calling them both to a meeting in his Parliament House office, where he refused to believe that the workers would ever back them. He insisted that 'only the cranks, long-hairs, academics and do-gooders' wanted this change. He accused Gough of being disloyal to him. Gough insisted that publicly he had always been a loyal deputy to him but if called before a party committee, he would give his own opinion. He repeated to Calwell his belief that 'it was morally indefensible for a social democratic party to have the words "Maintenance of White Australia" on its platform'.

Dunstan noted that Calwell was apoplectic with rage at these words.

Calwell lobbied intensely against the Whitlam/Dunstan paper and when it was put at the federal conference, it received only seven votes.

This did not deter either Whitlam or Dunstan, both passionate progressive reformers of their party, particularly because they knew public opinion was on their side. In response to this pressure, the conference established an Immigration Review Committee, hoping this would push the issue into the background. The eventual motion which the committee proposed deferred its consideration until the next biennial conference.

Still undeterred, Dunstan's proposal at the 1965 conference was sufficiently minimalist not to upset the delegates and the motion to remove the words was unanimously supported. Gough was elated. As an impatient man, he had found the long, slow road to achieving policy change of any kind very hard to endure. Margaret was always at pains to convince him that if he was patient, and took it slowly, success would eventually result, but moderation of any kind was just not in his nature.

Another failing of his leader that upset Gough was his allowing himself (in Gough's view) to be 'duchessed' by the *Sydney Morning Herald* in the 1961 election. He hated duchessing or influence-seeking or lobbying by any powerful group or person. He refused to spend time with anyone he even suspected of it.

Gough's concern was based on a potential conflict of interest. In his view, if you got into bed with the media, or any powerful interest, then you always owed them. Once he was elected Deputy

Leader Gough would not own shares and would not accept retainers for legal work. He thought it imperative that he never be beholden to anyone. His family background and upbringing had ensured that he was never impressed with the trappings of money, power or influence – wherever it came from.

Margaret was not as Baptist in her dealings with the ruling class or the powerful as he was, although she was always careful with what she said to the media. Neither was she as scornful of those who sought to influence her husband as he was; she saw no point in alienating them. Gough may have been brilliant at devising policies but Margaret had all the instincts of a true political operator because she had a deep understanding of people and their motivations. Gough had no real interest or curiosity in people's hidden motives. Any form of psychoanalysis bored him. He did not wish to waste his time sitting around chatting or being introspective; he wanted to make things happen. He never really understood that these two things were not incompatible.

Gough's outstanding parliamentary performances, however, continued to sting his opponents. Menzies' personal choice for Attorney-General, Garfield Barwick, had proved to be a fizzer. He was never at ease in the bear-pit of parliament, which had none of the strict adherence to legal conventions as did the Sydney Bar, his training ground. Barwick had been accustomed to being accorded the highest respect but found none of it in the raw, brawling nature of parliamentary politics. When Whitlam's scorching retort 'This truculent runt [Barwick was short in stature] thinks he can get away with anything' rang out, Barwick was seen to physically reel back and was led from the Chamber, weeping. His political career had effectively ended. His memory of the humiliation inflicted by Gough, however, did not.

Gough's battle both outside and inside his party continued. He was relentless. When he didn't win by force of argument he wore his opponents down by the force of his personality and his powers of endurance.

Meanwhile, back home in Cabramatta, more and more constituents lined up outside the brick fence of the Whitlam home every weekend. They had come to their local member for help, knowing that he would listen carefully, take notes and do all he could for them. This was an area where Gough seemed to have endless patience. These people needed his help and he always showed them great care and understanding. Most of them were immigrants who reflected the latest wave of immigration to Australia. There were Maltese, Greeks and Lebanese, but the majority who had already established themselves in his electorate were Yugoslavs and Italians. The Yugoslav houses were brick and often had the top storey unfinished until more of their relatives arrived to live with them. The Italians lived further out because they had established market gardens; they never arrived empty-handed. Tomatoes were very welcome as Margaret was always cooking up a cauldron of bolognese sauce.

Gough conducted his interviews in the living room as electoral offices were only open on weekdays. His knowledge of and interest in the different cultures of the constituents only encouraged their numbers. Margaret never complained about these strangers who invaded her home on the weekends. She often gave them cups of tea and a biscuit while they were waiting. They knew her interest in and concern for them was as genuine as Gough's.

Margaret and Gough spent most weekends going to local events in a variety of clubs such as the Polish White Eagle Club, the Club Marconi and, of course, the RSL Diggers Club.

In 1962, Tony brought home a girlfriend named Kate Shea to meet the family. She openly admits that while she was smitten with Tony, it was Margaret she came to admire. She was totally in awe of her ability to feed this 'house of giants'. Margaret had an enormous Sunbeam frypan and in went all the eggs and bacon and tomatoes. Into the Mixmaster went the Milo, ice-cream and a few pints of milk. There were always huge piles of sliced fresh fruit. And that was just breakfast.

Kate couldn't believe Margaret's calm response when just before dinner the phone would ring and Gough would tell her he was bringing home six extra blokes for dinner. What's more, when they all arrived she was warm and welcoming, totally unruffled.

The incident that stands out most vividly in her mind is the night that she and Tony were getting dressed for a formal dinner. She was attempting to tie Tony's bow tie with a finger that was bleeding. When she left blood on his tailored white dinner shirt, he lost his inherited Whitlam temper and punched the bathroom door. His fist splintered a hole in it. Margaret said nothing. She calmly went to the magazine rack, tore out two pictures of the fountains of Rome and proceeded to tape them over the hole in the door. When reminded of this incident Margaret laughed and said, 'They were probably still there when we sold the house.'

Whenever she stayed in the Whitlam home, Kate and Tony would have sex in his bed, after which she'd slip back into Gough's study, where she was meant to be sleeping on the divan. She knew that Margaret was totally aware of what they were up to, but she made no comment. At 4 am Gough would often come into the study to make international phone calls. He would sit on the bed so totally absorbed in his phone conversation that he would be oblivious to the fact that he was sitting on Kate's legs. She said she would lie there not making a sound, thinking, 'This is probably history in the making I'm listening to.'

Kate kept her relationship going with Tony longer than it really lasted because she couldn't bear to think she would lose Margaret's friendship. She needn't have worried. Once you were Margaret's friend, she never forgot you. Even when Kate was married to someone else and having babies, little hand-knitted singlets from Margaret would arrive in the post. Margaret always remembered her friends' birthdays with a small gift or a phone call but never considered that her behaviour was extraordinary. This was not her upbringing, but her natural inclination.

In 1963, Nick received a letter that informed him that he had been accepted to study at Harvard University on a scholarship. He had learnt through swimming friends who had attained scholarships from American universities that it was worth sending in an application. When the letter arrived from Harvard and Gough read it first, he seriously contemplated tearing it up because he knew that there would be many extra expenses and was worried that they couldn't afford them. Nick was so excited at being accepted that Gough and Margaret decided they would just have to find a way to make it happen. Although Gough had limited corporate connections, he managed to arrange for Nick to work his passage to America as a supernumerary on a P&O cargo ship.

Nick still remembers that seventeen-year-old boy, sailing out through the heads of Sydney Harbour with tears streaming down his face. He didn't know when he would be returning home but the adventure of it all thrilled him beyond his expectations. Standing on the dock watching the ship disappear were his parents, both of them wiping tears from their eyes as the first of their babies left the country.

A year later Gough was awarded a grant to travel to America for three months to investigate forms of government. This time, however, the grant did not stretch to him taking Margaret, nor did their family budget. Instead of sitting down and feeling sorry for herself, Margaret thought, 'Blow this for a joke, I'm going too.' She cashed in a small insurance policy, which, together with money from her savings and a secret loan from her father, enabled her to follow Gough. Tony was at the ANU so she farmed out Stephen and Catherine to family and neighbours and took off.

The first week she spent entirely on her own, travelling across the States in a Greyhound bus before meeting up with Gough in Washington. Many women would be terrified at the prospect of such a journey but Margaret was positively exhilarated. It was the first time since she had married Gough that she didn't have to think about anyone but herself. She chose where to stay, what to eat, what to do. The luxury lay in just being able to please herself. It was a real adventure for her and she revelled in her freedom.

Once she met up with Gough, she was once again the wife of the Deputy Leader of the Australian Labor Party and had to assume the role. She enjoyed all the interesting and elegant dinners in Washington and New York with politicians and ambassadors but, secretly, she couldn't wait to be on her own again, travelling and staying at cheap places.

When Gough continued on to England, Margaret went to Boston, where Nick was working at his summer job as a swimming instructor, pool attendant and tennis companion at a community club. He was sharing a flat with two Australian and three American students. They gave Margaret the big bedroom, in return for which she became their chief cook and bottlewasher for a week. She loved it all.

Nick was getting around Boston on a motorbike and talked his mother into hopping on the back for a ride. She had never been more terrified and yelled her head off, despite Nick's urgings for her to stop scaring the neighbourhood. Nick had never seen his mother fearful of anything.

Her final stop was Chicago. By the time she reached it via Montreal and Niagara Falls she was literally down to her last ten dollars. She directed the cab driver to take her to the YWCA hotel and chatted away to him on the journey in her usual warm manner. As they approached the hotel he turned around to her and said, 'Why don't you go in, drop your things in your room then come back down? I'll take you for a drive around the city and then we'll have a roll in the hay.'

Never, in her entire life, had she been propositioned. Stopping herself from snorting, cool and calm as ever, Margaret replied, 'I think I might take a rain-check on that.' When she eventually told Gough about the cabbie who had put the hard word on her, they both shared a big laugh. Gough was not in the least bit worried about Margaret traipsing around the world on her own. He knew she was capable of dealing with any situation, no matter how difficult. He had total trust in her and in her capabilities. And even though he wouldn't tell her, he was quite chuffed at the thought that an American cabbie thought she was eminently beddable.

In New Orleans she had spent the night in a place that she later discovered was actually a brothel. She didn't care as it was cheap and right above the bus station. When she asked the taxi driver on the rank what it would cost to be driven around the city he said he would even take her to see the 'gordens', which she finally ascertained were the gardens where *Gone with the Wind* had been filmed. She loved seeing it all for herself as she had adored the film.

In San Francisco, the YWCA where she had stayed was across the road from a broadcasting station where she was told they taped television shows with a live audience. As it was her last day of freedom and it was free, she willingly joined the live audience laughing and clapping on cue. When she eventually arrived at the airport and checked in, she was confronted by a very distraught staff member from the Australian Consul General's Department. 'Mrs Whitlam. We have been looking everywhere for you. We knew you were flying home today. We were very worried that something had happened to you.'

She assured him that she was fine and there had been no need to worry. While he was escorting her to the VIP lounge she was quietly smiling to herself about the adventures she had enjoyed all on her own. The VIP lounge was certainly more comfortable than the waiting area of the Greyhound Bus Depot, but not nearly so exciting. Already she was missing the frisson that her freedom had given her, that secret buzz that came from just being herself and being able to act on a whim. Not feeling responsible for her children's or her husband's well-being had been quite intoxicating. She had felt high on it.

Once she was home again and life returned to its usual round of duties and routines, she realised that she never did anything that was hers alone. She also had no money left of her own. It was her mother who suggested she should go back to work. 'They're crying out for social workers, Margaret. I've seen the ads in the paper.' Now that Stephen and Catherine were both at school all day she decided to apply for a job that was advertised at the Parramatta District Hospital, which was close to home. They were delighted to have her work three days a week, or the equivalent.

For the first time in twenty years, she was earning her own money again. The real joy, however, was that she was once again an independent woman. The children noticed immediately how happy she had become. She had dinner with Tony in Canberra, where he was studying at the ANU, and he said to her, 'You'd never not work again, would you, Mum?'

Gough was also happy for her. His innate feminism gave him an understanding that work wasn't just about the money; it was about being your own person.

On 7 January 1965, her firstborn turned twenty-one. Tony wanted to celebrate it with home-made food and kegs of beer in their backyard. Margaret agreed to produce all the food, Catherine handed it around and Stephen served beer from the kegs. Gough just stood around, a beer in his hand, smiling at everyone. It was a classic 1960s 'Aussie-swill'–style birthday. They all had a great time. Margaret and Gough snuck off to bed early.

Stephen, only fourteen at the time, was highly amused at how progressively unsteady many of the male guests became. One bloke particularly stuck in his mind. He had a beer in one hand

and was attempting to relieve himself with the other by waving his member in high circles 'like sparklers on cracker night'.

Tony gave his bed to a friend who was incapable of driving home and took Stephen's bed. At 5.30 am Stephen wove his way between all the bodies passed out on the living room floor until he found an empty armchair, where he caught a few hours' sleep. Gough and Margaret slept soundly in their bed, pleased that their son and his friends had enjoyed themselves, in their own fashion. Neither of them ever attempted to impose their own tastes upon their children.

The government had decided to conscript young men to join America to fight a war in Vietnam. They were chosen by a lottery based on their date of birth. Anti-war demonstrations were being held in large numbers in America and soon followed in Australia.

Gough was fully behind his leader in opposing the government's sending young men to fight in Vietnam. Respect for him in the role of Deputy Leader was gaining ground to the extent that it was assumed he would succeed Calwell. However, he still had spontaneous eruptions of temper on the floor of parliament, which did not impress Margaret.

On 30 September 1965, at 2.12 am, Gough rose to speak on a Labor amendment to the Repatriation Bill, which aimed to extend repatriation benefits to the Salvation Army, among others. Everyone was tired and tempers were fraught because the government had caused the House to sit for so long. Paul Hasluck, the Minister for External Affairs, was sitting at the table. Knowing Hasluck's father was a retired Salvation Army chaplain Gough said, 'If the Minister for External Affairs is prepared to deny his parents in voting against justice for the Salvation Army personnel who have served in the forces, then

I suppose we need not worry about persons with less propriety and pride voting against all the principles which they so loudly espoused during the daytime and on sacred occasions.' As he sat down, Hasluck leant across to him and said quietly, 'You are one of the filthiest objects ever to come into the Chamber.'

With that, Gough took up a glass of water and hurled the contents straight into Hasluck's face. Hasluck sat quite still for several seconds. Then he took out his handkerchief and slowly wiped his face and clothing. Uproar erupted. It was some time before order was restored. Whitlam was instructed to apologise and he did. He also insisted that Hasluck withdraw 'the unparliamentary and provocative terms which he used and which were heard by several of my colleagues'. Hasluck apologised but added, 'The remark was made in a personal and direct way, it was not part of the proceedings of parliament.' For the remainder of the debate there was heckling and shouts of 'Wetty Whitlam' and 'Water Boy'. His Caucus colleagues were not so much bothered by the actual remarks but more by the impulsiveness of their maker. So was Margaret.

Gough's biggest clash with his leader and the heads of the party machine, however, centred on his support for federal aid for independent schools, which had now become an open wound between them. Metaphorical blood was on the carpet.

In February 1966, on television, he described the federal executive as 'incompetent and irresponsible'. His biggest insult – which the media repeated ad nauseam – was his calling them 'the twelve witless men'. He went on to attack Calwell's leadership by emphasising that only a Whitlam-led Labor Party would beat the government. He'd had enough. It was time for him to 'crash through or crash'. It was a highly dangerous approach – much like his style of driving. Margaret questioned whether he knew what he was doing. He assured her it was 'the only way forward'. She had no choice but to trust his judgement; he was very sure of what he was doing.

One month later the federal executive responded by formally charging him with disloyalty. Calwell said to them, 'We've got the numbers to get rid of the big bastard.' The current numbers were seven to five against Whitlam but, due to his successful campaigning in a recent Queensland by-election, he was owed. The president of the Queensland ALP repaid his debt by ordering the two Queensland delegates on the federal executive to vote against Calwell. Whitlam was merely reprimanded. In July of that year, the ALP federal conference adopted the policy of federal aid for independent schools. Gough's tactics had succeeded and the 'big bastard' had remained cool and confident throughout.

The reason he was so sure of himself was that he had a Plan B. If he lost the vote he would resign and Margaret would have stood in the by-election as the new member for Werriwa. He was totally confident she would have won, with him campaigning for her. Then, when he was readmitted to the party after serving his penance, she would stand down and he would be re-elected. He had constructed this complicated and elaborate plan without informing her, or anyone else. He knew she would back him if he had asked it of her.

He was right. When Margaret finally learnt of Plan B she agreed that she would probably have gone along with it to help him. But she confessed that she would also have done it because it would have been another very interesting experience.

Gough had no doubt that she would have won the party's endorsement and the seat. He also thought she was more than capable of doing the job (with him helping her, of course). John Menadue is firmly of the view that 'with her strength, her warmth and her excellent common sense she would have made a better politician than Gough'.

Gough totally failed to take into account the possibility that the electorate of Werriwa might not have obediently gone along with Plan B. That thought had never crossed his mind. Nor did the fact that if they had, once she was elected, Margaret might have been more popular than him and they might have wanted to keep her.

Fortunately for his career and their marriage, Plan B was never tested. Dame Leonie Kramer, (now) former Chair of the ABC and Chancellor of the University of Sydney, agreed with Menadue. Even though Dame Leonie and Margaret were on totally opposing political sides, she was in no doubt that Margaret was 'a natural leader and would have been a distinguished MP'. She believed that Margaret 'potentially sacrificed a very important career to be [Gough's] mentor'. Dame Leonie was very admiring of Margaret's ability to be open-minded and totally lacking in prejudice. She considered that a rare quality.

Later on, when Margaret was in her fifties, she was often asked if she was interested in entering politics. She always replied, 'Good heavens, no. I'm far too old.' Looking back on it when she was in her eighties she said, 'How ridiculous of me to say I was too old in my fifties. If I'd been a man I'd never have said that.'

Plan A having worked ensured that what lay ahead for both of them was very exciting. Another adventure for Margaret. And for Gough, a goal fulfilled.

6

Hearts full of passion

In February 1967, Arthur Calwell lost another election. In April, Gough was elected Leader of the Opposition, with Lance Barnard as his deputy. Gough created a first in Australian history by appointing a shadow ministry. The mood in the party swung immediately from pessimism to optimism.

For some time the media spotlight had been firmly focused on Gough. With his elevation to leader and possible future Prime Minister, it was now turned towards Margaret. Most political wives are photographed in a family group or standing beside their husbands. For the first time in her life, Margaret was centre stage. The media was falling over itself to get to know the wife of the tall, good-looking, commanding Opposition leader. Margaret was happy to oblige. In her view, all she had to do was just 'be herself'.

'Do come in, Father's on the telly', was her greeting to one journalist who arrived, unannounced, at her Cabramatta front door. Having spent an hour or so with her, the journalist judged her to be 'an attractive and impressive person'. Another early report on her was 'a supremely contented woman, with a highly developed sense of humour'.

Feminism's second wave was very much in the news and Margaret was confronted with the inevitable questions about 'women's lib'. She said she supported the traditional values of the family unit and that she would 'support her husband in whatever he chose to do'.

Her sense of humour, always lurking beneath the surface, popped its head up when she was asked if she had any influence over her husband's political ideas. 'You must be joking. But if he gets out of line I give him a good thump, although he's bigger than me.'

She was aware, however, that behind these seemingly standard questions were tricks to get a headline. She was far too canny to say anything that would harm Gough's election chances. Gough never spoke to her about what she should say. He trusted her common sense and her good judgement. Margaret soon became well-versed in answering predictable questions.

'The first thing they ask a political wife is always about the children. "How many do you have? Oh, how lovely. What do they do?" Blah, blah, blah. "Can we take a picture?" Blah, blah, blah. And then they try and slip in a political question. I'd had no political training, no media training. Thank God for the Penguin Club, which gave me some confidence. Mostly I just answered, "Well, of course I'm not the politician." Sometimes they'd do a bit of homework and ask me, "Weren't you a swimmer?" And

I'd say yes and go through my swimming history, and they'd think that was a big scoop.'

Journalists always asked the 'really big scoop' question, 'What do you think about your husband becoming Prime Minister?' All Margaret ever said, with a beaming smile, was 'Wouldn't that be marvellous.'

Margaret was well aware that most people made up their own minds about you, regardless of what you said. She knew her husband was challenging over twenty years of conservative rule. Some people were very threatened by him and by the thought of change. The conservatives were already spreading rumours about him being a Communist because he referred to his colleagues as 'comrade'. This was another example of his sense of humour. He was sending up those who had labelled him a Communist. The problem was that many people, especially those who were looking for a reason to disapprove of him, were very literal-minded. Once after Margaret left the local store a friend reported that a woman had said to her, 'Do you know who that was? She's the wife of the biggest Communist in Sydney.'

Stephen and Catherine were often subjected to playground taunts that their father was a Communist. As the youngest, Catherine had the toughest time because her father was now in the full glare of the public and media spotlight. She often came home late declaring that she'd had to 'fight a kid' after school because they had said something vile about her father. Catherine was tall for her age and strong and used to dealing with older brothers. She would not tolerate anyone making cruel or ignorant remarks about her dad. She was very handy with her fists, as were many of the Cabramatta students. Margaret, however, hated the fact that her children were being taunted, through no fault of their own.

Now that Gough was leader, Margaret was expected to accompany him to many more events. She tried hard to juggle her social work commitments at the hospital with her political commitments. However, she found it more and more impossible to fulfil her commitments at work. Something had to go. She chose to resign from her job. This wasn't just a question of being 'a good wife' or even 'standing by her man'. She saw it as her responsibility to support and help Gough however she could. She also knew that underneath all his confidence and bluster was the shy young man she had married. He still had trouble initiating small talk or casual conversation with people. She knew that her skills in this area made it much easier for him. He felt much more secure and confident in social situations when she was by his side; his awkwardness was less in evidence when Margaret was charming people with her conversation. She had loved her job at the hospital but made the decision to leave freely and without any pressure from Gough. She was not being a martyr to the cause. She chose to be with him because he needed her, and she loved him. It was as simple as that.

In the middle of 1967 John Menadue left his position as Gough's private secretary to join the staff of Rupert Murdoch, the managing director of News Ltd. His reason was – exhaustion. Gough had literally worn him out, physically and mentally. It was not just the long hours, the frequent travel, the living away from home and family. Menadue found his relentlessly confrontational approach within and outside his party difficult to experience on a daily basis.

Gough did not have the patience for incremental reform. His lack of people skills meant that he forced every issue to a crisis. While Menadue understood and appreciated that this is sometimes the only way to take on vested interests who oppose change, he simply could not last the distance. Gough was involved in every portfolio, obsessively making notes on envelopes and scraps of paper which he kept in his suit pocket and which were then upgraded by his secretary, Carol Summerhayes, into index cards called his 'insights'. His own research was detailed and meticulous. So, too, his devotion to reading *Hansard*. 'More matter, less art' he would roar at his speechwriters. Gough only had one speed: full throttle.

At the 1967 conference, one of his 'insights' was endorsed as the new health policy. It pledged a future Labor government to establish a comprehensive, universal healthcare service. The creation of a national health service and a national hospital system available to all Australians without charge and without a means test was a goal from which he never wavered. Despite the ferocious opposition from several conservative governments and leaders, he eventually succeeded in its establishment. Most patients who rely on it today and would fight to the death to defend its survival have forgotten or never knew who initially fought so hard to establish it.

January 1968 found Gough and Margaret together in Cambodia, Japan, South Vietnam and Indonesia. Margaret visited schools, orphanages and hospitals while Gough had political meetings. They took Stephen and Catherine with them, together with Graham Freudenberg, who was now Gough's speechwriter and press secretary. At the end of one stop-over Stephen found himself sitting in his room waiting a very long time for his parents to pick him up and take him to the airport. Forty-five minutes of waiting was finally interrupted by a phone call from his father asking Stephen where he was. Graham had taken all the bags to the airport and his parents had assumed he had taken Stephen too. Gough's solution was to organise a police escort so they would not miss the plane. Stephen loved the sirens. They almost made up for the fact that his parents had left him behind. These stories became part of the family folklore which Gough and Margaret thoroughly enjoyed re-telling and chortling over.

In June, July and August of 1968 Gough and Margaret took advantage of the mid-year parliamentary break to take themselves on a whirlwind tour of America and Europe. Margaret used her time to catch up with Nick, who had graduated from Harvard in June. They travelled companionably together around Europe by train, stopping off in various cities to sightsee, eat marvellous local food and go to theatres and concerts in the evening.

Sometimes, in order to save money, they shared a room. One night in France, when their luggage had been lost, Margaret, practical as ever, simply washed everything they were wearing, going to bed wrapped in a sheet. Next morning when she opened the door the young woman with the breakfast tray stood there staring at her. And then at Nick, still asleep in his underpants. 'My son is still asleep,' Margaret said pointedly to the woman, taking the tray from her. The woman looked back at Nick as if to say, 'Who do you think you're kidding?' As soon as the door closed Margaret woke Nick up so they could both have a good laugh. They continued on to London and then to New York to catch up with Tony, who was working there.

She missed her boys. In the diary of her trip she wrote, 'Leaving one in London was a bit of a wrench . . . Now I've left another one in NYC. At least I'm on my way to my young ones at home.'

In October 1968, Gough spoke at the National Labor Women's Conference. He was the first Labor leader who had ever represented the outer suburbs but it was Margaret who had overseen the building of two houses, raised four children, arranged for them to travel over thirty kilometres to high school, nearly twenty to a swimming pool (until she helped build one), endured no municipal libraries, no paved roads within a kilometre or two of their houses and no paved footpaths. She had battled with these disadvantages on a daily basis and it was her experiences, related regularly to him, that resulted in his emphasis on the federal government providing these facilities to the outer suburbs.

Margaret kept him in touch with every aspect of how women struggled to live and work in Australian suburbs. Suburban women could not believe how deeply he empathised and understood their needs.

Nineteen sixty-eight was a year of international rebellion. It was the year in which Bobby Kennedy and Martin Luther King were assassinated. It was the year of the Prague Spring, the Chicago Democratic National Convention, the Tet Offensive in Vietnam, the growth of the anti-war movement, the civil rights movement and the beginning of the end of the Soviet Union. And the beginning of the rebirth of feminism and the Women's Movement. The youth culture of sex, drugs and rock 'n' roll demanded change. The earth seemed to be moving on its axis as large sections of the population protested and marched against the old order of things. Australia was no exception. No matter how loudly conservatives protested – no one heard them.

Following the tragic drowning of Prime Minister Harold Holt, who had succeeded Menzies, John Gorton was elected as Liberal leader. Gorton knew better than to take on Gough on the floor of parliament. Gough was more preoccupied with fighting a battle to reform the Victorian branch of the ALP. He resigned, recontested the leadership and won it back, but only by six votes, which was not enough to break the Victorian stranglehold on factional power. This time he had neither crashed nor crashed-through, but they were on notice that reform was still on the agenda.

The times, they were a-changin' and Gough Whitlam was in tune with them. The 1969 election campaign launch slogan was 'Into the Seventies with Labor'. Everything that Gough had researched, spoken, written and analysed was crystallised into his plan for the next decade.

His speech began: 'We wish to renovate, rejuvenate, reinvigorate and liberate.' Its focus was on 'opportunities, the taking of opportunities and the making of opportunities for all Australians'. He continued, 'We are opening tonight not only a campaign but a crusade – a crusade to give all our people the opportunities to which they are entitled in a rich and growing nation.' That visit to see the evangelist Billy Graham had left its mark.

Gough was a genuine crusader, armed with policies for education, health, urban planning, pension increases, reduction of housing interest rates, Aboriginal land rights – and a promise to withdraw all Australian troops from Vietnam by June 1970 and to end conscription. He concluded: 'The future is with Australia; the future is with Labor.'

Margaret had focused on all aspects of the election. She had discussed, absorbed and approved of all Gough's policy initiatives and had become personally involved in the campaign. She even coordinated a women's group called ALPS – a sorority for political wives and female party supporters. People wanted her to speak, and speak she did at every opportunity – with passion.

Gough's performance was as outstanding as Gorton's was insubstantial. All his university theatrical skills were on show, his timing was impeccable and his jokes against Gorton and the Liberals lethal. Margaret even allowed herself to believe that they would win.

On election night, all their friends, staff and supporters gathered together in the Whitlam backyard to await the results. Margaret had cooked all day to prepare the food; Catherine, Stephen and Tony had been on voting booths. Television sets were scattered throughout the house. When the numbers finally rolled in, the ALP gained back all the seats lost in Calwell's 1966 disaster. They dared to hope. The final call, however, left them four seats short.

Nevertheless, everyone was elated. It was clear that the wheel had turned, just not far enough. Gough was high on all the cheering, back-slapping and congratulations he was receiving.

Margaret was smiling and stoic, cheering along with everyone. After they had all finally left, she quietly took herself down to a dark patch at the end of the backyard where no one could see her, to cry. She had really allowed herself to believe that they would win. She knew how long and how hard Gough had worked towards this moment. It had been a hard slog for her too. His energy was seemingly inexhaustible and she was one of the few people who could match him. But she was exhausted. She would never allow him to see her crying but she needed to let it all go before she could recharge her batteries and start the long climb again. Just at this moment, in the darkness of the back garden, her disappointment overwhelmed her.

It was the largest anti-government swing since 1931. Jim Cairns, Gough's former leadership rival, told the media, 'Mr Whitlam has passed the test of leadership . . . I think his presentation has been more articulate and successful than any since the war-time days of John Curtin.'

This was the election that turned the party around, not only in the minds of the voters, but in the minds of the parliament. This was the election that David Williamson, the nation's most popular playwright, captured in his much applauded play *Don's Party*, later made into a hugely popular film.

Gough and Margaret Whitlam were now firmly centre stage in the public theatre of politics, side by side. Their arrival at the Lodge was only a matter of time. The conservatives were worried. Very worried.

In December 1969, front pages of all the Sydney newspapers announced 'Dead . . . Famous Judge'. Margaret's beloved father, her most devoted admirer, had died. She had been visiting him in St Vincent's Hospital in Darlinghurst on a daily basis. Seventy-five, suffering from advanced emphysema, he was taken to the intensive care ward and heavily sedated. The nurses and the doctor told her not to continue her visits, as it was only a matter of days and he wouldn't know her. They probably thought they were protecting her. She did as she was advised. However, when Bishop Hulme-Moir, who conducted the funeral service, came to see Margaret afterwards he revealed that he had seen him in his last few days in intensive care. He'd said, 'Bill, if you know I'm here, just squeeze my hand.' And Margaret's father had responded. She was devastated. That could have been my hand he was squeezing, she thought to herself. It remained the greatest regret of her life.

It is always very sad when one of your parents dies. Even more so when that parent has been your greatest supporter, your tower of strength. Margaret was bereft. So were her children. Nick was twenty-four and in New York. Margaret wrote him a letter that he still treasures.

> I know you will be sad that you haven't seen him over the past years but think of the good times — the grand times — you had with him as a little boy and a young man. And remember his pride in you.

This letter reveals not just a mother helping her son deal with his grief and sense of loss but a daughter dealing with her own. Nick had marvellous memories of being taken to the bowling club by his grandfather and being introduced, tongue-in-cheek, as his son. He particularly remembers a day when they were both in a taxi and his grandfather had asked the driver to stop while he popped into the bottle shop to get some whisky.

The taxi driver turned to Nick and asked, 'Is that Judge Dovey?' Nick said, 'Yes, he's my grandfather.' The taxi driver replied, 'Great bloke. He got rid of the wife for me.' (Bill Dovey had been the Chief Judge of the Divorce Court.)

Margaret followed her advice to her son and kept her father's memory alive by remembering all the grand times they had shared, his pride in her, his belief that she would always be top at whatever she did in her life. She knew that he would not have wanted her to dwell on his passing but remain strong with her memories. She gradually came to terms with the fact that she would no longer hear his deep, rich voice on the other end of the phone.

Her mother, however, a woman previously so strong and in control of her life, totally fell to pieces. She took to her bed with all the long and loving letters he had written to her when he was away during World War I. Nothing Margaret could do or say could console her.

Eventually, with time, her mother took back control of what was now her life as a widow, sold the house at Vaucluse and bought herself a flat in nearby Rose Bay, close to the shops and public transport. She filled her life with a diary of events and good works. Structure and an organised life were the keys to her revival. Margaret took note.

Now that she was no longer working and was free to spend more time with Gough in Canberra, they rented a government flat in Manuka with a spare bedroom where the children could stay. This was their little haven away from politics and the public glare. They loved it. Just the two of them.

Having become totally involved in the previous election Margaret was prepared to speak her mind more openly. In an interview about the expectations placed on a politician's wife, she foreshadowed that she was not going to follow the traditional role of the silent and smiling wife behind the great man. 'People must come to realise that wives of politicians are personalities in their own right . . . In earlier years we were not such outgoing people. Perhaps now we are becoming a bit more brazen.'

Margaret was in fact talking about herself. She was prepared to lead the charge of the emerging, outspoken political wife. Gough backed her all the way. In fact, he began to discuss with her political dilemmas he was facing. For example, the question of when Papua and New Guinea should be given independence from Australian rule. Margaret's response was, 'Well, you don't ask a baby when it wants to be weaned. You just do it.' Impressed with her analogy, he toured Papua and New Guinea during the 1969–70 Christmas break. Taking four journalists with him on the RAAF VIP plane, he briefed them regarding his plans to make the territory self-governing by 1973, if he won the 1972 election.

On his return he continued to argue that Australia should no longer be a colonial power. He reminded everyone of our undefined position among our Asian neighbours, the high infant mortality of our Aboriginal population, our involvement in the Vietnam War, our lack of opposition to the sale of arms in South Africa and our immigration policy based on colour.

These were shocking words to the conservatives who had ruled the nation since 1949. Headlines in every newspaper ensured that it was the main topic of conversation at work and at home.

Margaret had long before accepted the fact that as a future Prime Minister Gough would invite conflict and controversy. She continued to be the focus of media attention herself, especially when in 1970 she agreed to join the panel of the popular daytime television talk show *Beauty and the Beast*. A group of well-known women gave their honest advice to questions from other women. John Laws, the top-rating commercial radio presenter, was 'the beast'.

In an interview with a male television journalist at the *Sun-Herald*, after the first show went to air, Margaret immediately noted that for once, her height was not a handicap. The article was headed 'Tall Girl Makes It as a Beauty'. Other columnists described her as 'zippy, zingy and uninhibited' in her answers to problems such as noisy neighbours and why husbands leave home. In other words, Margaret was totally at ease, being her open, honest, witty self. She enjoyed it all – the challenge of answering the questions, the drama of the panel and their differences, the excitement of a television performance.

The question everyone immediately asked her was, 'What does your husband think about you being on the show?'

'Well, he hasn't seen it. He hasn't got time to watch television in the daytime. Anyway, I'm glad he hasn't because I thought I was dreadful.' Self-deprecating as always.

The second question was, 'What do you think about the beast?'

'Both charming and intelligent. And you don't always get those together.' Spoken like a real politician.

Stephen Whitlam was also appearing on television, in a quiz show called *Pick a Box*. Like his father before him on radio, he won a considerable amount of money. All that book-reading had paid off. When Gough asked him what he intended to do with the money, Stephen said he was going to marry Sheena, his schoolgirl sweetheart.

Gough said he thought he was too young and not in a position to support his wife. Margaret agreed with him. Stephen, well-versed in arguing a rational case to his father, pointed out that ALP policy gave eighteen-year-olds full adult status and he was nearly twenty. He also reminded his father that he had married Margaret when he was in his twenties.

Assured that Stephen had made up his mind, Margaret and Gough accepted his decision. They both believed that they did not have the right to interfere in the lives of their children once they were adults. The marriage proceeded and one year later they were grandparents to Alexander Whitlam. Stephen trained as a diplomat in the Department of Foreign Affairs in Canberra.

In 1971, Gough shocked the nation and the government by leading a Labor Party delegation to China. Billy McMahon, who had replaced John Gorton as Prime Minister, attacked Whitlam and continued to refuse to open diplomatic relations with China. When Gough conducted a two-hour conversation with Premier Chou En-Lai in the Great Hall of the People in Beijing in front of both the Chinese and Australian media, he knew it would be world news.

Margaret was at home reading about her husband in the papers and watching him on television, delighted that he had finally succeeded in defining the political agenda. It was a courageous move. McMahon mocked the event, calling it 'a stunt'. One day later, Nixon announced that he would visit China within ten months. This visit was the basis for the John Adams opera *Nixon in China* and was a world first. Gough could not stop himself from laughing at McMahon's gaffe. The media joined in the laughter. Gough had pulled off a huge diplomatic triumph that heralded a dramatic change in the relationship between China and Australia. Alas, there was never to be an opera titled *Whitlam in China*. Rather than returning home a hero, most Australians had no idea why he had wanted to start a relationship with China. The anti-Communists used his visit as proof that he was indeed in league with the enemy. His conservative opponents were stirred from their complacency to ask, 'What will this man do next?'

Rupert Murdoch, however, was impressed. John Menadue, who was working for him, was keen for the two of them to meet. It is hard to believe that Gough did not want to forge a strong bond with the man who controlled large sections of the Australian press, but he refused Menadue's entreaties. He was suspicious of Murdoch and his power. He told Menadue that he never wanted to be beholden to anyone with wealth and power. Gough hated to be lobbied by anyone who wanted to influence his policies for their own self-interest. On the other hand, he failed to understand that a bit of charm and grace might have been useful, if only to neutralise the media's power.

Menadue persisted and the dinner he arranged in July 1971 between Whitlam and Murdoch he described as 'polite but cool'. In September 1971, Murdoch put out a friendly hand and invited Gough and Margaret to dinner and an overnight stay at his country property at Cavan, near Canberra. Gough reported back to Menadue that 'it was one of the most excruciatingly boring nights of his life'.

Margaret totally disagreed and found Murdoch 'a most charming and hospitable person'. She was always bold and forthright about expressing her own opinions. She made up her own mind about people, regardless of Gough's reaction. In fact, she remonstrated with him over his treatment of Murdoch, not just because she thought his judgement of people was often wrong but because she thought it very foolish to alienate someone who had the power to help your cause. Gough insisted that he would never crawl to someone like Murdoch, no matter how powerful he was. 'Naïve' was the word she used in response. But Margaret knew that when he had so stubbornly resisted all attempts at a relationship with one of Australia's most influential men, she was not going to change his mind.

John Menadue was disappointed with Gough's dismissive attitude because he knew that Murdoch saw him as a winner and wanted to support him in the 1972 election. Gough wanted to win on his own merit and on the quality of his policies. He believed that men like Murdoch always wanted something in return.

In December 1971, Murdoch's *Sunday Australian* featured a full-page interview with Margaret by the tough-minded journalist Geraldine Pascall. Her aim was to trail around with Margaret for two days and report on the real life behind 'Labor's Leading Lady'. Margaret was firm in her insistence that while she and Gough shared the same values, her opinions were her own. She could see no reason why she should not be free to express them. She was adamant that he never tried to impose his ideas onto her, though he did explain the reasons for certain policies when she asked him to. 'Gough wants to do things for Australia and the only way he can do that is as leader of the government.'

What amused Margaret most, she told Pascall, was the alarm and fear some people were expressing at the reality of a Labor government. 'They seem to think something frightfully obscene is going to happen. I usually tease them by saying, "Come on, now, you'll be right. We'll look after you when the revolution comes."'

Amusing though Margaret found it to refer to a 'revolution', there were still many conservatives who believed Gough Whitlam as Prime Minister would be the end of civilisation as they knew it.

After exhaustive interrogation, Pascall summed up Margaret Whitlam. 'Upper-class background but a deep social conscience; strong individual personality and a traditional commitment to husband and family.' As for Gough, she concluded that Margaret was the best public relations agent he could have. From then on, the media named Margaret 'Gough's secret weapon'.

By the time the nation was reading this very positive article, Margaret, Gough, Catherine and Gough's sister, Freda, were already in Tehran on their Christmas break.

Gough had realised that the only way he could ever really relax was away from Australia, where he could immerse himself in another culture and gain knowledge from meeting other heads of government. His obsessive nature was such that only by physically removing himself from the day-to-day problems of federal politics could he be refreshed enough to take on the next challenge.

Of all the important and powerful leaders that they met during their political travels, Margaret's favourite was Golda Meir, the Prime Minister of Israel, who they met during this trip. Normally during such a visit, after meeting and greeting was over, Gough would disappear with the political leader for a personal conversation. Golda Meir insisted that Margaret join them, and included her in their discussions.

An excerpt from Margaret's travel diary gives an insight into her ability to capture her personal impressions in a vivid but succinct style of writing.

Standing in the centre of the room she made a stocky figure all in black – with lace-up shoes, black dress and jacket. When we sat down, she assumed a commanding air. She has big, strong hands which are used a lot as she talks in her rich American accent. No artificial aids grace her face and figure, but her hair, her face, her hands, her clothes are spotless and of the best quality. We liked her. We think she liked us. She gave us an hour of her time and a cup of coffee while she, the only smoker, had three cigarettes.

The closer they came to the 1972 election, the more Margaret took on a public role. The ALP organisers finally realised that her warmth, charm and wit were a perfect antidote to the perception of Gough as a cold, distant, intellectual loner. Gough was not really interested in projecting an image. His aim was to change the country, not to change himself to suit the PR machine. When the interviewer Mike Willesee had pushed him on his reluctance to talk about himself, all he would concede was that he was 'a bit inhibited'.

His office staff, like his family, were well aware of his outbursts of temper and stubbornness. But to them he was also warm, funny, familiar and caring. He was always a lively inclusion in personal staff celebrations and happily gave away his office receptionist at her wedding.

Those who had reported on his 'make-over' since his return from China never knew that the only reason his slicked-back hairstyle had been replaced with a softer 'fluffy' look was that he had been unable to buy his usual Brylcreem in China. His staff had admired his new look and so it remained.

ALP National Secretary Mick Young planned a brilliantly organised campaign, which had been practised and tested. The campaign theme of 'It's Time' proved to be an outstanding winner. The Murdoch papers threw their considerable weight behind the belief that after twenty-three years of conservative government it was indeed time for a change.

The more Margaret travelled around the country with Gough, listening to his speeches and giving many of her own, the more the former champion swimmer was determined that this time they would win the race. Three weeks before the election day was announced, Young and Menadue suggested to Murdoch, who was returning from overseas to be in Australia for the campaign, that they organise a cruise on the harbour with the Whitlams. Gough refused. 'I'm too fucking busy to see Rupert.' When they continued to pressure him he said, 'I'm not going, but will Margaret do?'

Such social events were never pleasurable for Gough but he knew Margaret would be a hit. Behind the scenes it was Margaret who convinced him he had to attend and behave himself. With Margaret by his side, even he could be persuaded to be courteous, if not relaxed. She knew there were times when she had to read the rule book to him in no uncertain terms. He trusted her judgement, even if it didn't suit him to do so.

Saturday 2 December was finally announced as the date of the 1972 election – it was to be a short, three-week campaign.

The well-oiled campaign launched into overdrive. From the moment Gough stepped onto the stage of the Blacktown Civic Centre and intoned 'Men and women of Australia' it was clear that this was the culmination of everything he had been working for since he first entered politics. The speech contained nearly 200 promises, covering every aspect of Australian life that he sought to improve.

The day after the launch, he started with interviews in Sydney, flew to Melbourne, where he gave a press conference at the Commonwealth parliament offices, recorded a segment for the ABC television current affairs program *This Day Tonight*, launched the Melbourne campaign at the Springvale Town Hall and attended a late-night supper. The following morning he left early for Brisbane and did it all again.

He never slackened his pace for three weeks. His policies were based on everything he had ever learnt from his parents, Curtin, Chifley, the 1944 referendum on post-war reconstruction and the Constitutional Review Committee. He even allowed himself a personal reflection. 'The basic foundations of this speech lie in my very first speeches in parliament because I have never wavered from my fundamental belief that until the national government became involved in great matters like schools and cities, this nation would never fulfil its real capabilities.'

Everywhere Gough visited and spoke, he was greeted like a rock star with cheers and screams and standing ovations. Margaret was by his side before and after these almost evangelical displays of excitement and hope. While he spoke she sat in the front row of the audience. He knew she was there, sharing it all with him, believing in him. That was what counted. They had come this far. Together, always side by side. They were both convinced that it was the right time for him to lead the nation.

No matter what the
future brings

On 22 April 1942, Margaret Dovey had married Gough Whitlam, a young law student in an RAAF uniform, before he left her to fight in World War II.

On 2 December 1972, Gough Whitlam led the Labor Party to victory after twenty-three years in the wilderness of Opposition. He was now the Prime Minister of Australia and she was the First Lady.

When they finally heard the news that victory was theirs, Gough and Margaret were in the salubrious Sunnybrook Motel in Cabramatta. Room 7 had been overflowing with his staffers and advisers. It was stuffy and humid with damp bodies and high expectations. Gough sat, crushed in the centre of them all, leaning towards one of the four television sets as if his life depended on it. And, in a way, it did. Not long after the counting began, he turned to Graham Freudenberg and said quietly, 'I think we're in.' By 10.30 the room was ecstatic with jubilation. They cracked open more than a few bottles of champagne.

With Margaret by his side, they emerged from the room to greet the press. At 11 pm Billy McMahon, the man Gough had once laceratingly described as 'Tiberius with a telephone', conceded defeat in a 'landslide vote for Labor'. Then they walked two blocks to their home in Albert Street. Gough and Margaret, towering as always above their advisers and campaign workers, smiled and waved at the hundreds of supporters who lined the streets, all chanting 'Gough, Gough, Gough'.

Their traditional election night party that Margaret had organised while she was on the campaign trail was in full swing. The front and back lawns and every room in their house was frothing with people already wild with celebration. Margaret put her arms around Gough, kissed him generously on the mouth and said, 'Darling, we've made it.'

Banks of flashing light-bulbs, thrusting microphones and blinking television cameras demanded his attention. At 11.30 pm Gough climbed a 3-metre-high scaffold which had been hurriedly erected in their backyard and gave his first televised address as Prime Minister—elect. 'It is a magnificent victory. The government will have a mandate from the people to carry out all its programs . . . Tomorrow is the first Sunday in Advent – the advent of the first Labor government in twenty-three years.'

He was remarkably calm and composed, even though he was surrounded by people who were overemotional, overexcited and over-the-limit. As he and Margaret cut the huge victory cake, hands together, he turned and beamed at her. She never forgot the feeling of total elation on that night.

It was wonderful to have that good feeling. Of course I felt proud of him. I wouldn't have been with him if I hadn't. I also thought he deserved to be Prime Minister – he had the looks, the talent and he had worked hard for it. I just kept saying to him, 'Isn't it exciting.' He just seemed to take it all in his stride so I wasn't at all fearful at the prospect of being the wife of the PM.

* * *

Looking out of the windows as the RAAF VIP jet landed at Fairbairn base, they could see nothing but waving hands and cheering crowds. Twice on their journey into Canberra the car had to stop because the supporters made it dangerous to drive on. Gough leapt out of the car to speak to them and shake hands before they cleared the road.

Margaret was amazed. Her husband was being treated like a hero. She found herself waving at them through the car window and then bursting into laughter. The car dropped Gough at Parliament House for his meeting with Lance Barnard. He was already preoccupied with the task ahead, while Margaret went to the Lakeside Hotel to relax.

On 5 December Gough called on the Governor-General, Sir Paul Hasluck, the man he had previously thrown the contents of a glass of water over in parliament. At 2 pm Gough announced that it would be another week before all the votes would be counted. His Excellency had agreed that it would not be possible or proper for the federal parliamentary party to meet before 18 December. In the interim he and Lance Barnard would form a two-man government. At 3.15 that afternoon Edward Gough Whitlam was sworn in as Prime Minister of Australia and the minister responsible for twelve other portfolios. Barnard was responsible for a further fourteen portfolios.

Immediately upon returning to Parliament House they set in train the end of conscription, the remittance of joint sentences and fines against national service objectors and plans for national servicemen in the army in Vietnam to be discharged. Gough announced the first step towards recognition of China. He had been waiting twenty years to implement many of these policies. In the first four days of this two-man government he took the nation's breath away. They had gone from a slow waltz to wild rock 'n' roll.

Margaret was determined to set her own stamp on the position of consort to the Prime Minister. She told a press conference of women journalists that she no longer thought that marriage as an institution was as important as she had thought thirty years before. This was a surprise to Gough as well as the assembled media. She also backed the reopened equal pay case and the legalisation of abortion. What really shocked them, and her husband, was her support for the decriminalisation of marijuana. She had been told by her medical friends that it 'does no more harm than drinking, not even to excess, nor smoking regular cigarettes'. Here was a PM's wife bold enough to state her own opinions. Never before in the nation's history had this happened.

When asked how she would decorate the Lodge she replied, 'With people.' When she was asked to compare herself with the previous PM's wife, Sonia McMahon, she answered truthfully, 'My main decoration is my conversation.' She did not engage in the kind of bland, 'stand by your man' comments or avoidance tactics that previous PM's wives had hidden behind. Some of them were in fact very powerful behind the scenes, but were never prepared to step out of their husband's shadow.

Gough was full of admiration for his forthright partner. The following week he made twenty-eight more announcements. He was charging ahead at his usual breakneck pace with no conception that many Australians were shocked at what they considered his unseemly speed. Margaret was concerned that because he had been waiting for this opportunity for so long he had forgotten that most Australians had not. She kept reminding him that he needed to take the people with him, especially in these early days. 'I am, Margaret, I am' was his only reply.

When the *Sydney Morning Herald* published a daily panel listing 'What the Government Did Today' Gough was delighted. Margaret again urged him to slow down a little. 'But Margaret,' he said, 'Australia desperately needs these changes. And the sooner the better.' He was a man on a mission and nothing, not even Margaret, could curb his pace, his enthusiasm or his energy.

Expressions of congratulations arrived in a deluge. They came from the most powerful through to the most powerless in the nation. A former neighbour in Canberra reminded him that his mother, Martha, had confidently predicted that her son would one day end up in the Lodge. A woman who had been helped by him when she had been evicted as an eighteen-year-old wife and mother wrote: 'I have always felt you were very sympathetic; kind and in no way felt that helping "little people" was below your dignity.'

Even Sir Robert Menzies, the man who had always hoped to woo him over to the Liberals, sent him a generous message of congratulations. 'Nobody knows better than I do what demands will be made upon your mental vigour and physical health. I hope that you will be able to maintain both and send you my personal congratulations. My wife who well knows the nervous strain of being a Prime Minister's wife joins with me in sending our good wishes to Mrs Whitlam.'

Genuinely moved, Gough replied with the same tone of graciousness.

No Australian understands better than you the private feelings of one now facing the change from the years of leading the Opposition to the burdens and rewards of leading our nation. You would, I think, be surprised to know how much I feel indebted to your example, despite the great differences in our philosophies. In particular, your remarkable achievement in rebuilding your own party and bringing it so triumphantly to power within six years has been an abiding inspiration to me.

Away from the rough bear-pit of Question Time on the floor of parliament, politicians can show that even though their political philosophies are very different, they can appreciate the skill with which others practise them.

Arm in arm, after dinner and the heat of the day, Gough and Margaret strolled around the garden of the Lodge. It should have been a peaceful, relaxing experience in the cool leafy surrounds after the turmoil of the previous week. But behind every third tree there seemed to be a policeman or a security guard lurking. Margaret tried to ignore them but they kept catching her eye and saying, 'Good evening, ma'am.' She got the giggles, elbowed Gough in the ribs and said, 'I can't believe this.'

He strode on, as if he had been doing this for the previous ten years. 'You'd better get used to it, darling. This is our life now.'

Margaret had begun to take mental notes of all that she was seeing and experiencing. Now that she had been offered and accepted a weekly column in *Woman's Day* magazine about her new life, it was all good material. Just as Eleanor Roosevelt had done in her daily newspaper column, titled 'My Day', Margaret was determined to adopt a chatty, down-to-earth prose style. Ever since she had refused Frank Packer's offer to become a socialite reporter, she had had a longing to write. Now, at last, she had the opportunity and the subject. She had always kept a diary of people they met and places they visited, but this was a chance to directly communicate with the Australian people, particularly women. She could share her experiences with them and give them an insight into what being the wife of the Prime Minister was really like. She would write as if she was personally talking with them. They could perch on her shoulder and see her world as she saw it.

Gough was, as usual, delighted that she would have a chance to be published and the public would get to know her.

Her first column shocked some of her readers. Not only did she describe their garden walk but she took them into their bedroom.

15th December 1972

We've replaced the twin-beds with the double bed from the McMahon and Holt-favoured suite, but we've stuck with the bedcover there. It's all pink and yellow flowers which somehow don't go with the beige butterfly wallpaper in our room. There's a little balcony off the room, a dressing room and one of the attached bathrooms has a proper shower recess – Gough's adamant about the necessity for that.

One of her first lunch guests was Germaine Greer, the infamous feminist author of *The Female Eunuch*, an international bestseller. Margaret agreed to let Greer interview her for the *National Times*. Greer confided to Claudia Wright, a journalist friend, that she thought Margaret was 'the best political wife in the world at this moment'.

The lunch-time interview lasted two hours, during which Margaret reaffirmed to Greer her belief that abortion should be legal. 'It shouldn't be a criminal offence for a woman to decide what she's going to do with her own body. You should be able to let it be known that you were having an abortion instead of a baby.' She revealed that both personally and as a social worker she had seen too many awful results from illegal abortions.

Greer was gobsmacked at her openness and her refusal to sidestep politically hot issues. She asked her whether she would stop giving these opinions if Gough asked her to because they were politically embarrassing to him. 'Absolutely not,' she replied. 'They are my personal and private views. I am entitled to them. And Gough would not expect me to hide them. Never.'

As for sex, even though Margaret had never been unfaithful to Gough, she did freely admit to being 'a mental adulteress'. She described her husband as 'a very groovy chap, very alive'. When Greer asked her how he had shown his appreciation for all her help in the election she said, her eyes flashing with mischief, 'He whispered sweet nothings or sweet somethings in the middle of the night.'

Margaret, as she had promised, told her readers in *Woman's Day* what she had thought of the outrageous and infamous feminist. 'Off-camera, off-microphone, off-tape-recorder she is feminine, shy and nervous. She wore a navy blue midi dress of simple design – long sleeves, tied neckline. She is romantic, pretty, has a desire to be a mother but has the uncertainty of her own selfishness that so many clever people have but don't own up to.' She entreated Germaine to return to Australia to live.

The press were generous in their praise of the new PM's wife. The *Daily Telegraph* said that Gough had 'made his best leap forward when he married Margaret Elaine Dovey'. It described her as witty, intelligent and not afraid to speak her mind. In Aussie-speak, 'Meg' was 'a bottler'.

The *Age* described her as a 'beaut bird'. The *Sydney Morning Herald* talked to one of her former neighbours in Vaucluse. Mrs Magda Challen, a Hungarian in the days when foreigners were 'reffos', said she was always friendly, bright and cheerful. 'You can't put on a show like that every day for four years.'

Margaret openly described her own faults as being 'loud, a terrible temper and a sulker'. Being tall, she said, didn't inhibit her as much as it used to but she would like to get rid of her 'double chin'. And when the journalist remonstrated she quipped, 'Perhaps I should wear them grandly like "jew-ouls".'

Gough continued his normal pattern of rising early, working long hours, meetings every evening, and reading papers, reports and documents until well after midnight.

They had their first family Christmas at Kirribilli House on Sydney Harbour in 1972 and took time out to see the film *The Adventures of Barry McKenzie*, in which Gough had conferred his one and only 'damehood' on Edna Everage. They also saw *The Mavis McMahon Show*, starring Gordon Chater. One of the targets of his satirical send-ups was Margaret Whitlam, who laughed louder than anyone else in the audience. 'I must ask Gordon for the wig he wore; it's just my shade of grey. Super.'

Rupert Murdoch was still totally on their side and *The Australian* named Gough 'Australian of the Year'. Even Molly Meldrum, in the pop music newspaper *Go Set*, awarded him the Australian Prize-Fighter Award.

Nick Whitlam was visiting from England and after a family lunch on New Year's Day they all took a sentimental journey back to Cronulla, to look at their first house and see some of their old friends.

Gough chose Australia Day to announce the new 24-member Australia Council for the Arts with Dr H. C. 'Nugget' Coombs as its first chairman. Artists of all genres were very excited at the prospect of a body like the British Council for the Arts, dedicated to developing them and their work.

The contract for the National Gallery of Australia was revived and the plans which had stalled under Gorton for the Australian Film and Television School were finalised.

Not only were the artists and all their followers in thrall to this Prime Minister who seemed determined to fulfil all their hopes, but what he managed to convey was that art was not something that existed overseas, in other cultures. Suddenly, Australians were being exhorted to be proud of themselves and their creativity. For many, it was the beginning of a new confidence to use our own voices, to speak and write in our own accents, and learn to celebrate being Australian. It signalled the end of the cultural cringe.

The first session of the twenty-eighth parliament opened on 27 February 1973, with all the established formalities and rituals. Gough looked serene, his head held high, above his Caucus. They were certainly very different from the grey-haired, grey-suited, grey-faced men of the previous government. Al Grassby wore a purple suit with lace cuffs, matched with platform shoes. Bill Hayden was in a suit of ice-blue, and white shoes. Twelve Labor members did not take the traditional oath but chose the affirmation of allegiance. This was, after all, the 'Age of Aquarius'.

The Prime Minister's guests were Margaret, Tony and Catherine (the other children were overseas), Margaret's mother, Gough's sister and several Labor colleagues who had shared the long journey with them.

It was two weeks before Gough passed his first bill in the House of Representatives, which was to grant an additional week's annual leave, making it four weeks for public servants. This set the standard for all Australian workers. In the Senate, Lionel Murphy, the Attorney-General, gave notice of a bill to abolish the death penalty, which it had taken him ten long years to get up. All the ministers in the new government lined up at the barrier, ready to take off. It was just a question of who would get a bill up first.

By the end of their first hundred days, the Whitlam government enjoyed a 1 per cent rise in the polls since the election. For Gough, it was a dream he had only dared to hope would come to fruition.

For Margaret, however, the first hundred days were not so rosy. For the first time in her life she felt she had no control over her days or nights. She was no longer the ruler of her own domain. The main problem was the lack of any established role for the Prime Minister's wife. She was just expected to organise the staff at the Lodge and be on call, whenever needed. There was no list of duties, no spoken or unspoken rules, nothing concrete of any kind. It didn't suit Margaret. She was happy to accompany Gough to official lunches and dinners. She was willing to stand in for him to open fêtes or attend functions. She was even willing to pour coffee and tea for those who dropped by the Lodge and failed to see him. She was not, however, willing to give up having a life of her own.

Her *Woman's Day* column of 11 January states:

Each day I try to talk with Pat, the cook, about what is happening food-wise during the next few days: how many people are coming to eat, their preferences for food and so on. She then makes out the orders and the butler telephones the grog. Accounts are paid monthly after a double-check by the butler, the cook and me.

And so the tedium of domestic detail dragged on.

She had no interest in redecorating the Lodge but she did insist on installing air-conditioning in the kitchen, which was extremely hot. She couldn't understand how the other wives had allowed Pat to work in such shocking conditions. She worked out how to extend the seating of the polished mahogany table in the dining room, which only accommodated twelve people. Even her own in Cabramatta could seat sixteen.

She dispensed with Zara Holt's hot pink linoleum in the kitchen, replacing it with black and white tiles. She also dispensed with the services of the butler. He had given her the creeps by staring at her when he delivered the breakfast. She thought he was trying to see what she was wearing in bed. (She said it was usually nothing.)

When he was caught taking a sip from everyone's drink before he served them, she rang the bureaucrat in charge of hiring and firing. 'I'm going away for a week or so soon. I don't want to see him here when I return.'

Already she found herself dreaming about returning to her old life. This new one was proving to be restrictive and somewhat tedious. She took herself and Gough back to their home in Cabramatta, which was just as they had left it. She cooked their favourite roast lamb and they sat down together to watch the telly afterwards. She concluded, 'There's nothing wrong with suburbia. I'm envying the life I left.'

Everywhere she went, people asked her, 'How are you finding your role as the wife of the Prime Minister?' Her droll but honest reply was, 'I'm still finding it.'

She had tried meeting some of the unwritten expectations of PMs' wives and they didn't suit either her life or her needs as an individual. She hated wasting time; always had. Her mother had ensured that most of her spare time as a girl and young woman was taken up with worthwhile activities. She was never going to be an accessory to someone else's life.

Suddenly she found herself, having run her own life for thirty years, sitting around 'like a tame poodle, all dressed up with nowhere to go, waiting to be told when she was needed'.

When Gough had business dinners in the dining room she was forced to skulk alone in the little sitting room, eat her dinner off a tray and be content to watch television. Even when she was finally alone in bed with her husband, she had to share him and the bed with a pile of red despatch boxes which he worked his way through late at night and early in the morning.

Fed up, she set about changing what she could envisage was going to be her life in the Lodge. She demanded to know at least a week in advance what events she would be expected to attend and organised a schedule for herself.

She told Gough and his organisers that she would never be available on Tuesdays in Canberra: that was her fixed golf day. On nights when Gough was occupied with working dinners she would arrange to go to the theatre or a film. She would go alone if necessary. No longer, she said to herself, would she sit around waiting, like 'an aged princess in a tower'. Being seen but not heard was just not her style.

One bright opportunity arose in the early weeks in the form of a satellite interview with David Frost, the well-known British journalist. Margaret loved the word 'diverting'. Frost provided a pleasurable diversion from her mundane life. 'He is a marvellous man to flirt with by telephone. The dialogue was full of double-meanings, but in the nicest possible way.'

Margaret loved to flirt, on or off the phone, and the charming Frost was a master of witty flirtation. She still hankered after the Noël Coward life, conveyed in his songs and plays.

One serious question, however, stopped her in her giggles. Frost asked her whether there was something the press hadn't uncovered about her husband. Margaret paused and then told the truth. 'Basically – he's a shy man. The press all over the world are so anxious to depict him as a viper-tongued, belligerent, unkind man, but he's not. He's really fairly soft and kind – and shy about revealing that.'

Another of her initiatives or diversions was to organise a party for the wives of members and senators of different political parties to meet her and each other. True to form, there was to be no sitting around with cups of tea, exchanging pleasantries. She organised for them all to play tennis and croquet, and swim.

She was the first to shout 'For God's sake, Margaret, get the ball in the court!' She was the first to get into her swimming costume and dive in. Betty Gorton gave everyone instructions on how to play croquet. Margaret had been forced to stand around, thoroughly bored, at too many ladies' garden parties. She had sworn that, given a chance, she would do it all very differently. She was a woman of her word.

She ensured that whenever the Whitlams entertained, their style, like that of most Australians, was casual and relaxed. Neither she nor Gough could stand those who were pretentious in any way, or who used entertaining as an opportunity to show off or 'put on side'. Such displays reduced them both to laughter. At times they dared not look at each other for fear of losing their poker faces.

April 1973 meant a visit to London to see the Queen. The British press were out in force to test them out. Margaret met them head-on. 'Ask me an outrageous question and I'll give you an outrageous answer' was her opening line. They loved it. 'One helluva beaut Sheila', said the *Sunday Mail*. 'She has broken the rule of the League of Prime Ministers' Wives which puts caution beyond spontaneity', said *The Times*.

When *Woman's Day* asked if she was worried she would be seen as too folksy in her chatty diary, she quipped, 'Better to be seen as folksy than not seen at all.'

Their first night in London was spent at Windsor Castle with the Queen and Prince Philip. Margaret described in great detail for the readers of her column all aspects of the experience. Protocol at the palace was pre-dinner drinks at 7 pm in a little sitting room lined with a vast number of royal portraits and French carpet. Prince Philip met her, then the Queen Mother entered in a lovely blue printed silk dress with an aqua cardigan draped over her shoulders. Finally the Queen and Gough entered, having finished their formal talk. Her Majesty sipped a tomato juice while Prince Philip had a gin and tonic. Princess Margaret joined them and Lord Snowdon soon after. The Princess said he looked 'as though he had just come from the stables' in his jeans and denim jacket.

At 7.40 they curtseyed and withdrew upstairs to their rooms to change. Gough and Margaret were in their private apartment and she couldn't resist having a second bath (she'd had one in London before they left), which had been drawn for her in her own pretty pink and white bathroom.

Imagine her luxuriating in its warmth, staring up at the framed lithographs of flowers. She was that young girl who once sat in a bath day-dreaming of a life spent meeting famous people and going to romantic places. Here she was lying in the bath in Windsor Castle, about to have dinner with the Royal Family on the eve of the Queen's birthday. It was a far cry from sitting on the train to Cronulla, shelling the peas for dinner. Gough, her husband, the Prime Minister of Australia, was lying on the bed reading the London newspapers.

At exactly 8.30, both of them suitably attired, they assembled with the others for another drink. This time Her Majesty had a sherry. This is how Margaret described it.

The Queen Mother was in a lovely white and gold dress. [Margaret judged her to be a pretty, feminine woman of enormous warmth.] Princess Margaret was in a deep red velvet pinafore, long-sleeved evening sweater; the skirt was flared. Every bit a Princess. The Queen wore an aqua-lace re-embroidered in silver and gold, gold slippers, diamonds at her throat and pendant diamond earrings.

The dining room was very grand – red and gold mainly with a vast ceiling. The dinner service was pale green, pale gold and white (Sevres) given to Her Majesty and Prince Philip as a wedding present by President de Gaulle. Prince Philip admitted to being very fond of it and having no intention of it being added to the official Royal Collection. He intended giving it to one of the Royal children. Three courses only at dinner. Sensible, beautiful and delicious.

First, fresh salmon, boiled potatoes and cucumbers in sour cream; then turkey with what seemed a million vegetables. The sweet was pineapple bombe with spun sugar – right up our Prime Minister's alley. White wine and/or red. There was coffee and port at the table before we left the room.

Margaret and Gough retired to their rooms delighted with how pleasant and relaxed the dinner had been.

They celebrated their thirty-first wedding anniversary on Easter Sunday as guests of Rupert and Anna Murdoch at their 'country estate' in Epping. Even Gough had to agree that it had been 'much more enjoyable than he had expected'.

All of their children had managed to be in London to see them, and Edward Heath had asked everyone to dinner at Number 10 Downing Street the following Tuesday evening. It was a jolly night and Heath asked Gough if he would read one of the lessons the following day at the Anzac Service in Westminster Abbey, to which they were all invited.

At a press conference prior to their leaving for Rome, Gough insisted that he would request the necessary repeal of British legislation in order to end Australian appeals to the British Privy Council. He could see no necessity for such a practice to be continued. The conservatives, of course, disapproved of his actions, but he was determined that Australia not only become but be seen as an independent country governing in its own right. Appeals to the British Privy Council were 'a relic of colonialism'.

During their brief stay in Rome, Gough and Margaret had a private audience with Pope Paul VI in the Vatican. Gough judged him to be 'a gentle and wise man'. Eric Walsh, Gough's media adviser, had brought three sets of rosary beads for Gough to take to the Pope for him to bless. Gough's droll riposte to him was, 'You needn't have gone to all that trouble, Eric. I could have blessed them myself.' This self-mockery was, of course, one of his signature forms of humour. It continued to vastly amuse Margaret but she nevertheless feared that those who didn't know him well enough would think he was serious.

After Rome came a brief visit to Mauritius, where Gough raised the question of French nuclear testing in the Pacific. When they took no notice of his protests he joined with New Zealand to institute proceedings in the International Court of Justice, seeking an injunction against France. This would become a landmark case in environmental and international law regarding the damage done by these tests.

When Margaret returned home she recounted more details in her column about what had undoubtedly been the highlight of her tour.

You can't imagine how relaxed and human the Royal Family are. When the Queen is away from photographers and pressmen she is so amusing and also easily amused. We've all heard about Princess Margaret's talents as an actress or mimic, but I was enchanted by several take-offs Her Majesty permitted herself – mostly gentle send-ups of people around her – even her own Mama. (Yes, she calls the Queen Mother either Mama or Mummy. The late Queen Mary was referred to always as Granny.) You would have loved the sight of the sisters sitting side by side on the deep-piled, cream sheepskin rug we gave Her Majesty for her birthday. They looked like 'the Little Princesses' on either one's teenage birthday.

When that was published there was a surge of letters to the editor from people who believed that she had broken protocol by divulging to ordinary Australians the intimate details of the Royal Family. They just didn't think it was proper.

Margaret was unrepentant about what she had written and continued to write about dinner in the wood-panelled, candlelit dining room of Number 10 Downing Street and later of their private audience with the Pope. Nothing and no one was going to stop her. She believed in what she was doing; she wasn't showing off or revealing private secrets – she was sharing her role with ordinary Australians. 'I came to represent all the ungainly people, the too-tall ones, the too-fat ones and the house-bound, as I had been, who'd never go to China or Buckingham Palace, and they all went through me.'

Apart from once again exposing her view of herself as someone, like many others, whose appearance made her feel different and set apart from the so-called norm, this statement also revealed her identification with those women who never thought they would get a chance to experience such things, except in their dreams. In her deeply ingrained democratic spirit, she wanted them to ride on her shoulders.

The general response to her visit to Britain by the local Australian press was very positive. Leigh Bottrell, from London, wrote in the *Telegraph*, 'You actually hear English women saying they would like to meet Mrs Whitlam. Considering the average time an Englishwoman takes to admit that she might like to meet even a new neighbour, the Australian Prime Minister's wife has gone over big in Britain. Meg, who rules the saloon bar of my local pub, actually confided, "Mrs Whitlam is the nicest woman we've had to see us since Mrs Roosevelt. Almost as nice as the Queen Mother."'

The first six months of government for Gough had been demanding and relentless, just as he had expected. What surprised him was the creative nature of the actual process and implementation of his much researched and discussed policies. He remembered his father discussing the same elation, stemming from his public service administration. He found a fellow traveller in Nugget Coombs, with whom he often walked from the Lodge to Parliament House. They both enjoyed this quiet time, away from the demands of the office, to actually discuss ideas and future visions for change.

Margaret continued her endless round of 'openings' and 'closings', always by her husband's side. When she had married him and supported his choice of career that's what she knew she was taking on; her attitude was, 'I went along with him, urging him and helping him . . . Why moan about it? I didn't find it strange. To me, that's what marriage was all about.'

Even though she now knew a lot more about politics, Gough never discussed his important political decisions with her. There is no sense in which she was an extension of government, nor even a direct influence on him. Not that it stopped her giving him her opinion if she felt so moved.

People did, of course, try to get at him or influence him through her and she would often pass on to him a petition or a letter or a document that she had been sent, but that was the extent of her political influence.

> *He is like an oyster now when he is planning something new. I am not received well if I try to comment on his turf. I am more on the outside than I was when he was in Opposition. He can be a vain, irritating man, but I can be irritating too. I am untidy. I talk too much and I interrupt. But if he does something that I think is wrong, I tell him so; that is the privilege of a wife of my vintage.*

One of his initiatives that she did approve of was his appointment of a special adviser to the Prime Minister on women's affairs. It took her by surprise, as it did most of his colleagues. Elizabeth Reid, who was the woman he appointed to this unprecedented and radical position with the PM's office, was struck immediately by Gough's 'tremendous awareness of women's issues'. He had been agitating for equal pay for women and the removal of discriminatory conditions in their employment for many years. The Women's Electoral Lobby (WEL) had been very influential in convincing him of many other areas of reform that needed addressing. He placed all such reforms in the context of human rights and was determined that Australia meet its international obligations, especially the UN 1952 Convention on the Political Rights of Women and the Universal Declaration of Human Rights. He immediately initiated a review of the conditions of employment for women in the public service, in order that it become 'the pace-setter' to promote the status of women.

The media reaction to the Reid appointment was shock and horror. Cartoonists and the tabloids had a field day, delighting in revealing that she was in fact a 'single' mother, married but separated from her husband, who preferred to be known as Ms Reid, rather than Miss. The Liberal Premier of New South Wales, Sir Robert Askin, scoffed that he had no need for 'a superwoman' since he already had one at home.

Despite these reactions, Reid monitored all cabinet documents, which were required to include 'a women's impact statement', like the environmental impact statements that Gough had already introduced.

Reid's office functioned as its own department within the PM's office. She became a successful advocate for federal funding for many services, including women's health centres, rape crisis centres, childcare, family planning associations, women's refuges and working women's centres.

Whitlam knew, however, that what women needed to become fully developed as individuals was nothing short of 'revolution'. 'We have to attack the social inequalities, the hidden and usually unarticulated assumptions which affect women not only in employment but in the whole range of their opportunities in life.' He knew this was not something that government action alone could solve; that it required a re-education of community attitudes and the uprooting of community prejudices.

While Margaret was full of praise for Gough's feminist sympathies and initiatives, she still found her own role very restrictive. Sometimes she wished Gough would turn his attention to her personal need for 'a revolution' in her own daily life.

There were limits to how far Margaret could be content to be an appendage to her husband and his job. At the end of her twelfth month as 'the Lady at the Lodge', Lee Patterson spent several weeks on the First Lady's trail and wrote an extended feature article for *POP* magazine, accompanied by a lurid caricature of Margaret, complete with fishnet stockings, lace suspenders and tassels attached to her nipples, leaping out of a birthday cake on which burnt one candle.

Margaret did admit that she had finally become used to Gough being referred to as the Prime Minister, whereas in the first few months whenever she heard it she used to laugh, dig him in the ribs and say 'That's you'. As for her public utterances, she had no intention of ceasing to make them. 'I say what I think when I want. I am not a mouthpiece for my husband or for the ALP and it's very frustrating for me when people assume that I am.'

Lee Patterson commented, 'If nothing else, Margaret Whitlam has shattered the porcelain image of the PM's wife as some sort of beloved, untouchable and inviolate lady of the flowers who appears and rubs a few platitudes together at fêtes before ascending again to the big house on the hill.'

She was trailing around observing Margaret's 'openings' and 'closings'. At the opening of the Australian Regional Conference of International Toastmistresses, she witnessed first-hand Margaret giving the person who introduced her as speaking about the role of women in Australia a totally unexpected roasting, rather than a toasting.

Margaret Whitlam stood up to her full 6 foot 2 inches, in itself an awe-inspiring and impressing statement, and said 'There was no mention of me speaking about the role of women when I was invited here, so I am not going to. If you want guest speakers, ask them to speak and give them a subject. I was first asked to open this conference officially and then I received a note of thanks when I accepted but nothing else. You therefore can't blame me for wondering what it is I am supposed to do.

There is nothing outrageous about refusing to give an off-the-cuff speech on a topic which the organisers have not mentioned to you before. Margaret was a stickler for doing things properly. If you asked her to do something and she agreed to do it, then you must stick to your original contract. She always prepared in advance for whatever she agreed to do; even if she was going to an opera or a concert she would play the music beforehand just to get herself 'in the groove'. This was, of course, a result of her upbringing, her parents, her schooling and her understanding of what constituted proper behaviour.

When Gough was first elected Margaret had been very upset by a letter that he received from a close friend of theirs, Alex, which said that Gough was a traitor to his class but that Margaret would always be welcome as an old school friend of his wife, Isobel. Gough and Margaret had lived among these people, been to school with them, studied at university with them; they had even been to some of their weddings. And yet they were appalled that Gough and Margaret, whom they saw as belonging to their own class, had jumped the barriers and taken up with the so-called 'uncouth rough Unionists and the sweaty workers'. There were many people who held these views. Many members of the Liberal Party never forgave them for joining the Labor Party and therefore never viewed the Whitlam government as legitimate. Gough and Margaret were not only class traitors but usurpers of what the Liberals, after more than two decades in government, believed was theirs by birth and entitlement. From the moment the Whitlams moved into the Lodge there were many who pledged to do whatever it took to eject them as soon as possible.

Even though Gough and Margaret were aware of these attitudes towards them, they never really believed that their political enemies were intent on removing them from government by whatever means they could engineer.

As the son of a top public servant Gough had the highest respect for the proper practice of parliamentary government. He assumed, somewhat naïvely, that though Liberal Senator Reg Withers denounced his mandate and assumption of the office of government as 'an aberration' and a result of the 'temporary insanity' of the Australian electorate, he would never act in any way to deny its legitimacy.

And yet the word 'illegitimate' became a common description of the Whitlam government by the Opposition. All those institutions that had defined themselves by the principles and policies of the previous twenty-three years of Liberal government now joined the Liberal party in its denunciations and slurs. They soon added to their accusations of 'illegitimacy' by using words like 'incompetence', 'improper', 'corruption', even 'criminal'.

Sir Robert Menzies was aghast at the changes and reforms of the Whitlam government, believing it to be 'carrying out a purely Communist policy'. Gough Whitlam's leadership was seen by the establishment members of the Liberal Party as a serious threat to the stability of the nation.

Gough rebuffed such statements. His undying belief in the proper processes of parliamentary democracy prevented him from taking those forces who were uniting against him seriously. He believed that they all shared in his rock-solid belief in maintaining proper political governance. Conservatives are there, after all, to conserve the status quo, not destabilise it. He even recommended his old nemesis Garfield Barwick to the International Court of Justice for its consideration of Australia's case against French nuclear testing. He never took his Attorney-General Lionel Murphy's actions in having his office swept for surveillance devices seriously. Neither did he take seriously Murphy's suspicions about a journalist he specifically asked ASIO to check on for attempted spying on himself and Whitlam. Gough considered this to be paranoid rubbish. He refused to sack the four top public service 'mandarins', who made no secret of their disdain for him and his government, in the belief that they were proper public servants above all else.

In July, Margaret promoted a series on Australia's wildlife for the Paul Hamlyn Publishing Group and she donated the fee to the Australian Conservation Foundation. People still complained in the media about her working. In her diary she wrote 'What am I to do? Stay in a cage – wide open to view, of course – and say nothing? That's not on but if I can do some good I'll certainly try. I'm trying.'

On 21 July Margaret celebrated her mother's eightieth birthday with her by taking her to lunch, after which her mother went to see the Kirov ballet with a friend and Margaret returned to Canberra. Margaret admired the way her mother, having now moved to the flat in Rose Bay to be nearer the shops, had carved out a full life for herself. The 'old girl', as she had called her affectionately for the previous twenty-five years, had organised a program for herself so she was never bored or lonely. She never complained if she didn't see her daughter for a month and simply got on with her bridge, her radio listening, her handiwork and her visits to the theatre.

On the weekends when Margaret and Gough were able to spend some time at Kirribilli House on the harbour in Sydney, Margaret was always amused when, echoing across the water to the wide verandah (where she often sat catching up on her correspondence or her accounts), she would hear the words from a loudspeaker on one of the tourist ferries announcing: 'This is where the Whitlam family live.'

The so-called Whitlam family now consisted of her and Gough. Tony was working as a lawyer in New York, Nick as a banker in London, Stephen as a foreign affairs trainee in Geneva and Catherine was living in a student share house near the University of New South Wales, where she was studying to become a teacher.

In August, Gough travelled with Nugget Coombs to Daguragu to celebrate the first handover of Indigenous land rights. People from Aboriginal communities from hundreds of kilometres away gathered together with bureaucrats and politicians. The Gurindji people called Gough 'Jungarni' – 'that big man'. They had struggled under the leadership of Vincent Lingiari to claim back their land. Gough ended his speech with the now famous words, 'I put into your hands this piece of the earth itself as a sign that we restore them to you and your children forever.' He then poured the earth from his hands into those of Lingiari, whose speech ended with the words, 'We will be mates. White and black ... They took our country away from us, now they have brought it back.'

Despite these wonderful healing acts, to be followed by legislation, Gough continued to battle with the Opposition and the 'prima donnas' in his own cabinet, saying, 'I don't care how many prima donnas there are, so long as I'm prima donna assoluta.' Margaret was planning the activities for the Royal Visit in October of the Queen and Prince Philip. In keeping with her own style of informal formality, she made the bold decision to have a lunch for them outside in the garden of the Lodge. Fortunately the day was fine and Margaret's chosen menu was a great success. Fresh asparagus (from the Lodge garden) followed by trout with almonds, savoury rice and a mixed green salad. Cheese was served in the French tradition before the dessert, which was gingered pears.

During this visit the Queen was formally declared 'the Queen of Australia', signing her assent to the *Royal Style and Titles Act* in Canberra. The rough diamond from Queensland, Jack Egerton, greeted the Queen with a smile and said, 'They tell me, luv, you've been naturalised.' Prince Philip chatted amiably with Bob Hawke while the Queen admired Al Grassby's wildly colourful tie.

Gough complimented Margaret on the outstanding organisation and success of the lunch. He always had complete faith in whatever she organised in terms of food, conversation and conviviality. They were areas which remained a total mystery to him in terms of their execution.

Also a mystery for him was the headline in the *Sun-Herald*. 'Poll shock for Labor'. It showed that if an election was held, the Coalition would easily regain government.

The big event of the Royal Visit was the opening of the Sydney Opera House, complete with music and fireworks, all of which was a huge success, except for the wind, which would have blown away the Premier's chair when he stood up to make his speech but for the quick thinking of the Queen and Prince Philip, who grabbed hold of it and held it down. When the Queen finally departed, Gough gave her a parting gift – Al Grassby's tie. By the time it was all over Margaret finally admitted in her diary to being tired. Very tired.

Nevertheless, three days later she and the PM were in Tokyo, where she lunched at the Imperial Palace, which, although she thought it rather forbidding from the outside – grey granite surrounded by a moat – was 'elegant and beautiful inside with its space and glass and wood and deep pile carpets of pastel-hue perfection'.

A series of banquets and lunches and visits to sacred places followed, including an evening of entertainment with the geishas. In all of the photographs Margaret and Gough look like giants compared to the Japanese. Margaret wished she had been able to have her photos taken without her shoes, which she removed in restaurants. 'One feels such an ox in the presence of these finely built people.'

Gough's early success at getting his monumental number of bills passed in both Houses had now ceased. The conservatives, now buoyed by the latest polls, decided to apply political pressure. There was a backlog of rejected or amended legislation in the Senate, including the Family Law Bill (no fault divorce), the Health Insurance Bill (free universal health insurance), the Petroleum and Minerals Authority Bill (government funding for Australia to undertake its own exploration and production in an attempt to stop more foreign ownership) and the bill dearest to Gough's heart, the Schools Commission Bill and States Grants Bill (needs-based funding directing money away from the most advantaged schools to those with the greatest need). This caused much grinding of teeth and popping of veins in the temples of the Prime Minister.

He was even more visibly upset when, after a disastrous by-election result in Parramatta in September, he was persuaded by his advisers to relinquish the portfolio of Foreign Affairs in order to focus on why Labor's stocks had slumped so dramatically, so early in their term of office.

Liberal Senator Reg Withers – who had made no secret of his strategy to remove this illegitimate Labor government by blocking the supply bills – urged Billy Snedden, the then Opposition leader to use their Senate numbers to enact his plan. This would deny the Whitlam government the financial means to govern, forcing another election.

Snedden refused.

An analysis of the government's problems revealed that raising interest rates to counter rising inflation before the by-election hadn't helped and that the electorate felt bewildered. 'They're going too quickly, too soon' was the general consensus.

In a confidential letter to the PM, a group of Caucus members said that the ministers had failed to explain the philosophy behind all their policy initiatives and that since Gough's personal standing and opinion poll ratings were high, he should become the major salesman for all the policies, preferably through more frequent television appearances. They also said they regretted the fact that they had to communicate with him by letter as he was always too busy to see them.

It was true that because they had been so long out of government many of his ministers were failing to perform well and Gough was spending more and more of his time trying to make up for their failings.

Early November found Margaret and Gough in China, where, in addition to Gough's excitement at finally meeting Chairman Mao, Margaret conquered one part of the Great Wall and saw the Ming Tombs which house the thirteen emperors of the Ming Dynasty (fourteenth to seventeenth centuries AD), which are an hour and a half from Beijing (then Peking). She had been looking forward to visiting the Forbidden City and was not disappointed.

This was the first visit of an Australian Prime Minister to Communist China. It symbolised, in Whitlam's words, 'the successful ending of a generation of lost contact between Australia and the most populous nation on earth'.

The fact that they were greeted at the airport by thousands of dancing schoolchildren waving scarves and singing 'Welcome' was testimony to the importance of Gough's earlier visit as Opposition leader. Gough engaged in twelve hours of talks with Premier Chou En-Lai and an hour with Chairman Mao.

In all his discussions, Gough emphasised 'the abiding virtues in Australian society which have given us a distinctive nationhood. The belief in fraternity and independence, the instinct for fair play, justice and freedom that Eureka signifies.' Australians at home were stunned by his ability to communicate their virtues so clearly and easily with Chinese leaders. It removed many of the fears and 'bogies' of the past.

Back on home soil Gough was being castigated and denounced for approving the purchase of the painting 'Blue Poles' by the American artist Jackson Pollock for $1.3 million. The conservatives went ballistic, which only served, in Gough's view, to emphasise their innate ignorance and philistinism. Gough was so amused by their reaction that he ordered a reproduction of 'Blue Poles' to adorn the Prime Ministerial Christmas cards – signed, of course, by himself and Margaret.

On 30 November, Margaret and Catherine were in London to celebrate Nick's wedding to 29-year-old Judy Frye. Gough had met Judy the year before, but political duties prevented him from being present at the wedding. Nick's brother Tony was his best man. They were married in London's Chelsea Registry Office and Judy's parents threw a huge black-tie dinner-dance the following night in a marquee connected to their large Dulwich house. There were more than two hundred guests, including Rupert Murdoch.

In January 1974, John Menadue had organised for Whitlam and Murdoch to meet for dinner in New York. By chance, Gough saw David Frost in the foyer of the Plaza Hotel and chose to have dinner with him instead. He cancelled Murdoch. Menadue was beside himself. Murdoch was understandably insulted. One of Gough's staff managed to get them together for breakfast at Murdoch's apartment two days later, but Gough did not go with good grace. He didn't feel it necessary to share his thoughts with Rupert Murdoch. Margaret admonished him for his rudeness towards Murdoch; she hated rudeness in any form. But she was much more sensitive to the power Murdoch wielded, and the stupidity of alienating him, than her husband appeared to be.

In the same month Margaret agreed to become the first woman member on the board of Commonwealth Hostels Ltd, but when it became known that she had accepted a payment of $1950, there was a media outcry. 'An imprudent appointment', announced the *Age*. 'Drop it Meg', suggested the Melbourne *Herald*. Margaret refused to bow to her critics and responded to accusations of 'jobs for the girls' by reminding them that she was a trained social worker and that having 'subjugated' herself for an entire year, she was very pleased to be doing something constructive for a change. The media were still of the firm belief that wives of Prime Ministers should not work for money.

In response to the blocking of supply by the Senate, Gough advised the Governor-General, Sir Paul Hasluck, on 10 April to dissolve both Houses in order to have an election for the whole parliament, and not just the half Senate, on 18 May.

On 25 April, Anzac Day, the *Daily Telegraph* ran a feature on 'the most exclusive girls in the country – the Prime Minister's daughters-in-law'. Pip Colman had married Tony Whitlam the previous weekend in a 'surprise Darling Point ceremony'. As a teacher before she began modelling, the *Telegraph* projected that she would find the world of politics 'a far-cry from the ultra-glamorous jet-setting life she leads as a model on the international fashion scene'.

Margaret and Gough, however happy they might have been with their son's wedding to Pip, now had another election to fight less than eighteen months after the previous one.

Reg Withers, after relentless persistence, finally got his way. Snedden capitulated and they blocked supply. Once the vote was passed, a seething Lionel Murphy stormed out of the Senate, crossed Parliament House and entered Gough's office.

An hour later, Gough emerged to convene a special Caucus meeting. He was coatless and wearing a pink shirt. The pink shirt, however, had no cuffs. Eric Walsh, his media adviser, had introduced Gough to his six-year-old son, who was visiting parliament that afternoon. Wanting to give him a memento of the special occasion, Gough spontaneously tore off both his cuffs, signed them and passed them on to the other ministers to sign. This act is an example of what Margaret was referring to when she told David Frost that Gough was a soft-hearted, caring man. What was a ruined shirt without cuffs when compared to a special gift for a six-year-old boy? Gough's action was that of a generous-spirited man; a man who generally covered up this side of his nature when in public. This was the man Margaret had fallen in love with and married.

The Caucus unanimously agreed to the calling of a double dissolution. Lionel Murphy told the reporters, 'The party is completely behind our great leader and we will go out and fight and win.'

It's still the same old story

It was only seventeen months since Gough had stood on that same stage in the Blacktown Civic Centre. He began with the same words he had used before: 'Men and women of Australia'. He explained how the new team they had chosen in 1972 had been unable to pass the laws to make the changes for equality of opportunities that the people had voted for.

The Labor campaign would emphasise the government's achievements and the 'obstinacy and opportunism' of the Opposition. This was an elected government which the Opposition had been determined by any means to obstruct. They continued to view the Whitlam government as 'illegitimate'.

Everything they had promised was now threatened by the actions of men elected to the Senate not in the last election but in 1967 and 1970. They were men who refused to accept the verdict of 1972. Therefore Gough chose the path of declaring a double dissolution of both Houses in order to prevent this happening again. It was up to the government to make it impossible for them to say once again that the result was a mistake.

Elected governments must have the right to run their full elected term and carry out the program for which they were elected. He emphasised that the world was watching, especially the countries in our near region, to see whether Australia was truly a nation where parliamentary government was a viable and fair mechanism for peaceful political change.

Gough's fervour and passion for persuasion was just as strong as it had been in 1972. His speechwriter, Graham Freudenberg, noticed a new edge of anger and frustration in his voice. He even noticed 'a kind of fierceness' among the Labor supporters who gathered to hear him speak. Gough was on edge because he knew that it had been his decision to take them to this election and if they failed, all would be lost.

Margaret travelled everywhere with him on the campaign trail. In her private journal there is no attempt at gloss or spin; it was not written for anyone but herself. Things were tense from the beginning of the journey.

> *Sydney 30th April 1974*
> *We're off. E. G. and I drove out to Blacktown at an early hour to collect ourselves. I was horrified to discover that the rooms that had been booked at the Blacktown Inn were at the back (easy access and privacy) but they had no television or radio. I had no newspaper or a book to read.*

The fact that no one had factored in Margaret's presence or needs annoyed her. How many years had she accompanied Gough on this political journey? No one – certainly not the men who organised the election campaign – ever thought of her as an important contributor. Wives, despite Gough's radical women's policies and appointments, were still treated as store mannequins. Look nice; don't speak.

Margaret demanded that someone find her a radio so they would know from the news headlines what was happening, and a newspaper. She absorbed herself in the crossword while Freudenberg and Gough worked on 'the speech'.

> *Now airborne to Melbourne. No-one talking much, especially not to me. This is likely to be the tenor of the tour. Expecting it I've brought along an enormous bag of work to do. Letters to answer, photos to sort, knitting. Blow everyone.*

Once again she was relegated to silence. Once again she busied herself with things to do, like a child told to sit in the corner and play with her toys. Even when she spoke her words were ignored.

> *We left Hobart this morning at 6.30 am — a hellish time with everyone tired from yesterday in Melbourne and Tasmania. As usual, my car companion — life partner — call him what you will uttered not one word on the way to the airport — except to ask the driver to change the car's radio station.*
>
> *I'm getting so the word wouldn't even have to be kind to be welcome. What a sad saga this has become. I wish everyone would smarten up and be friendly.*

The stress and tension of this election was much greater than that of 1972, which was a journey to a triumph they all knew they could expect. This had none of the singing, the razzamatazz, the jolly good-natured banter. It was full of the anger and frustration of a job half-done. A series of goals incomplete because of a game of dirty tricks and irresponsible treatment of the parliamentary system.

Inside, Gough was boiling with fury that he had been forced to go through all this again, after such a short time. He was reliving the previous seventeen months in his head. Going over and over it all, trying to see how he could have made it work. What really frustrated him was that he knew there was nothing he could have done. The Tories believed that a Labor government was a boil on the public rump that needed to be lanced. Those he had trusted to maintain correct procedures and proper practice had been intent on betrayal from the beginning. Bastards, all of them.

He did not discuss his thoughts with Margaret because they made him too angry and frustrated and he needed to remain calm and in control. Anyway, there was no need to burden her with it all. He was, however, guilty of taking her place at his side for granted. He did not have the emotional intelligence to realise that an occasional kind word would have been welcome. His mind was not on Margaret or her needs – it was totally focused on winning this election with a majority in both houses. He simply expected her to know and accept this.

Adelaide.
A lot of my time in the past few days has been spent in the bathroom. There is always someone else in our room when I'm about to dress or undress. Sometimes three or four people. Many times I wonder why I came along as my opinions are never heard. If I utter – someone pulls a face. And if I don't, I'm stared at accusingly. It's all a bit of a bore and not nearly the fun we had last time.

The 'someone' who is pulling faces at her if she speaks, or staring at her in an accusing manner if she doesn't, is clearly

Gough. She cannot win, whatever she does. He is taking it all out on her because he knows her love is such that he can; it is unconditional, even in the face of his rudeness.

> *E. G. tripped over something, a briefcase I think, and proceeded to take out his rage on the nearest door. When I demurred I was called 'a silly old bag'. 'Well you're older' I said, and inferred 'sillier'. 'But I don't look it' he said, then added 'Viperish woman'.*

The Whitlam temper was off its leash. The viperish tongue was his, not hers. 'Viper' is a particularly Shakespearean term often used in connection with women, because they are seen as creatures who betray those who take them to their bosom. In other words, viperish women are not to be trusted because they will ultimately betray you.

Gough's spitting out these words against Margaret was typical of his defensive mode of attack. Having kicked a hole in the motel door he was feeling foolish. He did not need Margaret to add salt to the wound. His crack about not looking older than her, even though he was, was an arrow aimed directly at her vulnerable point: her concern with her appearance.

After he had spat it out, he would immediately forget it. Margaret was meant to forget and forgive him for any such outbursts as he was under great stress. She knew that and would never have packed her bags and returned home like many an insulted wife. She would sulk when they were alone and maintain a calm and controlled presence when they were on public display. But there was a limit to how much of this poor behaviour she would withstand until she really took him to task. For those who believe in star signs, she was a Scorpio, and there was definitely a sting in her tail when she decided to use it. Gough was well aware of this and was usually careful never to push her too far. At fifty-five she was also menopausal and it didn't take too much rudeness for her disturbed hormones to take over. She had, like many menopausal women, put on weight around her stomach. This was particularly galling because the fashion at the time was tailored waists with belts. Gough would have heard her complaining, many times, about her displeasure with her appearance, especially at a time when she was among the most photographed women in the nation.

Gough knew he had gone too far. Margaret's subsequent journal entries report that Perth was rather pleasant. She had also been given something useful to do other than change her clothes in a small bathroom.

> *My part was large enough and very interesting — the child-care centre at Garden City and a visit to an Aged Person's [sic] Retirement Village. A good night at the Savoy Plaza Hotel with much support by Yugoslavs and Italians as well as expected Labor people.*

> *Friday 3rd May*
> *Adelaide Park Royal Motel*
> *Somebody's got to make the coffee. Let it be me. Now I know my role in this campaign. Keeping the coffee coming in motel rooms. And ironing the shirt of the Day. Good girl.*

She had also prerecorded two interviews on Adelaide's most popular commercial radio station, 5AD, with Pat Hudson and Andy Thorpe. She was happy to do whatever she could to help.

> *Sat 4th May — Evening*
> *Bomb scare at the meeting in Norwood Town Hall. After a rousing welcome, I began to wonder what was going on with Barry Brown and Reg Bishop*

conferring and much movement at the side. Finally Reg came up on stage, whispered to Don Dunstan and gave me a card which read 'Security. Leave soon without panic.' He asked me to give it to Gough when he finished speaking. Five minutes later, he did, I did and we did. A bit scary and a bit abrupt as an ending to a successful meeting. We drove away swiftly instead of meeting people and attending the Mayor's reception.

What this journal entry also records is that early the next morning after the bomb scare, Margaret actually confronted Gough and asked him to explain why he had wanted her to accompany him on the campaign. Gough was never easy with personal questions which required him to explain the emotional reasons behind his actions. His answer was brief.

'Because you're an asset.'

It was the first real compliment Margaret had received on the campaign trail. Out of his mouth, it meant a lot to her. And then he added, 'And for company.'

That is about as much as he could reveal of his real emotions and personal need of her. Knowing him so well, she was content with his answer.

By Thursday 9 May they were a much happier couple and team.

The mood has changed. Tempers have improved and morale is high. Enthusiasm at meetings is beyond belief. Attendances have created records — the performance of EGW is masterly. No doubt he carries the burden and the team but how well he wears.

She was back in love with him again.

On 10 May, *The Australian* recorded the huge crowds that her man was attracting, even in Liberal seats.

On Monday night in the Liberal seat of Bennelong, he drew more than 3500 people. The next night he attracted a huge crowd of more than 10 000 in the heartland of the very marginal seat of Cook. The next night Mr Whitlam got one of his biggest orations ever from a crowd approaching 4000 in the outer Melbourne seat of La Trobe.

The Murdoch press was not taking sides in this election. Gough and Rupert had gradually parted ways, as John Menadue, who was still general manager of News Ltd in Australia, confirmed. *The Australian*'s editorial pages featured one senior journalist writing 'Why I will vote Liberal' and another writing 'Why I will vote Labor'.

The election result was patchy in that Queensland showed a 4 per cent swing against the ALP, and the greater weighting given to country votes through unequal electorates resulted in a swing against the government. This was countered by the swing to the government in the suburbs of Melbourne and Sydney. Al Grassby suffered the shock of a defeat after what many condemned as a racist campaign against him.

For Gough, it was nevertheless a great victory. He became the first Labor PM ever to win consecutive terms. The government lost only one seat in the House of Representatives but with the addition of two new seats, its majority was reduced from nine to five. Gough's assessment of the election was that the double dissolution still did not give them control of the Senate. Both major parties held twenty-nine seats and there were two independents. But for the first time in its history, the ALP added three women to its Caucus.

The six bills that provided the grounds for the double dissolution would finally be passed.

Gough allowed himself to feel both angry at the hostile Senate which had caused the election and yet politically secure for the next three years.

The Opposition, however, felt even more determined to push their claim that the ALP still did not have a mandate to govern. They continued to insist that because they did not control the Senate, the government was illegitimate.

Within days of the election result the senior figures of Treasury warned Gough of a frightening economic outlook. Inflation was out of control, wages were out of control, public expenditure was far too high. All of this was exacerbated by the international oil crisis. Treasury's prescription was to cut spending, increase taxes on petrol, spirits and tobacco, restrain wages and increase unemployment. This was, if followed, to be the end of all of Labor's promises. Gough accepted their advice, believing it to be non-political, knowing that his decision would split both the cabinet and the Caucus. Cabinet became – in the words of Paul Keating, who had just become a minister – 'a basket case of undisciplined self-absorption'.

By 11 July 1974, Gough's fifty-eighth birthday, his government was destroying itself from within.

This was the day that Australia's eighteenth Governor-General was sworn in. His name was John Kerr and he had been entirely Gough's choice. Judgement of the right person for a particular job had never been his strong suit.

It had taken Kerr six months to consider Gough's offer and during that time he had insisted that the salary be increased by 50 per cent to equal that of the NSW Chief Justice, a position Kerr had only occupied for a year. He wanted his tenure increased to ten years, a clothes allowance and various other top-ups.

Gough agreed to all of these conditions. What he didn't know and was never told by Kerr, however, was that despite having assured Gough of his absolute confidentiality during these negotiations, he had discussed his possible appointment with at least three top legal figures, including Sir Garfield Barwick, Chief Justice of the High Court of Australia.

Gough never discussed his choice of Kerr with Margaret. If he had, she would have been highly critical and attempted to talk him out of it. She had overheard him discussing terms and conditions of the appointment with someone called John and wrongly assumed it to be Mr Justice John Moore, the president of the Australian Conciliation and Arbitration Commission. She was shocked when she discovered Gough had actually appointed John Kerr. She thought of him as a weak man with a high-pitched voice, and a bit 'suss'.

She said to Gough, 'Oh dear. You could have done better than him.' Gough would have none of it and listed off Kerr's achievements. Margaret told him that there was more to making the right appointment than listing the facts. There is knowledge of what motivates a person; knowledge of their strengths and weaknesses; knowledge of what lies beneath the public façade. Gough had never been very strong on subtext. Margaret wasn't the only one to have doubts about Kerr as Governor-General. When Bob Hawke and David Combe heard about it, they took off for the pub to drown their sorrows, utterly dismayed by what they considered to be 'a terrible appointment'. Hawke had encouraged Gough to consider Sir Richard Kirby. Lionel Murphy was also alarmed. 'It's your appointment, Gough . . . I only hope we don't live to rue the day.'

Margaret and Gough lunched with Kerr and his wife Peg at Yarralumla the day after Kerr had been sworn in. Gough and Kerr had known each other as colleagues over the years, but Margaret and Peg had trained together as social workers and been loyal friends for over thirty-two years. Margaret had always thought Kerr pompous compared to Peg, who was so unpompous. She knew that Peg was not well, having had a stroke, and suspected that the main reason Kerr had taken the job was that if something happened to Peg, there would be servants there to look after him. Margaret said, 'He actually admitted this. He was purely thinking of himself and that only increased my dislike of him.'

Not long after that lunch at Yarralumla, Peg was admitted to hospital. She died a few months later. Margaret was very sad, but not surprised when Kerr married again soon after. 'Of course he then married wife number two, who had been girlfriend number one for years and years.'

The fact that Gough had totally ignored Kerr's past associations with B. A. Santamaria and the DLP, and the fact that in 1963 he had tried and failed to win pre-selection to the Liberal Party, showed how much of an ingénue he was in the games of power and intrigue. Even Kerr's one-time friend, Liberal leader Billy Snedden, said, 'Was he a person you could trust? Oh God, no!'

During the late 1950s Kerr had become heavily involved with the Australian Association for Cultural Freedom, the publisher of the magazine *Quadrant* and the local offshoot of the Congress for Cultural Freedom, which was financed by the CIA. He was elected president of the Law Association for Asia and the Western Pacific, later to be revealed as 'a total CIA front'.

Margaret did not dwell on her husband's poor choice of Governor-General, firstly because she knew that once he had made the appointment he would never admit to having any doubts and, secondly, because she was off with her secretary, Barbara Stewart, to Japan to launch a new container ship for the Australian National Line.

On 9 August she stood on the dock in Kobe and declared, 'I name this ship the *Australian Emblem*. May God bless her and all who sail in her.' Her little axe cut the cord that released the bottle of champagne that baptised the ship in the traditional manner. It was the same day that President Nixon resigned, which killed off any media coverage.

Returning at 6 am the following morning she found the press waiting for her. Tired after her ten-hour flight, she ignored the advice of her secretary to just say 'no comment'. She stopped to answer their questions, 'out of politeness'. After a few cursory questions about the ship launch, they asked her about inflation in Japan. She answered that there was a problem with inflation there and added, 'But I think you people do not help with all the hoo-hah you go on with. Australia is in a much better position than the rest of the world.'

Headlines in all the papers the next morning shouted 'PM's Wife Thinks Inflation a Lot of Hoo-Hah'.

The words 'Hoo-Hah' opened the floodgates when she arrived at a lunch in the Green Valley Community Centre in Sydney's western suburbs, where she was to be guest speaker. Three housewives were waiting for her with placards that read:

'INFLATION DOESN'T MATTER? NOR DO WE?'

'MRS WHITLAM YOU CAN AFFORD TO IGNORE INFLATION – GREEN VALLEY CANNOT'

'MRS WHITLAM COULDN'T CARE LESS'

She swept past them. When she stood to give her speech she emphasised that she had been misquoted and had her words taken out of context, adding, 'Please don't believe a word you read in the newspapers. The press is an ass.' She went on to accuse them of being 'vultures, praying mantises, uninvited guests and intruders'. It was her temper that was now on display.

She was definitely on a roll, especially when 150 housewives clapped and laughed. She even turned towards the bank of television cameras aimed at her and said, 'You wouldn't be here today unless you hoped I'd put my other foot in it. I don't suppose the gentlemen of the press would even know where Green Valley is, or how the other half lives.' Her green eyes were flashing. The media was lapping it all up.

She calmed herself down a little and pointed out that not far across the creek was Albert Street, Cabramatta, where she and her family used to live. When she was asked whether the federal government understood how fed up everyone was with inflation she gave the answer she should have given the day before. 'My husband is sick at heart about the whole situation. And so am I.'

But it was too late for her to salvage her situation. The next day the newspapers reported everything she said, especially the comment that they were all 'vultures'. What followed were letters to the editor from members of the AJA (Australian Journalists Association), of which she was a member, calling her comments 'red-neck'. One female AJA member demanded she apologise, resign her union membership and stick to social work.

Margaret Whitlam's honeymoon with the press was over. Gough never berated her for her intemperate words. He had been in the publicity game long enough to know that the press can make you a rooster or a feather duster.

Having done it, Margaret did not lose too much sleep worrying about the incident. She was too excited about the prospect of presenting her own, one-hour television program, to be called *With Margaret Whitlam*. It was to be produced by David Frost's company, Paradine Productions, and recorded in Melbourne.

Her first program went to air on 5 September, her subject was pornography and her first guests were David Frost and Leonard Bernstein, in Australia to conduct a series of concerts. She presented herself not so much as an interviewer but as a host. 'It's not a show, it's a conversation piece.' It certainly was a topic of conversation among the Australian population, amazed that the wife of a Prime Minister would agree to present her own television program.

In general, the television critics were not kind. They claimed David Frost 'gushed all over her saying "she's so good, so lovely, *so divine*".' They complained that she talked over the top of Bernstein. Headlines like 'All So Much Hoo-Hah' were predictable.

Margaret was pleased with the show and determined to ignore the negative comments. 'I suspect that most bad comments were written by people who didn't see the whole program. Anyway, that's what I like to think. It makes for a happier way to deal with it.'

Gough thought she was simply marvellous for giving it a go. He always admired her spirit of adventure and positive attitude. He knew she was genuinely interested in other people and said she was 'addicted' to conversation.

The critic from the *Age* said that 'she was so amusingly erudite that I won't be surprised if her show outlives the Labor regime that, indirectly, spawned it'. Words like 'warmth', 'witty', 'ironic' and 'wry' were often used, showing that Margaret approached this new role of television presenter in the same way she approached life – by being herself.

In her *Woman's Day* column she admitted that she had 'fallen in love with' Leonard Bernstein. She was quite smitten with him. After Margaret had taped his interview he invited her to accompany him to a cocktail party that Dick Hamer, the Victorian Premier, was having for him. She demurred. He insisted. Margaret could not resist his charms. Hamer was surprised but delighted to see Bernstein arrive with the PM's wife on his arm.

> Lenny was absolutely gorgeous. In the taxi he was rabbiting on and asking me about music. He was touchy but not feely. I confessed that I liked music to float over me. He said, 'Oh no, Margaret, it's got to be more than floating' and went into a long dissertation about the power of music.

He was vivacious, funny, intense, charismatic, intelligent and sexy. Perhaps this is why when he asked her out to dinner after the cocktail party she refused. She said that she might have had an affair with him if she'd had the time and circumstances had been different. Another woman might have seized this opportunity to have dinner and a one-night fling, but Margaret was essentially a true and faithful woman who loved to flirt but was not prepared to break what she saw as 'the rules'. She told Gough about her visit to the cocktail party and he seemed more amused by it than worried. It would never have occurred to him that Margaret would be unfaithful.

Breaking the rules was, however, the main topic of the media regarding Margaret. Now they were complaining that with her $400 per week from her television program, $250 for her diary column and the salary from her directorship of the Commonwealth Hostels, her weekly income was only a few hundred dollars less than her husband's. The *Sunday Observer* insisted she refuse the payments as it was an embarrassment for her husband and the Labor Party. The *Sunday Mail* ran headlines like 'Big Big Purse for Big Marg'. Some said Margaret was guilty of cashing in on her husband's good fortune. She was called 'the voluble hoo-hah political madam'.

Her secretary issued a press release assuring everyone that all her earnings would be donated to charity.

Inevitably there was the predictable, anachronistic argument from Mike Gibson in the *Daily Telegraph* that it wasn't 'proper' or 'dignified' for the wife of the PM to do such work. 'I don't want to be represented by the compere of a late, late TV show or someone who writes a housewives' gazette in a women's magazine.'

Margaret simply ignored such comments and continued to enjoy doing her program, in the process interviewing, among others, an Antarctic explorer, a racing driver, a pop music composer, a photographer and a US Ambassador. The second series was moved to a later, less popular timeslot, which always means lower ratings. Her contract was eventually not renewed.

Gough's ratings were sliding too. Mostly due to Australia's increasing inflation rate. At 14.4 per cent Australia's inflation rate was lower than that of Japan (22.5 per cent), Italy (18.9 per cent) and Britain (17.7 per cent). However, America, West Germany and Canada all had much lower rates of inflation than Australia, despite being hit by the same increase in oil prices.

He was also attacked for his frequent trips overseas. The *News* in Adelaide wrote:

> With the economy at a most critical stage, the Prime Minister is packing his bags for North America. He could hardly have chosen a worse time to be away – with massive unemployment looming, the effects of the budget and devaluation still to be tested and with wage indexation in the balance. Later this year Mr Whitlam will be away again – on a tour of Europe.

Gough never took such attacks seriously. There was a sense among voters that he was away too much and that he used the position of Prime Minister as an excuse for travelling and cultural pursuits. It was true that Gough had discovered a passion for travel. He found it relaxing, restorative and stimulating. The tougher it became at home, the more he needed to recharge his batteries through combining travel with international leaders' meetings. It was not as if he was lounging around drinking Piña Coladas in the sunshine, but that was how the public perceived it.

He was fortunate that John Menadue had left his employment with Murdoch and returned to take over as the Head of the Department of Prime Minister and Cabinet. Gough had finally become suspicious of the senior bureaucrats who had worked in the Treasury for the conservatives for the past twenty-three years they had been in office. He needed Menadue because he could trust him and his judgement absolutely.

On 15 December, Gough and Margaret left Australia for their Christmas break. It was Gough's usual breakneck itinerary – thirteen countries in thirty days, including Sri Lanka, Belgium and the United Kingdom.

On 25 December, Cyclone Tracy hit Darwin. Devastation and chaos on Christmas Day. Australian newspapers depicted Gough and Margaret surveying the ancient ruins of Greece rather than the recent ruins of Darwin. They were, in fact, at King's College, Cambridge, listening to Christmas carols.

Menadue and Acting Prime Minister Jim Cairns were shocked and horrified by what greeted them in Darwin. They rang Gough and advised him to fly home immediately. Margaret agreed with them. Her diary records her instinctive reaction. 'My first impulse was to fly home with my husband but I was told that my duty lay with the maintenance of the planned program of visits.'

Freudenberg was a witness to the very heated argument between Gough and Margaret over this issue. Margaret was adamant that their duty was to be with the victims of this disaster. Gough failed to grasp the political implications of them not both ending their trip and returning home. Personally, he felt he had worked very hard and desperately needed the break that the trip afforded.

Once again, he lacked the ability to see it from the viewpoint of the Australian people. His continuing with an overseas trip of which they were already critical was seen as a totally selfish act. The public believed his duty was to be with those Australians in need and to be seen to be helping them through this crisis in whatever way he could.

Margaret argued her case from every angle but he refused to agree with her. The social worker in her knew the people in Darwin needed to feel that the Whitlams were on their side. As a director on the board of the Commonwealth Hostels she knew the necessity of being there to ensure the quick supply of shelter and food. And even more importantly, to provide a sense of security. All her instincts cried out for them to fly straight back to Darwin. Gough simply did not understand her arguments; he did not want to even entertain them.

As someone who had fought in World War II, he should have remembered the strength and courage, not to mention respect, that King George VI and the Queen Mother afforded those whose homes had been destroyed by continuing to live in London and survive in the rubble with them.

Gough's eventual compromise with Margaret was that he would fly home for a few days while she carried on with the meetings already planned, as his deputy.

Right up until he left for the airport she continued to plead the case that she should accompany him. In the end, as Prime Minister, he had made his decision and that was that. She knew it was the wrong decision, but also knew that he was absolutely determined to carry on with the trip after he had dealt with the disaster. There was nothing else she could say or do.

Margaret followed his orders and flew on to Sicily and Malta. When he finally arrived in Darwin, he was shocked not just by the devastation of the cyclone but by the intensity of the hostility of the people towards him. Nothing, however, would have made him change his plans. He told Brigadier Alan Stretton, who was in charge of restoration and was complaining about federal ministers who wanted to make their own decisions, 'They give me the shits as well. Do what you have to do. If you have any problems, give me a ring and I will fix it.'

When Gough returned to Kirribilli House for cabinet meetings, Menadue took up the argument that he should give up the overseas trip and return to Darwin with Margaret by his side. He pursued it with relentless fervour as, like Margaret, he knew that it was the right thing to do. Eventually Gough looked him in the eye with a cold stare and said, 'Comrade, if I am to put up with the fuckwits in the Labor Party I have got to have my trips.'

This may well have been true, but this situation was not about him. It was about the thousands of people in Darwin who were homeless and in need of his help and support. He should have been seen to be putting them first, even if he resented it.

The resumption of his trip to Crete to meet up with Margaret did not gain him any friends. It did, however, please his enemies on both sides of the House. Despite all the good that so many of his policies had done for so many people, they never forgave him for choosing Europe over being with those shattered Australians in Darwin. Like all human beings he had his blind spots, and this decision highlighted one of them. It did him more damage than he could ever have imagined.

* * *

In 1975, Gough appointed Margaret to chair the Australian National Advisory Committee for International Women's Year. Even though she was not sure about the aggressiveness and the shrillness that often accompanied the burgeoning women's liberation movement that was sweeping the world and roaring through Australia like a bushfire, she was a firm believer in their cause. She called upon all women to take control of their own lives.

The political year began with the ALP federal conference in Terrigal. Margaret spent most of her time swimming in the pool. Photos of her diving appeared in all the newspapers, together with descriptions of her swimming 'queen-like' laps. Gough was busy undermining the power of his enemies in Treasury by gaining support for his proposal for the creation of a new Department of Economic Planning. His other aim was to gain support for Rex Connors' plans for 100 per cent ownership of all energy resources in Australia. Gough shared Connors' vision and encouraged him to search for overseas loans, which resulted in a meeting late in 1974 with a shady London-based commodities dealer by the name of Khemlani. Jim Cairns also decided to tell the *Sunday Sun* that he 'felt a kind of love' for his sexy office manager Junie Morosi. Inflation was rising and support for Labor was falling.

The February parliament was a powder keg just waiting for a match. The Opposition persisted in their deliberate strategy of creating chaos and disorder. Their aim was to convince the voters that there was a national crisis and therefore a desperate need for a change of government. The Speaker, Jim Cope, struggled to control the rowdy mob and was finally convinced by Whitlam to resign. It was the beginning of resignations and sackings of men in the ministry whose surname began with 'C'.

In March, Snedden was replaced as Opposition leader by the steely-eyed Malcolm Fraser, who had been responsible for undermining Gorton's leadership and was widely distrusted among his own colleagues. They did, however, recognise his strengths: ruthless determination and relentless ambition. His aim was clear. First he would take control of the divided Liberal Party, then he would control the parliament, which was already self-destructing under Gough's leadership, and finally he would destroy the government.

At 6 feet 5 inches, he was the first Liberal leader to match Gough's towering presence. However, Gough never matched Fraser's cunning.

April 1975 saw Margaret and her secretary, Barbara Stewart, quietly visiting the victims of Cyclone Tracy. Margaret praised their resilience and their determination to get on with their lives. She met young women bringing up their children in tents and caravans and told them how much she admired their calm and their optimism. She also told them she looked forward to playing a part in the planning of the new Darwin. Happy though they were to see her, they had no praise for her husband.

June was spent in Jamaica for the Commonwealth Heads of Government Meeting (CHOGM), where Margaret joined the wives from Jamaica, Britain, Canada, Nigeria, Guyana and Western Samoa in a mini-conference to discuss the role of women in society.

This was followed by the big International Women's Year conference in Mexico, where Margaret never sought to assert herself as the wife of the PM and involved herself in all the discussions and activities with great humility. Susan Ryan, a candidate for the Senate, described Margaret as 'a beacon of sanity and common sense'.

Back home Gough was sinking further into conflict and fighting adversaries on many fronts. The Bass by-election had resulted in a 17 per cent swing against the government and the loss of that seat to the Liberals for the first time in twenty years. Fraser was a formidable opponent and Gough set about trying to put his ministry in order. Clyde Cameron was moved, and Bill Hayden replaced Cairns as Treasurer.

Margaret spoke to Gough about Cairns' relationship with Junie Morosi, but he said it was Cairns' personal business and all the rumours were tabloid beat-ups. Margaret did not agree. She argued that Cairns was making a complete fool of himself, his wife, Gwen, and the government. She urged Gough to talk to him, though she must have known that this was the last thing Gough would do. He avoided personal, one-on-one discussions with her, let alone his colleagues. He either avoided them, delegated someone else to talk to them or tongue-lashed them in the throes of a temper tantrum. He never developed the skills necessary to deal with the management of his ministers.

July brought an end to Margaret's employment as a columnist with *Woman's Day*. Joan Reeder, the editor, wrote, 'You may think that this decision is somehow mixed up with the present problems of the government . . . The fact is, Margaret, that we think the column has run its course.'

Margaret accepted her sacking with her usual calm stoicism, not seeking to retaliate or punish anyone. It was not her style or her inclination.

Hayden produced a budget in 1975 of which the media approved. Despite the fact that accusations and allegations were escalating about what became known as 'the loans affair', Australia had for the first time in its history received a triple-A credit rating.

Just when Gough began to hope that his defiance against the allegations that the government was in chaos had started to pay off, the Opposition produced evidence that Rex Connor had continued to pursue loans with Khemlani after the date Gough had told him to cease. Connor was obliged to resign. Cairns' sacking followed when a document which he claimed he could not remember signing was produced, showing that he too had been pursuing loans behind the PM's back. Fraser described the government as 'the worst in Australia's history' – thus paving the way for him to ultimately convince the Senate to block the supply bills.

One night in September found Gough alone in his office with Elizabeth Reid, his Women's Adviser. She was there to protest Menadue's suggestion of moving her unit out of Gough's office and into the Department of Premier and Cabinet. She paced the room as she talked, becoming more and more emotional. When tears began to run down her face Gough's embarrassment manifested as a stony silence. When she could see her words were having no effect she blurted out, 'And you should know that Kerr told me personally that he was intending to dismiss you and force an election. He also told Clifton Pugh the same thing when he was painting Kerr's official portrait.'

Gough did not respond. He simply did not believe her. She was clearly overcome with emotion and he wished she would leave his office so he could get on with his work.

Reid said, 'It was as if I hadn't spoken. I walked away feeling that I was the wrong messenger, that in Gough's head I was this woman who was his adviser on women, so how could I possibly have something as grounded and shattering as that to say to him.' She left his office, never to return.

Gough claims not to remember that conversation. It is possible that he totally dismissed it as the ravings of a woman out of control. Nor did he repeat what Reid had told him to Menadue or to Margaret. Even if Margaret had believed Reid, Gough would have remained certain in his own belief that Kerr would never betray him or the government.

Day by day, the Opposition, under the leadership of Malcolm Fraser, turned the heat up on the fact that Gough would be forced to defer the supply bills in the Senate because of what Fraser described as 'extraordinary and reprehensible circumstances'.

On 15 October the Senate voted to defer the budget, by twenty-nine votes to twenty-eight.

Murdoch's *Australian* reported that 'If Mr Whitlam continued to stay in office without seeking a general election, the Governor-General had the power to dismiss him as Prime Minister.' Margaret was alarmed when she read this. She rang Gough immediately. He assured her that she had no cause for worry. It was just media muckraking. He would sort it all out. She believed him because he had successfully negotiated so many political crises in the past.

Nevertheless, she took herself off to the visitors' gallery to witness parliamentary proceedings for herself. What she saw was her husband delivering rousing, fighting speeches as a forerunner to the half-Senate election he was planning. Her morale lifted.

On 18 October, the headline in *The Australian* read, 'Governor-General Will Act Soon, Says Fraser'.

Violent demonstrations against the Opposition's blocking of supply were being held in every capital city.

On 21 October, Fraser met with John Kerr. He had clearly sensed Kerr's insecurity regarding his position and after that meeting he never wavered in his belief that Kerr would intervene on the Opposition's behalf if Gough refused to call a general election. There were, however, those in Fraser's own party who were very uneasy about the stand-off that Fraser had engineered. He told them not to waver, certain that he would win through.

Sir Robert Menzies was encouraged by Fraser to enter the fray and publicly support the actions of the Opposition. On 22 October, Menzies released a public statement aimed not only at attacking the government but killing off public support for the Opposition. He urged the Governor-General to step in and act unilaterally.

As if he did not have enough enemies, Gough also embroiled himself in a fight over CIA influence in the National Country Party, which resulted in the CIA believing that Gough would reveal in parliament that Pine Gap was in fact a CIA operation. Telexes to and from the CIA and their operatives in Australia which focused on how to deal with this crisis were revealed in a later film titled *The Falcon and the Snowman*. The former CIA operative Christopher Boyce, following his recent release from prison, revealed in his book *American Sons: The Untold Story of the Falcon and the Snowman* that the reason he decided to betray the CIA was their deception about their interference in the politics of a parliamentary democracy, namely Australia, who had fought next to the United States in two world wars. He also claimed that he heard the project CIA resident refer to the Governor-General of Australia as 'our man Kerr.'

Gough was courting danger by threatening to close down Pine Gap. And yet at no stage did Gough's faith in Kerr falter. He believed that by standing his ground he would win through because everyone involved, especially Kerr, would follow proper and correct procedures according to the Constitution.

Unlike Gough, Fraser had a far more perceptive grasp of Kerr's failings and insecurities. He also knew how to play on them to his own advantage. He admitted later, 'I knew Sir John fairly well, something Whitlam had forgotten.'

Gough had no interest in the inner workings of Kerr's psychology. He seemed incapable of looking beneath the surface of the man's behaviour and relied instead on the political rules and constitutional requirements of the position of Governor-General in relation to the Prime Minister. He also failed to notice how Kerr's recent marriage to his second wife and former mistress, Nancy, had changed him. She was as desperate as he was to be reassured that her life at Admiralty House was secure. They both adored all the pomp, privilege and ceremony that accompanied the role of Governor-General. It never occurred to Gough that Kerr might be feeling personally threatened and insecure because of this crisis.

In fact, on 16 October at a state dinner at Government House, the Prime Minister of Malaysia, Tun Abdul Razak, had openly asked Gough what the role of the Governor-General would be if the Senate did not pass the budget. Gough quipped, 'It all depends on who gets to the phone first, he to dismiss me or I to have him recalled.'

Everyone laughed but Kerr. This was exactly the question that obsessed him, day and night. Margaret joined in the laughter but she was not convinced that Kerr was on their side. His new wife, she had noticed, was at great pains to emphasise her status and her sophistication. Gough referred to her in private as 'fancy Nancy'. One of her most obvious pretensions was her insistence on having the dinner menus for Admiralty House printed entirely in French. (One of her previous roles had been to look after French officials from French Polynesia, Tahiti and New Caledonia.) At a recent formal dinner Gough had pointed out a mistake in her menu in his typical blunt manner, in front of the other guests. 'Nancy,' he said, 'I'm surprised. You've made a mistake in your French.' She bridled a little but tried to laugh it off. 'Oh, Prime Minister, you can't mean that.' But Gough would not let it go and laboured his point of correction.

Later on at home, when they were alone, Margaret said, 'That was not a very clever thing to do. Did you notice the expression on both their faces? It won't stand you in good stead. No one likes being corrected and embarrassed in public.'

Gough dismissed her comments, once again displaying his total lack of understanding of other people's reactions to his behaviour. Margaret, however, was very attuned to the effect his words had on other people. Vain and pretentious people are often insecure, and hate to have their mistakes pointed out, especially in public. She continued to argue that he should not be so sure of Kerr's undying support.

'It was just a little thing, Margaret. Don't labour the point. Besides, I was right.' Margaret snorted, 'That only makes it worse. You will not be forgiven for it. Mark my words for once.'

After the Opposition blocked supply once again, Kerr asked Gough if he could discuss the impending situation with Fraser. Suspecting nothing untoward, Gough agreed, ignorant of the fact that they had been in contact several times.

On 6 November, Gough met briefly with Kerr to confirm that he would call a half-Senate election, to be held on 13 December. Kerr went ahead and chaired the Executive Council meeting as if nothing was amiss. Later that afternoon Gough even suggested that Hayden, as Treasurer, fully brief Kerr that supply funds would last until about 11 December.

'He's one of us. You can trust him,' assured Gough.

During this briefing, Hayden was suspicious of Kerr's disinterest. Instead of going to the airport as he had planned, he asked the driver to go straight to Parliament House where he ran down the corridors. Bursting straight into Gough's suite, he said, 'My old copper's instinct tells me he's going to sack us.'

'No, comrade, he wouldn't have the guts to do it,' was Gough's only reply.

This showed that apart from the fact that he believed that proper procedure would not allow it, Gough considered Kerr to be a weak, gutless man. It therefore followed that he would be too weak to go up against Gough. At this point Gough might also have considered the possibility of a weak man caving into the conservatives in an attempt to save his own skin. Judas was a weak man.

That night over dinner in Canberra with Margaret, Freudenberg and friends, Gough was so buoyed up at what he foresaw as his future success and Fraser's impending failure that he leant across the table to Freudenberg, raised a glass and proposed a toast to John Kerr. Margaret did not drink to it.

9

A fight for love and glory

The eleventh day of the eleventh month of 1975 is a day etched in the minds of many Australians.

It was one of those rare occasions when Gough awoke alone at the Lodge. Margaret had spent the night at Kirribilli House as it was the last board meeting of the year for Commonwealth Hostels Ltd and she had invited the board members over for drinks and lunch as a Christmas treat. Gough was already in his office at Parliament House by 9 am. He had ignored the bevy of reporters buzzing with the rumours that he would soon be announcing a half-Senate election. Fred Daly and Frank Crean joined him for a thirty-minute meeting with Fraser, Phillip Lynch and Doug Anthony. Gough offered a compromise, whereby he would delay the half-Senate election for six months if the Opposition would allow the Senate to pass the supply bills immediately. Fraser said that he would consult his senior colleagues about the offer, but that he did not think they would change their position. He then requested that the government not reveal anything of this meeting to the media. Gough's obsessive belief in following correct protocol – which was that the Governor-General be told of a half-Senate election before the media – led him to agree to this request without questioning Fraser's motivation. It worried Frank Crean, who asked Gough before he left the meeting whether the Governor-General was still onside.

'Of course,' replied Gough, reaffirming his belief that the Constitution stated that the Governor-General must act only on the advice of the elected Prime Minister. Fred Daly did not share Gough's confidence that the Governor-General would always stick to the rules. He smelt a rat.

Gough contacted Kerr just after 10 am to make an immediate appointment to see him and have him sign the official letter. Kerr delayed the meeting until 2 pm. Gough then proceeded to the Caucus meeting where he announced there was to be a half-Senate election. They all burst into cheers and spontaneous clapping. He told them that this had been a fight against the blackmail of the Senate that they had been duty-bound to win, not just for their government but for all future governments.

At 11.45 am the House of Representatives met to debate an Opposition censure motion against the Prime Minister. Fraser reiterated once again his repeated belief 'that there are circumstances where a Governor-General may have to act as the ultimate protector of the Constitution'. Gough ignored this statement as he was certain that the Governor-General's announcement of a half-Senate election was assured. He moved an amendment to censure Fraser. In the middle of Gough's attack on him, Fraser stood up and left the Chamber. Gough was momentarily thrown by Fraser's departure, but continued to debate the censure until the House adjourned at 12.55 pm.

Gough returned to his office to pick up the official letter for the Governor-General, then hopped into the prime ministerial white Mercedes.

* * *

When the car pulled up at the Governor-General's residence at Yarralumla, Gough did not know that Fraser was already inside, waiting in a nearby room. His car was parked around the back of the building.

Kerr and Gough were face to face in Kerr's study. As Gough took out the letter from his pocket, he said, 'I have the letter advising a half-Senate election.' Kerr interrupted him.

'Before you say anything, Prime Minister, I want to say something to you. You have told me this morning on the phone that your talks with the leaders on the other side have failed to produce any change and that things therefore remain the same. Are you prepared to recommend a general election?' Gough said he was not. Ignoring the letter Gough was holding towards him, Kerr handed him a letter of his own, already signed, which dismissed him and his entire government. Gough took it and read it quickly. He could not have been more shocked if the Governor-General had taken out a gun and threatened to shoot him.

He sat there staring at Kerr in stunned disbelief.

Kerr's high-pitched voice broke the silence. 'My reasons are set out here.' He then handed him a statement that Sir Anthony Mason had drafted days earlier, which Kerr had signed.

'Have you discussed this with the Palace?' asked Gough, suddenly finding his voice.

'I don't have to,' Kerr replied, 'and it's too late. I have already terminated your commission,' adding, 'the Chief Justice approves of this course of action.' The Chief Justice was Gough's old nemesis, Sir Garfield Barwick.

'I advised you that you should not consult with him,' Gough asserted.

Shrugging his shoulders, Kerr responded, 'We will all have to live with this.'

'You certainly will,' said Gough.

Kerr stood up and stretched out his hand.

Dumbfounded and dazed, Gough shook it, out of habit and courtesy, turned and walked out of the room.

They would never speak to each other again.

Minutes later, Fraser walked in and eagerly accepted and signed the letter outlining the conditions offered to him as the newly appointed caretaker Prime Minister of Australia.

On returning to the Lodge, Gough's first thought was of Margaret. She and her board were just finishing their pre-lunch drinks overlooking the harbour when she was informed that there was an urgent call for her from Canberra. When she picked up the phone in the study it was Robert Millar, Gough's driver, who spoke.

'The boss asked me to tell you that he's been sacked.'

'What do you mean "sacked"?'

'He told me to tell you that he can't ring you at the moment but he's been sacked. That's all I know. He said he'll ring you later.'

Margaret put down the receiver and returned to the dining room. The word 'sacked' stung her ears.

One of her colleagues, noticing her worried expression, asked, 'Anything wrong, Margaret?'

'No, no, let's have some of this delicious food.'

Thirty minutes later she heard the phone ring and raced to answer it.

'He's sacked me,' said Gough.

'Who's sacked you?'

'Kerr.'

'Don't be ridiculous. He can't sack you, you're the elected Prime Minister.'

'I walked into his office, he asked me whether I was going to agree to an election of the House of Reps. I refused. He said, "In that case I have no alternative but to withdraw your commission." And he handed me a sheet of paper.'

'How ridiculous. Why didn't you just tear it up?'

'Because, Margaret, it was a legal document.'

'So what! You should have torn it up. There were only two of you there. Or you should have slapped his face and told him to pull himself together.'

Margaret was serious.

'I have to go, Margaret. There are people I have to see. I'll ring again later.'

Margaret returned to the table and somehow continued to smile and nod and chat in a normal fashion. When they had finished their coffee, she returned with them all to finish the board meeting in North Sydney.

No matter how hard she tried she simply could not concentrate on the agenda. Sacked! What was she meant to do? Why hadn't he called her back to say he'd fixed it. Sacked! But he had been elected – twice. He'd fix it – he always fixed problems in the past. Sacked! Couldn't be right.

Eventually one of her fellow board members sensed from her expression that something was definitely wrong.

'Why don't you buzz off home, Margaret? We'll finish the meeting.'

* * *

At 1.45 pm John Menadue was eating a sandwich in his office at West Block, waiting for Gough to call him and confirm a half-Senate election. When the phone rang, it was the Governor-General's private secretary, David Smith, eager to pass on the news of Gough's dismissal.

When Menadue arrived at the Lodge, Gough was sitting at a table in the sunroom, eating a steak. While many of his colleagues found it hard to believe he could eat anything, given the circumstances, they did not realise that food was always a steadying and comforting influence on him.

'The bastard's done a Game on me,' he shouted at Menadue, referring to the previous dismissal of the New South Wales Lang government by Governor Sir Philip Game.

The Lodge suddenly erupted into chaos as everyone burst into the sunroom, confusion and shock on their faces. Amid the chaos, they decided that Gough should draft the necessary resolutions to fight Kerr's actions for the afternoon sitting of the House of Representatives, where he still retained confidence. Gough did not know that Kerr had already appointed Fraser as caretaker Prime Minister.

* * *

Margaret's doctor was waiting for her when she arrived back at Kirribilli House. He had heard the news on the ABC.

'I thought you might be suffering from shock. I called around to see if you needed anything.'

Margaret was touched. She was not in need of medication but poured herself a generous Bloody Mary while the two of them sat in the living room, waiting for the phone to ring.

* * *

As Gough drafted his motion, the blood that had drained from his face with the shock began to return. He became more convinced that if he played this properly, he would defeat Fraser and be restored as Prime Minister by the People's House. He rang Margaret when he had finished to assure her that he would fix it. She said she was pleased to hear the energy back in his voice, and he said he was pleased the doctor was with her.

'I'd better come down straight away,' Margaret said. She knew that he needed her in times of crisis. Even if there was nothing she could actually do, they would be together. They were both stronger when they were side by side.

'No, you stay where you are. I'm driving to Sydney tomorrow,' he replied.

His voice was so firm and assured she thought it best not to argue. She desperately wanted to be with him, but did not want to upset him.

He told her again that everything would be fine by the end of the day, told her he loved her, to stay calm and that he would ring again later.

* * *

Nick Whitlam and his wife Judy had only returned from the United Kingdom to live in Sydney five days before. Nick heard the news bulletin in a taxi on his way back home from lunch. The bulletin said that a vote of no-confidence in Fraser was being put to the House of Representatives. He thought to himself, 'Dad will be back in power before the day is out.'

Margaret received another call from Gough's driver to pass on the same news from Gough. She was almost reassured.

Unfortunately, in all the shock and confusion swirling around the Lodge, no one had bothered to inform Ken Wriedt, the Leader in the Senate, what he should do.

At 2 pm, Reg Withers was sitting there 'grinning like a Cheshire cat', knowing his tactics had won through.

At 2.20 pm, having had no communication from Gough or anyone else, Wriedt moved that the appropriation bills be brought forward.

At 2.24 pm, the vote was passed. The Senate of the twenty-ninth parliament of Australia adjourned, never to sit again.

In the House of Representatives the motion of no-confidence in the new Prime Minister moved by Gough was carried, sixty-four votes to fifty-four. The Speaker, Gordon Scholes, announced his intention to convey the House's message to the Governor-General and the sitting was suspended until 5.30 pm. When Scholes rang Yarralumla to seek an appointment with the Governor-General, he was told that Kerr was too busy to see him.

No one in the Labor Party could believe that the Governor-General had placed himself above the elected Prime Minister and the House of Representatives to remove a Prime Minister and a government before an election had been called. There were even those in the Coalition who were shocked. They would have accepted some kind of intervention to demand a general election, but not the sacking of a democratically elected Prime Minister by a Governor-General whom he himself had appointed.

As the news spread, hordes of shouting, angry, emotional crowds surged around Parliament House. A continuous communal chant of 'We want Gough!' boomed down the corridors.

At 4.45 pm, the Governor-General's secretary, David Smith, stood on the steps of Parliament House. He read a proclamation from John Kerr announcing that he was dissolving both Houses. He concluded with the words 'God save the Queen'. Gough had pushed through the crowds and was standing right behind him. When he took the microphone there was deafening cheering and whistling. Towering over them all, he began 'Ladies and gentlemen . . .' There was silence. And then, his eyes flashing with the fire of revenge, he boomed, 'Well may we say, "God save the Queen" – because nothing will save the Governor-General.' Thunderous applause followed the confident upward tilt of his head.

He continued. 'The proclamation which you have just heard read by the Governor-General's official secretary was counter-signed "Malcolm Fraser", who will undoubtedly go down in Australian history from Remembrance Day 1975 as Kerr's cur.'

And finally, because he simply couldn't resist putting it on the record, 'I'm the first Prime Minister to be sacked since George III sacked Lord North.' He urged everyone 'to maintain their rage' for the next four and a half weeks until election day.

Gough rang Margaret to tell her that it had been agreed they would stay in the Lodge until the election. She said, 'Well, I'm leaving Kirribilli House before midnight. It's not proper that I stay here. If you're sure that it's not necessary for me to be with you, I'll go to the flat.'

They had purchased a small flat in Darling Point as their secret retreat from the rigours of life in the public eye. There, the two of them could spend time with each other. Margaret would cook the roast lamb while Gough sat nearby, proofreading his papers. They thought it would be a lovely place to live when they eventually retired.

'If you think that is for the best, my darling, then do it. I'll be there tomorrow. I have to go now; there are so many things that need to be done. I'll see you tomorrow. Give my love to the kids and tell them everything will work out for the best.'

When he hung up, Margaret felt a strange panic begin to rise in her throat. Knowing she had to get a grip on herself she rang Nick and asked him and Judy to come over. Tony was working overseas; she would contact him later. Catherine suddenly appeared on the doorstep, wide-eyed with shock.

'Are you okay, Mum?' she asked, enveloping her in a big hard hug.

'Yes, darling, I'm fine. I'll need your help moving some of our personal stuff to the flat. Dad thinks it's best.'

Stephen was between diplomatic postings and was working in his office at the Department of Foreign Affairs when Sheena, his wife, rang him. He decided not to visit his father that night, as he knew he would be too busy. He rang his mother to check that she was with the rest of the family. The next day he called in to see his father twice, just so he could reassure himself and his mother that Gough was coping with the shock. Gough put on a brave face so the family would not be as distraught as he felt.

Margaret and her children sat down together at Kirribilli House for the last time to eat the wonderful dinner that the women on the staff, who were very upset, had cooked especially for them. Margaret took control and set the tone of the evening. The rules were – no more questions, no going over and over what had happened, no speculations, no anger. That way madness lay. They would wait for Gough to ring and be optimistic about the future. Shock insulated them from the bomb that had struck them. Deep down, they all believed that he would fix it. Somehow.

Margaret desperately wanted to be with him, to hold him, to kiss him, to comfort him. She knew his mind must be in turmoil and when it was he needed to be alone to think things through. She had to put his needs above hers.

Rationally, this all made sense but nothing quelled the horrible sinking feeling in her stomach. She needed to hear his voice.

When he picked up the phone she knew that his brusque replies to her questions were merely his way of saying, 'Please leave me alone to sort this out.'

'I know you have a lot on your plate at the moment, my darling, but are you sure you don't want me to fly down in the morning? I just need to be with you.'

'Absolutely not. I will have solved it all by then. You have to believe in me, Margaret. I know what I am doing. I hate us not being together but I need this time alone to think through all the alternatives. I love you but you must let me choose what is best. I will ring you in the morning.'

'Well, if you are sure. I don't want to disturb you any more than you already are.'

'It's for the best, darling. Please believe me.'

As soon as she put down the receiver, she wanted to ring him again. They were always at their best when they solved problems together. But she knew that there were times when he needed to blot out everyone else, be totally alone and inside his own head. She did not want to put any more pressure on him than he already had. But left to his own devices, he could spin right out of control. She should be there just to make sure he managed to get some sleep.

That night, Margaret slept alone in the flat – tossing and turning, constantly waking up to wonder if it was all a bad dream. How could this be happening to them? She desperately wanted to ring Gough and several times reached for the phone, but did not want to wake him up. He would need all the sleep he could get, just to cope with whatever lay ahead.

Gough was so disturbed he did not even bother to undress, let alone go to bed. He paced around and around the room, unable to settle. The events of the day swirled like a tornado inside his head. He wanted to ring Margaret but did not want to wake her up. He knew from her voice how distressed she was, but he also knew that she would be more distressed if she was here with him. He did not want to inflict more pain on her. Somehow, he alone had to find a path through this chaos. Different scenarios flashed through his mind like traffic lights on speed control.

At least the kids were there to help her. Eventually he sat down at his desk, always a place of calm, and recorded the events of the day, just to get them straight in his own head as well as for the historic record. The more words he wrote, the more unreal his predicament seemed to become.

Later, on 15 November, he told the interviewer Kerry O'Brien that he had never had a bigger shock in his life.

The next morning, having been up all night, sleepless and in shock, he made some notes for his regular weekly broadcast which he intended to fulfil. He rang Margaret, who said she was going into the city with their daughter-in-law to buy a television so she could at least keep up with the media coverage. He read his opening sentences to her:

When I last gave one of these broadcasts I spoke to you as Prime Minister of Australia, as head of the twice-elected government of this country. Today that office is held by another man, a man who has never faced an election as party leader in Opposition or in government: and Australia is ruled by a party twice defeated, twice rejected by the Australian people.

Margaret said, 'That's wonderful, darling, but I think you should speak more from the heart. Let them know how shocked and hurt and betrayed you feel. Everyone who has supported you must be feeling the same way.'

For once, he took her advice.

In his first broadcast since his dismissal he gave them a small glimpse of what he was going through:

Politics is not a life for faint-hearted people and we get used to the hard knocks; but you must forgive me if I betray some natural emotion at these events and the way they came about. I imagine that many of you – not necessarily Labor voters, but typical Australians of every persuasion – will have shared a sense of shock and incredulity at the developments of the past week. That such things could happen in Australia could seem beyond belief; but they have happened in other countries. It is possible for an elected government to be removed by the stroke of a pen.

The next night, 12 November, in his last phone call to Margaret he promised her he would unplug the phone and go to bed. No matter how hard he tried, sleep eluded him and he found himself at his desk, making notes for the most important election campaign he had ever faced.

Although Gough and Margaret had rung each other constantly she hated the fact that they were apart. Even though his staff and his cabinet were with him, it seemed chaotic to her. She knew that together they would have been able to create some order, make some sense of their bomb-blasted lives. She should have insisted on being there with him, but she knew he hated to be bossed around when he was in a state.

It was two full days before she saw him. By that time he appeared to be focused on the campaign and the task of convincing the voters to 'maintain the rage'. She knew that inside he was bleeding. That night, when they were finally alone and together in bed, she took him in her arms and held him very close. She wanted to pour all her love into him to stop the hurt. She also knew, however, that no amount of love from her, the children, his staff, his supporters would be enough until he had been reinstated as Prime Minister once again.

Gough no longer had the advantage of incumbency with which to fight the election. Nor was there much money in their coffers. Despite the plethora of reforms in education, the law, consumer protection, childcare, the arts, land rights and many more areas, the party's internal polling revealed that the only positive achievements for which the voters gave the Whitlam government any credit were Medibank and Legal Aid. The fact that Gough was the first Prime Minister in Australia's history to have been dismissed by the Governor-General hung around his neck like a dead albatross. Many people believed that there must have been more to it for Kerr to have taken such drastic action. Suspicions of corruption, scandals and conspiracies were rife.

Margaret threw every last bit of energy and love she possessed into keeping Gough buoyed up during the campaign. Never before had he felt so loved, not just by her but by the Australian people, who cheered him on in their thousands wherever they went. Surely, they thought, the wrong that had been inflicted by Kerr would be righted by the Australian people.

They were both quietly confident. Throughout the campaign they had been together, hip to hip. There was no bickering between them this time. She had become Gough's 'open missile' as opposed to his 'secret weapon'. She played a very prominent part in this campaign, speaking with passion at rallies, meetings and smaller groups. She was happy to do whatever she was asked – and more.

She told the *Age*, 'The whole business got my dander up so much I was ready for anything. I travelled the country with him and everywhere we went we were greeted with hordes of onside, loving, articulate, supportive people.'

In between these euphoric bouts of public adulation she kept Gough's spirits high. She regarded Kerr and Fraser with absolute scorn – not just for what they had done but for the dishonourable manner in which they had done it. 'I was very, very angry. How could those conservatives act against the proper conventions and everything they always said they held dear?'

Margaret was still in a state of shock and disbelief. She, too, was naïve in believing that the pursuit of power at any cost did not involve breaking the rules and deceiving your enemies. She had always thought she was more worldly and cynical about people's real motives than Gough. This time, they had deceived her as well as him.

Four and a half weeks later, after the masses of cheering crowds who had supported them all over the country, after the endless early mornings and late nights, after the desperate strategy meetings and the total exhaustion of meagre party funds, after all the 'Maintain the Rage' and 'Shame Fraser Shame' posters, Gough and Margaret retired to the Lodge to await the results of the election.

* * *

It was clear to both of them by 8.30 from the tally room results that they had lost. By 10 pm the loss was not just bad, it was catastrophic. They lost twenty-nine seats in the House of Representatives. Their five-seat majority was now a fifty-five-seat deficit. The chaos of the loans affair, the undisciplined behaviour of his ministers, the accelerated pace of change, had all taken their toll. The electorate had quite simply endured enough instability, trauma and conflict.

The Liberals had achieved a clear majority in both Houses. Six former ministers in the Whitlam government had lost their seats. It was the single greatest loss since Federation. The only small consolation was that Tony Whitlam had won the seat of Grayndler.

When it was clear that they had been savaged, Margaret moved away from her family and friends and hid herself in the butler's pantry. Graham Freudenberg saw her leave the room and followed her. Finally, amid the canned tomatoes, the regimented jars of chutneys and jams, she leant on her friend's shoulder and let her tears flow.

She sobbed for Gough. She sobbed for the loss of her desperate hope that they would be vindicated and return, triumphant, to the Lodge. She sobbed for the loss of the vision that Gough had cherished for the future of their country. She sobbed from sheer exhaustion.

Soon after 11 pm, Gough arrived at the tally room with a dry-eyed, composed Margaret by his side. The now familiar chant of 'We want Gough' rang out. He raised his hands. The chant eventually died down and the man who spoke was clearly gutted by the loss. He conceded defeat, congratulated his opponents and thanked everyone who had worked so hard in recent weeks. He was quiet, dignified and, above all, controlled.

It was Bob Hawke who, with tears streaming down his face, expressed the emotion and the words that Gough was repressing.

'We've had the guts ripped out of us.'

A case of do or die

Gough was a deeply wounded man. He had remained the leader of the party only because Bill Hayden refused it. John Kerr was now officially a national pariah. Not one member of the ALP Caucus attended the opening of parliament. One way or another, the nation was licking its wounds. Whitlam supporters still recovering from the loss of their leader, vowed revenge. Whitlam haters were just glad it was finally all over and the conservatives were back in control. Fraser was widely despised, despite his victory. Kerr was forced to face demonstrations, egg-throwing and public vilification wherever he went. He increased his drinking and was often visibly inebriated at official functions.

In April 1976, Fraser reintroduced the imperial honours system that Gough had replaced with the Australian system of honours. Sir John Kerr became the first Knight in the new system. Privately, whenever Gough railed against Kerr, Fraser and the Murdoch press, Margaret's general response was not to indulge him. 'It's done, my darling. There's no use in crying over spilt milk. We have to move on.'

She knew there were times when she had to take a tough love approach but secretly she was devastated for this shadow of the man he once was. His parliamentary performances had lost their fire and passion. Every parliamentary sitting was an ordeal to be endured.

Early in 1976 Richard Butler entered their lives. He had been based in Singapore in the diplomatic service when he was assigned to look after Gough, who had arrived for the funeral of the Malaysian Prime Minister. So impressed was Butler with the man who had been so viciously betrayed, he decided to take on the position of Gough's principal private secretary. Hawke had warned him off. 'Gough's finished. Don't go near him.' But Butler was determined to try and help Gough get back into power because he believed that what had happened to him was outrageously unjust.

On his first day in the new position Margaret popped into the office. They hit it off immediately. They shared cultural interests, a sense of humour and, most importantly, a devotion to Gough.

Butler witnessed, first-hand, how essential Margaret's strength and steely resolve were to Gough's fragile sense of well-being. Butler saw Gough as 'a divided soul'. A part of him was all anger, gritted teeth and clenched fists. The other half was a man who had been smashed with a sledgehammer. One day Gough would be barking orders at Butler in a ferocious, imperious manner. On other days he would arrive in Butler's office, slump into a chair and just sit there, as if to say, 'Help me, please help me.' He was totally lost.

Butler did his best. He is adamant, however, that it was Margaret and her deep, unconditional love that saved him in those difficult times. 'Where he was rocky, she was stable. Where he would lose his grip temperamentally, she would remain equable. Where he would feel clearly that people hated him, she would love him more. She kept the faith of their marriage. She kept the faith of their love. She kept the faith of Labor.'

Sometimes Gough would turn his anger on to Margaret and give her a tongue-lashing about arrangements or opinions. She knew it really wasn't about her. She would respond with, 'Oh shut up, you silly old goat. Go and have a shower and cool off.'

Gough clung to her, emotionally and physically. She stood proudly by his side wherever they went, declaring to the world, 'I love this man.' She did not do this with any sense of duty or martyrdom. She was never the self-effacing, stand-by-your-man wife. She had stature and authority. But she always maintained genuine humility.

Butler believed that it was Gough's pig-headedness and his temperament that did him harm on 11 November when, rather than seeking to defeat the motion of denial of supply in the Senate, he barred himself in his office and wrote the speech that he would give in the House. He was more concerned with the historical quality of his speech than getting to Ken Wriedt, the Leader in the Senate, to tell him to refuse to pass the Supply Bill. There were people knocking on his door saying, 'Stop writing the speech and turn your mind to what's happening.' Gough's temperament often prevented him from making the right decision. Everyone is wise with the advantage of hindsight.

Butler never regretted working for him. Gough was everything he had hoped he would be.

* * *

There's nothing like a public humiliation or failure to sort out who your real friends are. After the dismissal, Nick and Judy were blackballed from joining a small swimming club at Bondi Beach. Catherine resigned her membership in protest. Margaret immediately renewed Catherine's membership and her own, explaining to her that you never let your enemies think they have destroyed you. You can, however, let them know that you know what they did. The first time Margaret met one of the known perpetrators she said, 'Don't expect me to talk to you, because I know all about your part in blackballing Nick and Judy.'

While Margaret was openly vocal in her disdain for Malcolm Fraser, when Tamie had her party for the political wives at her new home at the Lodge and asked Margaret to attend, Margaret accepted with warmth and civility. In fact, on the day she moved into the Lodge, Tamie was very touched to find a letter of good wishes from Margaret, who would have thought it extremely rude not to have left such a note, despite the political warfare between their husbands.

As soon as Gough was no longer PM the rumour-mongers had a field day. Vicious rumours about their marriage started to spread through Sydney's exclusive eastern suburbs, especially among those who believed the Whitlams never should have been in the Lodge in the first place.

Margaret's brother, Will, a barrister and later a Family Court Judge, who lived in Vaucluse, rang up to tell her that he had been to three separate 1975 Christmas parties where he'd been told Margaret and Gough were getting a divorce. Many of the rumours were more lurid – either Gough had bashed Margaret or she had stabbed him.

Margaret knew that their political enemies had been waiting to get their revenge but she could not believe the depths to which they would sink.

In 1976, she toyed with the idea of writing a book about her husband, the private man, as only she had known him. Handwritten pages torn out from a journal and dated 26 March 1976 reveal her motivation.

> This seems a good day to begin. For once again I was shocked and hurt by the attitudes of an outsider. Outsider? Unbeliever? Enemy? Now I wonder why I was so polite to the over-dressed, ridiculous woman who came up to the official table after lunch and said something like 'I didn't appreciate being jostled on the stairs by your demonstrators.' My demonstrators? What was she talking about?
>
> Well there was a small gathering of people outside the Hilton as we came to the opening of the American Centennial celebrations and some of them did wave that excellent Eureka flag – but my demonstrators? Who does she think she is? What does she know of me? Or mine? It's obviously time to speak up – to let them know of the gentleman I married – to react. I'm sick of hearing how he beats me – how we're divorcing, how much money we've stashed away in foreign countries, how many ruins we've visited or caused. Oh what rot it all is but at the same time how offensive and how hurtful that people should believe it.
>
> Wasn't it enough for the G.G. to ruin our lives? Is there to be no end to speculation and jubilation?
>
> The man that I married is, as he was, a gentle man. Two words or one, take your pick. Both apply.

To a romantic such as I, letters are always important — there have been many over our nearly 34 years together and they read well even now.

Next week the old man and I will have been married 34 years. We shudder at the headlines commissioned by enemies we thought we'd never have but glow in the knowledge of our steadfastness.

My God, they're talking about the man I married. I won't have it. Who do these people think they are? Is this Australia?

Where am I? In the flat that we (emphasis on the 'we') bought over a year ago as a weekender. Put that in your pipe and smoke it as the coarser kids used to say at school. Officialdom was okay most of the time but Gough and I yearned for a part of our town where we could disappear, where he could read in the sun and I could cook and potter, all without surveillance.

Well it was all made possible in the second week of November 1975. What I mean is the flat was furnished adequately and the occasion was afforded inappropriately. It was never our intention to live in the Cabramatta house again. It is too large for our now dispersed family situation. And no brickbats to Cabramatta. Some of my best years were spent there. I enjoy very much returning there. When we lived in that much maligned suburb our children were part of the scene and I like to think contributed to it.

I was part of the extracurricular routine in that over seventeen years I must have participated in everything from school canteens, Red Cross activities to political policy meetings. There was a time which many Australians shared with me when as the wife of the P.M. I had entrée everywhere and it indeed exceeded every expectation ever dreamed about with regard to the role of wife of the P.M.

Well, now it's stopped. Someone else has that job. Good luck to her and luck is needed. More than ever I want you now to know the man that I married, the sometime P.M. . . . .

I have to tell you that he is a perfectionist. Nothing is started if it has no prospect of completion and preferably successful completion.

When we were first married he, Edward Gough Whitlam, was in the reserve of the RAAF. I could never really understand why his parents chose not to call him Edward. My brother Bill has always called him Eddie instead of Gough. To me it's a very unchristian name but it does have a lot of meaning to the family whose antecedents served under General Hugh Gough at India.

I have resented the last six months because of the vicious lies and rumours that have been circulated mostly because of the victimisation of a good man.

I know. I married him.

I have not regretted it.

Thirty-four years is a long time. During this time I have hoarded — treasured, saved much memorabilia — call these love letters if you will, but look at them, think about them. Could this man be the danger certain interests are conjuring up? It's not on, mate. Here is a dedicated, honest man. People with the upbringing of EGW are excused selfishness, arrogance, greedy incompetence and lack of charisma if they belong to the Liberal Party, that most conservative group. Can't we have a bit too?

Well anyway you can have a look at some of his letters, mainly to me. I like them, I treasure them, I now share them with you.

Clearly, this was intended as a preface to the collection of his war-time letters to her, which she intended to edit and have published.

Regrettably, not only did she never write the book, she destroyed many of Gough's most personal letters to her, as she wanted to be the only one ever to read them.

After rereading these original faded notebook pages, scribbled in her own handwriting, more than thirty years before, she remarked, 'Oh dear, I really had my dander up, didn't I?' The fact that such an even-tempered, calm woman as Margaret allowed herself to express these emotions of distress and hurt is a testament to their depth at the time. It is a pity that events and time prevented her from writing the book and publishing the letters. Like her journal of 1941, started but never continued, the practicalities of everyday life intervened. And she buried the emotions.

In order to write a book, large, uninterrupted sections of time have to be allocated to the project and the author has to have the confidence to dedicate that time to writing. Margaret had the desire but not the urgent need nor the time to write that book. Neither did she really wish to make herself vulnerable by exposing those old wounds.

Judy and Nick continued to be ignored or snubbed by many of their neighbours in Woollahra (one of Sydney's poshest eastern suburbs). Gough continued to rail against 'the bastards'. Margaret, although upset by the rumours, was determined to get their lives back into a set routine. She didn't miss living in the Lodge as she enjoyed the freedom of having a flat in Canberra and one in Sydney and being able to see more of her friends. It had been hard to keep up with them while they were at the Lodge because her friends didn't ring, not wanting to impose; they always thought that Gough and Margaret had much more important people to entertain.

Knowing that the hurt and rejection they both felt after the dismissal and the election would take time to heal, she kept reminding Gough that they had lives to live and experiences to begin to enjoy. The more they were vilified, the stronger their marriage and their determination not to let their enemies win.

Margaret enrolled in classes in modern Greek at both the ANU and Sydney University. Her lectures were at the Law School in Phillip Street on Mondays from 6 pm to 8 pm, after which she and Gough would catch the 9 pm plane to their flat in Canberra, to return again to Sydney on Friday. Sometimes she would have forgotten to do the shopping and when she went through security she'd slap a large parcel of meat on the table for scrutiny. The security people would joke with her: 'Have you got the meat today?' they'd ask.

This is the real Margaret – no airs and graces – wife of the former PM and now Leader of the Opposition, cracking jokes about the chops and the roast as she boards a plane. She was constantly on the move. She had two small cars, one in Sydney and one in Canberra, and she buzzed around in both, visiting friends and fulfilling obligations in both cities.

Gough was soon back to his usual routine, which gave him a sense of security. He and Margaret spent much more of their time together. She never missed a parliamentary sitting. He could look up to the gallery and see her sitting there.

Margaret openly enjoyed attacking commercial radio talk-back broadcasters as being 'all dyed-in-the-wool Liberals' who daily urged suburban housewives to support the conservatives. She suggested women listeners free themselves from the 'mental thraldom' of the broadcasters' 'pernicious influence', which she believed had, together with an inherent snobbery, helped bring down the ALP the previous year.

In the mid-year parliamentary break they found some respite and restoration in travel. In China, Gough was feted because they recognised that he was the one who had introduced Australia to them. Stephen Fitzgerald, Australia's first ambassador there, was struck by how much the experience of the dismissal had 'knocked the stuffing out of him'. Even a visit to the History Museum, which once would have had him in a state of ecstasy, failed to move him. He lacked the vibrancy and excitement he once exuded.

Then, as if their world hadn't been shaken enough, an earthquake struck Tientsin (Tianjin) while they were staying there. Margaret woke at 4 am with the strange feeling that someone was trying to hit her on the head with a hammer. The walls shook, the windows blew out and a dressing table crashed onto her leg, gashing it open. Gough raced into the bathroom, grabbed a towel, wrapped it around her injured leg and scrambled around trying to find their clothes. Margaret's underclothes were drying in the bathroom so she grabbed a shirt, a pair of slacks and her sneakers. With a staff member shining a pathway for them by torchlight they scrambled down the stairs in the dark.

After spending two hours sitting in the gutter across the road from the hotel they were finally gathered together in buses and cars and taken to the middle of an athletics ground, where no buildings could collapse on them. They were among the lucky survivors.

Over 400 000 people died as a result of the earthquake. Margaret refused to have her leg stitched but agreed to a tetanus injection.

The next morning when it was in the news, a Nicholson cartoon appeared in the *Age* showing Margaret and Gough in bed together. Margaret is asking, 'Did the earth move for you too, dear?' Outraged readers complained that the cartoon was disrespectful. But it appealed so much to their sense of humour that Gough requested the original, had it framed and placed it above their bed in the flat.

The Chinese hotel had bundled up all their personal belongings from the shattered room and delivered the parcel to them.

Among Gough's official papers and the bowl of fruit from the sitting room were Margaret's knickers from the bathroom. At least they could still have a laugh.

The year 1977 heralded yet another election. Whenever Margaret was asked whether she and Gough would like another term back in the Lodge, she would answer, 'We do hope to go back. It would be very nice as a vindication.'

The truth was, she didn't really want to go back to the role of being wife of the PM. It was for Gough that she wanted the people to vote Labor back in. It would also be a confirmation that betrayal, hypocrisy and lies are not rewarded.

She did make it clear that, given another chance in that role, she would be even more her own person. 'I don't mirror my husband's views. It's so absurd, just because you are a politician's wife to sit around like a dummy, saying nothing, or echoing him. You might as well give up living.'

She freely admitted that she was more cynical and 'more of a wake-up to people'. When asked by the media to comment on her husband's government, she didn't try to avoid the question. 'The problem was they went at it like a bull at a gate. They worked too hard and tried to do too much too soon . . . but they could see what needed to be done. When I think of all those red boxes of government papers always beside the bed. It used to be lights on at 5 am and Gough was right into the red boxes.'

Election night was 10 December. This time Margaret and Gough, with their family and friends, gathered together in Gough's Sydney office in Westfield Towers. Early on, the mood was buoyant, but as the night wore on, their spirits quickly deflated. Margaret made no effort to jolly everyone along. Nor did she weep at the loss. It was his staff who had tears streaming down their cheeks when he announced he would be standing down as leader. He had been the longest-serving leader in the history of the ALP. The Whitlam years were over.

Gough had not seen the enemy coming. Perhaps because he had been ambushed, dismissed and then rejected, he had that dazed look that asks: 'How did this happen to me?' Ever since Kerr's betrayal, he had firmly believed that the Australian people would eventually back him. If only, he thought, long enough for him to finish the plan of reform he had laid out for them and that they had supported in 1972. And 1974. He could not understand why their rejection of him and his party had hardened into such a devastating and lasting defeat. He knew he had achieved many great reforms in health, education, equal opportunity, discrimination, Aboriginal recognition – he could reel off all the achievements of his government. Why had they turned their back on him? He was hurt, deeply hurt.

Anger still burnt inside him like a furnace that would never run out of fuel. His immediate instinct was to retreat, back home to his favourite chair, to his government office, to his loyal staff. And to the nurturing concern and love of his wife.

Margaret was having nothing of retreat. She knew Gough was an impatient man who had charged ahead with change, leaving others in his wake. If he could see what had to be done, he could never understand why others could not. Once having explained it to them, he expected them to 'get it' and follow him. She knew that change was a two-sided weapon and that, if not handled slowly and carefully, it could blow up in your face. Gough had been working hard on his policies for the past ten years, but to the Australian people they were new and sometimes threatening. He never understood that.

She rang their friends and family to reassure them that they were both fine. She knew the last thing they needed was people sobbing over their defeat or ladling out pity for their plight.

Margaret had tasted and swallowed the bitter pill of defeat very early in her life. She had come last in her swimming race, representing her country in the Empire Games. It was both a private and a public humiliation. Even though her family and friends had known of her illness before she dived into the pool, she knew that many of them believed she should have withdrawn. She knew that she would have had to physically collapse before considering not giving it her best shot; that even on that fateful night, in the full gaze of the spotlights splashing off the pool, she would give it everything she had. And she had. She'd used every last ounce of mental and physical energy just to finish the race.

It was the same when the nurses told her that baby Stephen was probably not going to make it through the night. She used every ounce of her own will and strength of belief to assure herself that he would live. In that instance, the baby did live. It was nevertheless her attitude towards loss and defeat that really counted, irrespective of the eventual result.

Gough had never faced real loss or defeat in his life before the dismissal. He had worked long and hard towards his goals and eventually achieved them. He had never faced the kind of defeat he faced now. He knew it was unjust and unfair, but he was powerless against its force. No matter how much he raved and ranted, no matter how many doors he kicked, no matter how often he asked himself 'What did I do wrong?' it wouldn't change the result. Nor would it make him feel any better.

Margaret understood his pain and his anger, and his sense of the injustice of it. She knew also there would be no 'closure', no catharsis, no resolution that would heal the wounds; that the only way forward was to pick yourself up and keep going. There was no point in dwelling on the past; no point in going over and over the details. That would change nothing. She knew that she must not allow Gough to sink into a deep depression through getting bogged down in the quicksand of the past.

Her goal was to help him get over what had happened so that they could move on with the rest of their lives. It would not be easy. Politics was his passion. But they were both relatively young – she fifty-eight, he sixty-one– with a great deal to offer whatever opportunities came their way. Something would turn up; it always did if you were positive. She would not allow any indulgence in self-pity or wallowing. She was a strong woman – stronger than Gough emotionally. Stoicism had been an important part of both of their upbringings. Now she would have to teach him that other skill of survival – resilience.

She had not forgiven the traitors, those people who had always claimed their ownership of proper behaviour and high-minded principles. In her view, they had behaved shabbily. Their greed for power and self-interest had exposed them for what they were. Time would prove her right. And if there was such a thing as karma, they would get back what they had dished out.

She was also aware that, truthfully, she would not miss many aspects of the political life. She could look forward to being an individual in her own right, to what she considered to be a more personally useful and productive life.

She could indulge her love of writing.

She could play more golf.

She could decide on a whim to see more films, theatre and ballet.

She could see a lot more of her real friends, rather than the hangers-on and courtiers.

Perhaps she could live a more fulfilling personal life.

Just as she had predicted, once they were no longer at the centre of power and influence many of their so-called friends faded away. Those who had been pretending their friendship for their own advantage exposed themselves.

Their true friends and their family formed a secure circle around them. The Whitlam name itself had become a problem. Tony Whitlam, having secured a seat in the 1975 election, had been defeated in the 1977 election. Gough had managed to maintain an aura of control, despite what had happened to him in the previous two years. However, as the figures came in against Tony, Gough briefly broke down, telling Graham Freudenberg, 'It's his name.'

Gough's sister, Freda, had been the principal of PLC (Presbyterian Ladies' College) for nearly twenty years when, after years of friction, her resignation was suddenly announced in October 1976 by the council chairmen. Her difficulties with the council had begun with the election of the Whitlam government and increased during the next three years. She had had to withstand snide remarks and open attacks about her brother, the Schools Commission and funding for private schools. A former student even told her, 'Your name is a disgrace to the school.'

Gough was apoplectic with rage and guilt over Freda's forced resignation. Nothing was more distressing, however, than Catherine's treatment in 1978, when she secured her first teaching appointment at a Catholic school near Bathurst in country New South Wales. No sooner had she accepted the offer than a letter from the school arrived, announcing its withdrawal of the offer. The Bishop of Bathurst had decreed that no daughter of Gough Whitlam would ever be employed in his diocese. This vicious action shocked both her parents. Catherine decided that it would be easier for her to change her name to her mother's maiden name of Dovey. Gough was devastated, even though he understood why she did not want to be subjected to further brutal behaviour. He felt he had failed his party, his country, his son, his sister and now his beloved daughter.

When parliament opened in February 1978, Gough Whitlam was sitting on the backbench for the first time in seventeen years. The party had elected Bill Hayden as its leader. With Margaret's urging and encouragement he did not sit quietly with his head bowed. Within weeks he had placed 381 questions on the notice-paper.

Prime Minister Fraser faced his first challenge when he appointed Sir John Kerr as Australia's ambassador to UNESCO (United Nations Educational, Scientific and Cultural Organization). Kerr's package included an ambassadorial salary, tax-free living, entertainment allowances and residence in the new embassy in Paris, overlooking the Seine. Designed by the architect Harry Seidler, it had been commissioned by the Whitlam government. Gough had even turned the first sod in January 1975.

Fraser's own cabinet was divided over the appointment. The media was universally against it. Paul Keating, the member for Blaxland, accused the Prime Minister of being 'an insensitive totalitarian toff' who had 'made a mockery of our major institutions'.

Gough remained dignified and aloof from the furore, rising to remind the government that Kerr's Governor-General pension, which he would receive on top of the lucrative UNESCO package, had been negotiated by him 'so that he could act without fear or favour, because he knew that in retirement he would have an ample pension which would not require him to seek other employment'.

The most withering attack on Kerr was made by his former friend Senator Jim McClelland, who referred to the fact that Kerr was an embarrassment to the government, especially when he fell over in the mud while opening a country fair and 'conducted himself like a drunken lout before half the population watching him on television present the Melbourne Cup'.

The next day, on his arrival to take up the UNESCO position in Paris, Kerr resigned.

As parliament rose for its autumn recess, Gough and Margaret left for an extended overseas trip that became their farewell tour. It was a very crowded travel agenda, with visits to over twenty countries. Work combined with travel was one of Gough's greatest pleasures. Margaret knew he would have no time to dwell on the past. At the end of this two-month sojourn he accepted an offer to be a visiting fellow at the ANU in Canberra.

On 31 July 1978 he announced his immediate retirement as the member for Werriwa. He never returned to the parliament he had served in for the previous twenty-six years. Margaret considered it best that, in order to move on, he not be there to witness his formal farewells.

It was probably just as well, because few of his parliamentary colleagues rose to speak of him. His faithful followers were sure that the judgement of history would view him as 'a messiah', 'a great reformer' and 'one of the greatest Prime Ministers who ever stepped into the House'.

Barry Jones, a fellow parliamentarian, intellectual and another former quiz champion, gave a balanced view.

> He was, by universal consent, the greatest member of the present parliament – the largest in spirit, the loftiest in aspiration, the greatest orator and the member with the widest interests . . . Gough Whitlam was, I think, a man for all seasons, not especially for this one. He made many mistakes. He offended many rich and powerful groups. He was not always easy to work with and he liked to get his own way. The expression that he often used – 'crash through or crash' – is something we often have thought. His judgement was not infallible. Nevertheless, in a political Lilliput he was our Gulliver.

Not a single member of the Fraser government rose in the House to give him even the acknowledgement he formally deserved. Neither did Bill Hayden, nor his deputy, Lionel Bowen. They clearly did not wish to be tainted by using his name.

The Whitlams had moved into an apartment at University House at ANU and returned at weekends to their own apartment in Darling Point and their life in Sydney. Gough found academic life very different from that of parliament. He missed the energy, the buzz, the dynamism. Despite his contribution to seminars and colloquia, and speaking at luncheons, he found himself to be stultifyingly bored. Politics was the big picture, academia the small. He could not believe the emphasis on the minutiae of obscure research projects without any contemporary relevance or political context. Most of his colleagues shied away from betraying even a hint of their political beliefs and focused on projects that were safe and dull. Despite what had happened, he was very glad he had chosen politics over academia.

With the exception of Nugget Coombs and Professor Manning Clark he found the whole atmosphere deadening and uninspiring. Unless he was having lunch with them in the staff club he came back to the apartment to have his sandwiches with Margaret. She still prepared his favourite sandwiches for lunch, wherever he was. His mother had pampered him with his favourites and Margaret continued the practice. In both cases, it was an expression of love and devotion.

Margaret busied herself by taking on a course in literature and Greek. Tuesdays were golf. She joined a bushwalking group and a women's group that organised visiting lunch-time speakers. If she was busy, she left the prepared sandwiches for Gough. He was happy to read his reference books and think about the book he intended to write. Soon after Gough arrived at the ANU, Nugget Coombs' book *Kulinma: Listening to Aboriginal Australians* was launched. Gough had a special inscription by Coombs in his copy which read: 'To Gough Whitlam, whose government was the first and so far the only Commonwealth Government which has listened to Aboriginal Australians'. Gough was very moved by those words.

He also had great respect for Manning Clark and his work. He believed that Clark belonged to 'a select band of historians, who by writing Australian history . . . changed a people's perception of itself and its past so that the new perception becomes a living force in the present and future life of that people'. This was exactly what Gough, as a thinker, a politician and a policy-maker, had tried as a Prime Minister to achieve. Like Manning Clark he had tried and succeeded in many ways to change the way we thought about ourselves, which would result in changing the way we acted and shaped our nation.

He did, however, in a letter to Manning Clark after the electoral trouncing in 1975, concede that 'the simplest explanation of 13 December is that any government that presides over a recession and inflation, whatever the cause or its response, is headed for electoral defeat. Perhaps we are too fond of believing that Australians would behave differently from any other people.'

At this time he was also awarded the highest order in the Australian honours system that he had initiated to replace British imperial honours – the Companion of the Order of Australia. It was the first time he had visited Yarralumla since that fateful day on 11 November 1975. Margaret noticed he looked pale and clammy when Sir Zelman Cowen pinned the medal on his jacket. The past for him was not yet 'another country'.

For three years they had not attended any function at which Kerr was also present – not the opening of parliament or dinner with the Queen. They were rock solid. They would never see Kerr again. Margaret was very open about this decision. 'The man is dishonourable . . . When I think of the times we were in his company just before he did what he did to Gough and how he said nothing right up until that last moment. I'm disgusted.'

On 2 December 1978, Kerr's defence of his actions was launched in a book titled *Matters for Judgement*. The day after the launch, Gough sat down with Graham Freudenberg and began planning his own book as a response.

At the end of that year Margaret had also to deal with the death of her mother, Mary Dovey. Mary had been gradually fading but was determined to 'maintain her standards' right to the end. She was in hospital and Margaret rang up early in the morning to see how she was before she visited. The nurses said, 'She must be all right today, she's got the lipstick on already.'

Fortunately for Margaret, Mary was jolly right up until the end. Margaret missed her most around the cocktail hour when they would usually ring each other. Long after her loss Margaret would find herself picking up the phone, thinking, 'I must tell Mother about this.'

Now it was Gough's turn to comfort Margaret. He didn't let her down. He knew how much Margaret had loved her mother and valued all she had taught her.

For the next two months, Gough worked around the clock. On 8 February 1979, *The Truth of the Matter* was launched. No longer constrained by his political position, he let rip. He said that the former Governor-General's behaviour at the Melbourne Cup reminded him of the recent ABC television series *I, Claudius*, in which Claudius's nephew Caligula proposed to make his horse a consul. 'As many thousands were fortunate enough to see in the flesh, ample as it is, Sir John Kerr wove down from the Imperial box, so reminiscent of Caligula, to salute the winning horse, I couldn't help reflecting how much better a pro-consul the horse would have made.'

His enemies described Gough's comments as 'in poor taste'. Gough took them on – full frontal.

Let's cut through the humbug on this matter. In the orchestration of the destruction of my government, no rumour, no innuendo, from moral turpitude to financial corruption, was deemed outside the rules of the game . . . In this country the establishment makes its own rules and sets its own canons of taste. And if there was a time, when because of the nature of my role and my position, I thought it best to 'cop it sweet', I am prepared to do so no longer.

Even though the media took the high moral ground against his personal insults of Kerr, Gough needed to say it, not just for the public record but for resons of catharsis. He needed to dispel his fury.

The book sold 150 000 copies and Gough accepted a position at Harvard University as the third Visiting Professor in Australian Studies. This was a chair he had endowed to Harvard as part of the government's contribution to America's 1976 bicentennial celebrations.

Both Gough and Margaret really enjoyed the month they spent there. Gough's public lectures focused on his belief in the necessity for developing relationships not only with China, but Indonesia, India and Japan. Fraser had let the work Gough had done in regional development languish. His theme was the dynamic economic growth in the western Pacific, 'where expanding and enormous potential markets exist' and where 'China's emergence as a significant trading nation and financial power is of greater consequence to the industrialised nations of the region.' Even he did not know how prescient his words were for the nation. His lectures at Harvard were so successful and well received that they were published by Harvard University Press and titled *A Pacific Community*.

Margaret not only attended his lectures but met and listened to many famous and revered American writers. Her favourite was Eudora Welty, whose books she had always admired. 'She had a big voice and a little frame. She wasn't retiring or self-effacing but exuded the kind of confidence that comes from knowing what she was talking about. The students adored her.'

They returned to their combined life at ANU and in Sydney with more confidence and calm than they had left it. In 1980

Gough became ANU's first national fellow and in 1982 an honorary fellow of University House. Margaret began to find herself being invited to join the boards of various organisations. She was being asked to make a contribution in her own right, not because she was Gough's wife. In 1977, she became a director on the board of the Sydney Dance Company. In 1978, she became president of the ACT Council of Social Services and was also appointed to the council of Sydney Teachers College. She loved them all.

In 1979, after one of their regular European trips, Margaret stayed on in London for a few days to see friends and shop at leisure. Just as she was crossing Bond Street, her leg suddenly refused to move. The only way she managed to cross the street was by manually lifting her own leg and placing it down. She struggled to a nearby shop and bought a walking stick.

Gough was shocked to see her struggling to walk towards him with the aid of a cane when he met her at Sydney Airport. She had always been able to match him, stride for stride. The doctor informed her that the pin which had been inserted many years before when she had slipped in the laundry had worked its way out of her hip and had to be removed and replaced. After the operation Gough insisted she keep the old pin and wear it as a pendant. She did as he advised, put it in a safe place and never found it again.

Even though she continued to walk with a cane she readily agreed to become the chair of the Opera Conference, a national voice for all of Australia's opera companies. Now that they had so much free time they never missed an opera. So easy were they to spot on opening nights, two white heads together, they became known as 'the twin icons'.

In 1980, however, the stress of the preceding years took their toll on Margaret's health. Having previously suffered from arrhythmia of the heart she was prescribed new medication, ordered to lose weight and take life a little more slowly.

She immediately accepted an offer from the Australian National Railways to travel all around the nation, gathering material for a travel diary to be published in *New Idea*. She justified this adventure by saying that train travel was the best method of taking things slowly.

The real pleasure for her was that she was enjoying the experience of having a life of her own, separate from that of her husband. She revelled in her new-found sense of freedom and autonomy.

In 1982, she agreed to chair the board of governors for the NSW Law Foundation. On Australia Day 1983 she was made an Officer of the Order of Australia in recognition for her work in the community, education and the arts. She was delighted and couldn't wait to make an even greater contribution in her independence.

Gough was appointed the Visiting Professor of the Adelaide Law School for its centenary. Some of the karma Margaret had wished for seemed to be coming around. In February of that year, Gough's threat to Fraser that one day he would catch the Prime Minister with his pants down came true in a seedy motel in Memphis. Bill Hayden, who had not been gracious enough to speak about Gough after his resignation from parliament, was pipped at the post by the party's replacing him with Bob Hawke just prior to the election. One month later, on 5 March 1983, Hawke defeated Fraser and became Australia's twenty-third

Prime Minister. Fraser dropped his bottom lip and blubbered on television. Revenge is a dish best eaten cold.

Early in May of that same year, Gough and Margaret were relaxing in bed in a hotel room in Adelaide, when the phone rang. Gough answered it. Margaret heard him laugh loudly and then say, 'I'll have to ask Margaret about that. Can I ring you back?'

He put the phone down, came and sat on the end of the bed and said, 'That was Hawke. He's offered me the UNESCO job that Fraser gave to Kerr and Kerr had to abandon. What do you think?'

Margaret's heart sank.

She forced herself to reply, 'Well, it's a bit of an opportunity, isn't it?'

She knew that even though her current life would come crashing down around her, she could not prevent him from accepting the offer. It would be too mean and selfish on her part. A voice inside her head was screaming, 'Oh no, not again!'

By August they were at Villefranche-sur-Mer in the south of France, taking an intensive, month-long course in French. They had a delightful apartment overlooking the bay, and a driver who picked them up in the morning, took them to their classes, then returned later in the day so they could do a bit of shopping. Margaret and Gough sat on the balcony every night with a drink and did their homework. Margaret's accent improved rapidly. Gough mastered the grammar but not the accent. Not that it really mattered, as he would always have interpreters.

Once settled in their luxurious ambassadorial apartment in Paris, they were the envy of Parisian society because of their magnificent view of the Eiffel Tower and the Seine. Margaret should have been overjoyed. Here she was living in a huge, beautiful apartment in the middle of Paris, the city of her dreams. No matter how often she told herself that, she still felt strangely subdued.

Eventually she was forced to admit – only to herself – that she was, in fact, a bit depressed by it all. Gough was back to his old self – energised, excited, bursting with ideas. What was wrong with her? Why was she not equally elated at this change in their fortunes? Why couldn't she just be happy for him? She let none of this show and carried on with her hostessing duties, meeting and greeting and smiling. But her depression didn't go away. It nagged at her, always present at the back of her mind, numbing her pleasure.

When the *Australian Women's Weekly* sent an interviewer to talk to her about her glamorous new Parisian life, she heard herself saying, 'I had quite a career of my own in Australia before I left . . . sometimes I feel as if now I'm *rien*, nothing, a has-been.' As she heard these words coming out of her mouth, she knew that was what was wrong with her. She had spoken the devil.

Quickly changing the subject she told them the story of Al Grassby's tie, which Gough had given to the Queen. Years after the dismissal, when they were lunching privately at Buckingham Palace with just the Queen, Philip, Andrew and Edward, in the middle of the first course Andrew had suddenly unbuttoned his jacket and revealed Grassby's tie. The Queen roared with laughter and said, 'I wondered why you had your jacket all buttoned up.'

The journalist lapped it up.

Even when feeling a bit low, Margaret had an irrepressible sense of humour. When she and the journalist were settling down for coffee in the sitting room Margaret remembered that a few nights earlier she and Gough had seen a flasher. 'I kept looking at him,' she said, 'and Gough kept telling me, "Don't look, Margaret, don't look." Then I saw he was looking as hard as I was.' Chortle, chortle.

That night the journalist reported seeing Margaret at an evening reception. 'She was the ideal hostess, moving from group to group, introducing strangers, keeping an eye on the caterers, always warm and smiling.'

Though she was not by nature an introspective person, Margaret was forced to face up to what was causing her depression. Here she was again, living the life she had been forced to live at the Lodge. She missed the autonomy of her life in Sydney. She wanted to be Margaret, not Mrs Whitlam. She was back on the old treadmill. Having admitted all this to herself, she refused to wallow in it. She would not be a victim to others' expectations. It was up to her to change her own role, and her own life.

She set about planning her days and making her time in Paris work for her, as well as her and Gough. Without Margaret, Gough would have spent most of his time reading at home. She would have to plan some adventures.

Margaret joined their cook on her regular excursions to shop in Passy, a very old and chic shopping area in Paris. Once the cook showed her where to buy the best cheese, fruit, vegetables and bread, Margaret began to feel more at home.

One Sunday she persuaded Gough to go to the market. She kept saying to him, 'Why don't you go and look at the cheese stalls.' He refused, not because he didn't like cheese but because he didn't want to go anywhere without her.

On weekends, when the French go to their country houses, Margaret gave the staff time off and would cook at home, just for the two of them. Gough couldn't have been happier. She planned weekend escapades for the two of them, like picnics in the country or informal lunches at special little restaurants she had discovered. On Saturdays they often went to the theatre or the opera. Often they just crossed the river and walked for miles, exploring the city like young lovers there for the first time.

She also organised a weekly meeting in the apartment with her conversation group: seven French women and seven English-speaking women, all wanting to learn the others' language.

She missed her Sydney friends and her children, despite the fact that most of them had been keen to take the opportunity to visit them. And there was always a mid-term leave back home.

In 1985, while on leave in Sydney, they attended an open-air performance of *The Tales of Hoffmann* in the Domain. When they arrived, the crowd suddenly leapt to its feet and gave them a totally spontaneous standing ovation. They stood there, quite gobsmacked. Smiling and waving, they were filled with surprise and joy at the warmth of the gesture. Journalist for the *National Times* Kristin Williamson described the feeling in the hometown crowd. 'If there is political royalty in Australia then the emeritus emperor and empress would have to be Gough and Margaret Whitlam.' In the history of political couples, particularly Prime Ministers and their wives, there has never been such a spontaneous communal outpouring of warmth and welcome as there was for Gough and Margaret that evening.

Back in Paris, one of the many guests who came to stay in the embassy was a young man called Mark Latham. He was brought over by Gough as his research assistant for his 'magnum opus',

The Whitlam Government 1972–1975. Latham called Gough 'the great man', which, of course, he loved. Margaret, however, was not as impressed with this young acolyte as her husband. She was a much more astute observer of people than Gough, who had a tendency to make quick judgements and refuse to reconsider them. She thought Latham was brash, overconfident and rude. She tried to teach him some of the table manners and social graces that he lacked, but he was only interested in impressing Gough. His flattery and devotion paid off, as Gough anointed Latham as the next member for Werriwa, his former seat, and a future Prime Minister.

Margaret had her own followers and admirers, one of which was Kathy Lette, who also came to stay with them in Paris. Kathy had worked with Catherine Whitlam when they were much younger, selling books at Angus & Robertson in Pitt Street, Sydney. Kathy was at that time writing her first novel, *Puberty Blues*. She had left school at fourteen and when Catherine took her home to meet her mother, Kathy was impressed with the way Margaret took this 'surfie chick' seriously as a writer and encouraged her to read widely. 'I loved the way she treated everyone the same. Whether it's the Queen or the cleaning lady, she treats them as she likes to be treated. She has no tickets on herself.'

Margaret became her role model. On this particular visit to Paris in 1978, Kathy was amazed by Margaret's ability to be 'cool' and 'suave' in embarrassing circumstances. They had all arrived at the front of a very posh restaurant called Le Prée Catalan, in the Bois de Bologne, for lunch. Gough was in the front seat of the embassy car next to Henri, the chauffeur. In the back seat were Margaret, Kathy and Catherine. The maître d' and the head waiter were already waiting for the Australian ambassador and his guests out the front of the restaurant. Henri got out first to open the car door for Margaret. Never one to stand on ceremony, Margaret was already halfway out herself. As she stood in front of the restaurant waiting for the others to alight, her skirt suddenly fell down to her ankles.

Kathy and Catherine, both out of the car by now, stood still with shock like Stonehenge monuments. The maître d' and the head waiter also appeared to be frozen. Everyone was waiting to see what Margaret would do. The diners inside the restaurant were staring, open-mouthed, through the windows of the restaurant.

Margaret did not appear to be the slightest bit embarrassed or confused as to how to act. She simply looked down, said 'Oh, hello' then turned around, with her unskirted bottom towards the restaurant's windows and its maître d' and head waiter, bent from the waist, picked up the skirt, zipped it up, turned back to Kathy, Catherine and the chauffeur and announced, '*En avant!*' – Onward – and strode towards the restaurant.

She was not even slightly fazed. Once she had zipped up her skirt and spoken, Kathy and Catherine erupted with laughter. The maître d' and the head waiter, being French, greeted Margaret as if nothing unusual had occurred. Kathy and Catherine could not control their loud Australian hilarity.

Gough, on the other side of the car, was totally oblivious to what had happened and, ignoring the screaming girls, followed Margaret into the restaurant. Kathy thought it was one of Margaret's finest moments. She had 'out-suaved' the French.

It was Margaret's turn to laugh at Kathy a few nights later, at an embassy cocktail party. She had been trying to teach Kathy some French conversation by taking her to plays, believing that you can absorb a language through osmosis. Kathy mixed up *jolie* (pretty) with *gelée* (frozen) and spent the entire evening telling the sophisticated French ambassador that his wife was '*très gelée*'. When she told Margaret that he hadn't responded as she had expected, it was Margaret's turn to dissolve into hysterics.

During the time she spent living with the Whitlams, Kathy concluded that all of Gough's success was based on Margaret being his rock, his constant companion, his compass. In the years she had observed them as a couple she had seen that Gough's ineptitude at social interaction was always ameliorated by Margaret's ability to put everyone at ease and provide the social lubricant for every occasion.

In her own inimitable style, Kathy once said to Margaret, 'I can't believe you have only had sex with one man in your entire life.' Margaret laughed. Catherine immediately jumped in to defend her mother.

'Do you know how old my mother is? And what generation she's from? Of course she's only had one man in her life.'

Kathy, still unbelieving, replied, 'Well, I hope Gough's not a dud root, Margaret.'

Without blinking, Margaret replied, 'Absolutely not, darling.'

It was in Paris, however, that Margaret sought out a man with whom she had fallen a little bit in love.

One morning she read in the paper that Leonard Bernstein was conducting several concerts with the Israeli Symphony at the prestigious La Salle Pleyel in Paris. She immediately bought a ticket and was excited about seeing Leonard again after their brief flirtation in Melbourne, when he had taken her to Premier Hamer's party.

The day before the concert, she found out she was needed to accompany Gough to an important diplomatic dinner the same night as the concert. Ever the dutiful partner, she gave the concert ticket to a friend and wrote a note to Leonard telling him of her disappointment at not being able to see him. She invited him for a drink at the embassy.

The next morning she received a call from his personal assistant to say that unfortunately he had another concert performance and several rehearsals. Why didn't she come to a rehearsal?

Given the time, place and details regarding security, Margaret moved her other appointments around to make sure she could be there. Unfortunately, by the time she arrived the rehearsal was already in progress and the security guards refused to admit her. She wrote another note to be delivered to him which read, 'I came, I saw but I was conquered.'

The next morning a huge bunch of flowers was delivered to her with a personal note. She picked up the phone to express her thanks and was put through to the man she called Lenny. He had a bad cold and was very worried about the performance but he said, 'Margaret, be not concerned about our inability to talk. We will meet again. And we will embrace.'

Those words struck a chord in the heart of this romantic woman. She confessed, 'I was his forever.'

Unfortunately they never did meet again and embrace before he died. He lived on, though, in her romantic heart.

Gough's time as UNESCO ambassador had not been easy. His main task was to turn back the growing media tide against UNESCO, due largely to the US decision to withdraw from the organisation. He was determined to take on a rescue role in the resolution of the crisis that President Reagan's decision had created. The Hawke government was strongly opposed to the US decision. What alarmed Gough was the flow-on effect Reagan's decision had engendered in Prime Minister Thatcher. She was threatening a UK withdrawal.

This, Gough could see, was a strategic attack on the United Nations as a whole. The aim was to knock out UNESCO first, then garner support for the dismemberment of other specialised agencies and ultimately the United Nations itself.

On one of his visits home, he attacked Australian journalists at the National Press Club, where he was giving the address, for their ignorance about UNESCO and their repetition of America's attacks on him for being 'anti-American'. Gough was back to his old feisty self and Margaret clapped loudly, as did the audience at the lunch.

During question time, political commentator Mungo MacCallum asked him whether he was having as much fun in Paris as he did in Canberra. Gough quipped, 'The fun is where I am,' his talent for self-parody as sharp as ever. Even though he enjoyed the audience's laughter, his message was a serious one. 'The world of UNESCO is the world we live in. We in Australia cannot be indifferent to our particular place in that world . . . If the brave idea of UNESCO fails, the world will be a more dangerous place.'

His father would have been proud of him. His wife certainly was.

At every opportunity Gough continued to defend UNESCO with the intellect and passion for which he was famous. He reminded them of its largely unrecognised work against discrimination in education, and its work for heritage protection, literacy and cultural preservation. Before his term as ambassador ended, Gough had been elected to serve on the executive board of UNESCO.

On 11 November 1985, Bob Hawke launched Gough's new book, *The Whitlam Government*. It was the tenth anniversary of the dismissal. What emerged after all this time were what Gough called 'confessions'.

Four former Liberal Senators had publicly confessed, independently of each other, that in 1975 they had been having second thoughts about Fraser's tactic of blocking the government's budget bills – which Fraser had denied to Kerr. They all stated that on 11 November 1975 within twenty-four to forty-eight hours they would have crossed the floor to vote with the government. Neville Bonner had actually told Fraser of his intention to do this on 9 November. These confessions proved that Gough had been a very short time from having the bills passed when Kerr dismissed him from office. Gough's unemotional reaction to these confessions showed how far he had managed to deal with the betrayal and injustice that had been inflicted on him. His only statement was 'It is now a matter of public record that the action against my government on 11 November 1975 was not only wrong and unconscionable; it was simply unnecessary.'

He was no longer a broken man.

On 11 July 1986, Gough celebrated his seventieth birthday in their apartment in Paris with all his family, friends and former staffers, who had flown in specially for the occasion. They relived their decade together and its Shakespearean conclusion with camaraderie and celebration. With Margaret by his side, lifting her glass, Gough toasted them all. 'There are many minders, many speechwriters, many back-room people but there has never been an association of such intensity and value in terms of public affairs as there has been between us.'

The lights from the Eiffel Tower sparkled back at them from across the Seine.

They lifted their glasses in unison to toast Gough on his birthday, delighted to witness their old friend back in form.

Having travelled, side by side in their seats on the Qantas plane from Paris to Sydney, on their final leg from Sydney to Canberra Qantas was unable to seat them together. Gough was not pleased. He liked having Margaret next to him. He spoke to the CEO of Qantas, James Strong, at Sydney airport, personally asking him to rectify the problem. Strong patted Gough on the back and said he would do his best. After Gough shook his hand and bade him farewell, Margaret called Strong aside. In a quiet voice she said, 'I wouldn't try too hard, James. Quite frankly, I could do with a break.' A long plane journey with one's beloved could sometimes be too much, even for Margaret.

Once back in Sydney, they each slipped back into their busy schedules. Gough was now chairman of the National Gallery, a fellow of the Sydney University Senate and a member of the Constitutional Commission and the Australia–China Council.

Margaret was appointed to a six-member committee to review the state government's role in adult education. On the committee was John Wellings, the head of the New South Wales Board of Adult Education, and Anne Krone (later Wellings), an adult educator. These two people were to become crucial participants in Margaret's next decade of adventures.

She was also a judge on the National Book Council's Awards and involved in fundraising for the Australian Opera. She had an open invitation to write articles of her choice from several magazines and enjoyed freelance book reviewing for the major newspapers. It was a full life and she was happy to be back home among her family and friends, playing golf and swimming at Bondi.

The Whitlams were also back on everyone's invitation list, the dismissal a distant memory and considered a political blunder on the part of the Liberals. The Whitlam-haters, however, were still lurking in the bushes, and as soon as Gough and Margaret had settled back into their Darling Point apartment, the rumours about their marriage again began to swirl around the eastern suburbs. This time they focused on Gough's relationship with a man called Andrew, forty years his junior. His family had migrated from Argentina to live in Cabramatta. Andrew had met Gough through his family when he was twenty-two and immediately looked to him as his mentor. When he decided to become an Australian citizen, he asked Gough if he would mind if he changed his surname to Whitlam, because he had such admiration for him. Gough, always susceptible to admiration and flattery, agreed. He did not think to ask his wife or his children whether they would approve; it never occurred to him that they would be upset. They certainly would have liked to have been consulted and were generally not pleased that this stranger now bore their surname. Gough took Margaret to Andrew's women's fashion shop in Double Bay and she even wore a few of his dresses. She wondered if Gough was allowing himself to be used as a form of publicity and self-promotion by this young man. Knowing that his greatest weakness was his lack of judgement regarding people, she nevertheless refused to be swayed by their old enemies.

Now that Gough had his old chutzpah back, he not only scorned the vicious rumour-mongers, he taunted them by sitting at a table outside Andrew's shop, sharing a coffee with him. Defiant and amused by the looks they gave him as they passed by, he refused to be cowed by their innuendoes. He was a free man now, and he could choose with whom he wished to spend time or have lunch.

Still naïve in many ways, he saw nothing wrong with adding fuel to their fire. He hated to give in to his enemies or let them see that he cared about what they were saying about him. Margaret, however, found it all very distressing, as so many of her friends reported back what was being said in those leafy, privileged suburbs. Whenever she mentioned it to Gough, he snorted with derision and said he was not going to give in to them by changing his behaviour. When he announced that Andrew was accompanying him overseas because of the problem with his legs and his decreasing mobility, Margaret spoke to the children. Tony, as the eldest, was selected to speak to Gough. He explained to his father that this would only give greater fuel to his enemies and the media gossips and greatly distress Margaret. With much grinding of teeth, and glaring eyes, Gough agreed that Stephen would accompany him on his overseas trip in order to help him get around.

Paul Keating was assailed by similar rumours from the same quarters when he was seen dining with a young, good-looking man in Paris. It was Patrick, his son.

When a friend asked Margaret what she would have done if the rumours had in fact been true, she said, 'Tell him to pull himself together and not be so stupid.'

Would it have ended their marriage?

'Absolutely not.'

Nineteen eighty-seven also included a hip replacement for Margaret, which meant a month in hospital and rehabilitation and walking on crutches until it was totally healed. She never complained as she loathed older people who whined constantly about their health problems.

It seemed that their time away from Australia had increased the media's interest in them. In 1988, the *Sydney Morning Herald* 'Good Weekend' magazine had a front cover and a feature article titled 'The Whitlam Dynasty: Inside Our First Political Family'.

By anyone's standards they were a tall, good-looking, intelligent and accomplished family who had stuck together and were close, with the children very committed to their parents. Even they could not believe how much energy both their parents still had for going out, meeting people and enjoying working in their various roles. In their seventies, their individual and combined schedules would have exhausted people twenty years younger. Neither of them was prepared to spend their days relaxing in the sun, enjoying some form of retirement. Gough's membership of the executive board of UNESCO took him to Paris four times a year for the next four years. He visited China for two weeks every year for the next decade as chair of the Australia–China Council. He was always welcomed with great enthusiasm and deference as the political leader who had first established relations between Australia and China.

Despite all her work on boards and committees Margaret did not neglect her duties with the women of the Labor Party. In 1989, the *Canberra Times* reported that over two hundred women had paid to have tea and sandwiches and listen to the speaker Margaret Whitlam, who was helping to raise money for the five women on Labor's ticket in the next federal election. Ros Kelly, the federal member for Canberra, told them that Mrs Whitlam was 'a great personal inspiration' and Rosemary Follett claimed she was 'not only one of Labor's great women, but one of Australia's greatest-ever women'.

Even though Margaret would rebuff such praise with the response that she had only done what had been asked of her, she knew that she had done a great deal more than that. Even though she had never seen herself as a political figure, there were many different ways to be 'political'. Even though she may have appeared to be playing a supporting role to Gough's main role, she was in fact carving out a role for future partners of Prime Ministers to be open and equal contributors, if they chose to be.

Broadcaster and columnist Phillip Adams believes that Margaret and Gough were a very successful double act. 'When you think of Gough, you think of Margaret. It is impossible to think of one without the other.'

11

Woman needs man, and man must have his mate

Early in 1990, John and Anne Wellings, who had worked with Margaret on the adult education inquiry, decided to start an international study tour business. When they asked Margaret if she would help plan and lead the tours, she leapt at the opportunity. At seventy-one, she was being offered her dream job.

The Wellings had noticed what an even-tempered, easy-going person she was, but even more importantly they saw the 'good-time girl' that emerged when she was away from Gough and her public responsibilities. She revelled in being free to be herself and couldn't wait to lead her first tour.

In July 1990, however, while on a visit to China with Gough, she tripped getting out of bed and broke her right wrist and her right leg. Osteoporosis had caused her bones to become brittle and thin. Gough called for help but the attendants were unable to fit their stretcher into the hotel lift. They decided the only solution was to roll Margaret up inside the rug she had fallen on and carry her down the fire exit to the ambulance. Once inside the hospital, with the help of an interpreter they rejected the offer of having her wrist set without anaesthetic and it was done under a full anaesthetic. She said she would have the leg fixed when she returned to Sydney, even though she was in agony. As it was going to take another day to arrange her transport to Hong Kong and then Sydney, they wrapped her up in the rug, carried her back to her room and placed her, still rolled up in the rug, on the bed.

If she hadn't been in so much pain she would have enjoyed the Marx brothers antics. Gough carefully placed a blanket over her and that was how she spent the night.

Once inside the plane she was positioned across three seats in the very back of economy, next to the toilets, curtained off from the other passengers. She could hear them outside the toilet saying, 'I wonder who's behind those curtains. Poor thing. Fancy being stranded back here.' Little did they know that it was the former First Lady of Australia, who was feeling very much 'a poor thing'. A doctor had been sent to accompany her. All he could do was ask, 'Do you want some juice? Do you want a wee?'

What made it much worse was that her husband, who was sitting in the front of the plane, did not walk down to the back to see her. Not once. He said he was too embarrassed to walk the length of the plane, past all the passengers. And that it would only cause a fuss for her. She was very cross with him. It was the only time in their marriage that she said he did something that really disappointed her. Once in nearly seventy years is a pretty good effort.

Gough panicked when anything was wrong with Margaret. She never encouraged him to visit her in hospital as he was hopeless. He didn't know what to say or do. He interrogated the nurses and the doctors and paced around the room in an agitated state. When he was not there, he rang her constantly. Just hearing her voice calmed him down. Fear of losing her stalked him until she was home and they were back together in the same bed.

On arrival at St Vincent's Hospital in Sydney, Margaret was met by her orthopaedic surgeon and her GP. A month later she left the hospital with a new pin and a plate in her thigh. When Catherine was getting all her mother's belongings together she pulled out what looked like an old piece of hessian from the hospital cupboard.

'Mum, what on earth is this?'

'My magic carpet,' replied Margaret.

While she was in St Vincent's her brother, Will, had been admitted to the hospice across the road. He was only sixty-six and suffering from oesophageal cancer. The day before he died the staff took Margaret in a wheelchair across the road to his room. She was very upset.

Now she was the only one left of the original Dovey family.

The prospect of leading an international study tour to France in September 1991 was something to lift her spirits. Instead of sitting in the back seat of an embassy car being transported from Charles de Gaulle airport into Paris she found herself in a coach with people she didn't know. She was very excited. Gough was on his own for the next three weeks. He could have moved into a club or a hotel but he preferred to stay in the familiarity of the apartment, surrounded by his reference books.

Margaret had put all his home-cooked meals in the freezer, with instructions for reheating. She had organised 'the kids', as she always called them, to check up on him and invite him to their homes on weekends.

From her first tour in 1991 until her last in 1999, Margaret led eighteen trips to twenty-four countries. She called this time her years of indulgence as they were so different from her many years of being housebound and practically a single parent to four children in the western suburbs of Sydney. She wrote a book about these trips and called it *My Other World*. She dedicated it to Gough with the inscription, 'To my dear husband, who still says he taught me everything I know.'

The dedication to her in his book *The Whitlam Government* is 'To my best appointment, Margaret Whitlam'.

The dedication to her in his later book *Abiding Interests* is 'To my most constant critic, Margaret Whitlam'.

In his book *My Italian Notebook* the dedication is simply, 'To my prima donna'.

When the Wellings decided to plan a tour to Eastern Europe, they asked Margaret if Gough would like to lead the tour with her, as they wanted to make use of his vast knowledge of the region and all his contacts. Gough agreed immediately. The only problem with his encyclopaedic knowledge of the history of most parts of the world is that he found it difficult to fit it all into a thirty-minute talk. Margaret took responsibility for reminding him when he went over the time limit.

Once, when they were in Thailand, Gough said to John Wellings, 'Don't let Margaret sit near me when I'm speaking. She makes these clicking noises with her tongue and it puts me off.'

On another occasion, when Gough was droning on and on over the microphone, John noticed that most of the travellers were asleep. Margaret offered to sit up the front and get him to wind up his lecture. After some time, John noticed that Gough was still talking. He snuck down to the front of the bus to discover that Margaret had also fallen asleep. Gough was lecturing to an entirely comatose audience.

On the trips they shared, the Wellings noticed how lovingly Margaret looked after Gough. They also noted that, caring though she was, she would not stand any nonsense from him. If he was being difficult she had no hesitation in ticking him off publicly like a schoolboy who was misbehaving. He never answered back; he always went quiet and toed the line. When Gough led tours on his own, like the one to the Black Sea, the Wellings noticed he appeared to be quite lost without Margaret. He rang her constantly but was not at ease chatting with anyone else unless it concerned a historical point of discussion – a conversation for Gough was usually a one-way lecture or a debate. Whereas when Margaret was without Gough, she was a real party person who displayed an almost girlish enjoyment of everything. She had a 'naughty girl' side to her, like enjoying a Bloody Mary at 11 am. She loved to clap her hands together to the music, eat German sausages and drink beer, getting everyone to join in with her.

Before every tour began Margaret learnt everyone's name. By the end she would know the names of their children and their grandchildren. She welded the group together by constantly taking photos. After the trip was over they would receive hand-written letters including photos of themselves. It was never a chore for her.

Neither Margaret nor Gough ever let politics cloud their judgement of people on the tours. They both made a point of treating everyone equally and with respect. There was only one man who had initially objected to Gough being included in the tour but by the end they were spending a lot of time together in discussion and had formed a great respect for each other's intellect.

Sometimes even Margaret was astounded at the depth of Gough's knowledge and off-the-cuff recall. On one occasion, when he made an impromptu presentation which led to an hour's detailing of the British monarchs and their intermarriage, from King Egbert to William the Conqueror, with every date and coronation described in perfect detail, Margaret was amazed when his audience burst into spontaneous applause. At these moments she would call him 'her favourite man' but still wonder why he had such trouble remembering their phone number.

On a trip to Turkey and Greece, Gough generously paid for his sister, Freda, to join them. Usually they only got together at birthdays and Christmas, but with advancing age Gough made a commitment to ring her every Sunday at 7 am, just to touch base.

Freda says they were more like only children brought up in the same house than brother and sister. Both of them, however, shared a deep belief in their responsibility to serve the community and help those less privileged than themselves.

Freda was never close to Margaret. 'I know she thinks I'm a wowser and it's true I don't drink.' But she was very admiring of Margaret, and aware of how much she had contributed to her brother's career.

He's not really a sociable person. She can talk to anyone and that has made it a lot easier for him. He is very devoted to her, in his own way. And very dependent on her. Margaret was brought up to be social and loves going out. We were brought up to serve the community first. After that, we would prefer to stay home and read.

Freda lives alone, teaches Latin and religious studies and helps people with their legal problems.

Nineteen ninety-three was particularly busy for the septuagenarian Whitlams. On top of all their other commitments, they were asked to be part of the lobby team to help Australia win the bid for the 2000 Olympics. They spent a few days in each place that needed persuasion to vote for Australia, which included Cameroon, Kenya, Mali, the Ivory Coast, Uganda, Swaziland, Zimbabwe and Botswana. Margaret particularly loved visiting people in their own homes and swears that the mashed pumpkin made by the wife of the UNESCO representative from Zimbabwe, which included peanut butter, was delicious.

In Swaziland the Australian delegation was taken out to a smart restaurant by the King of Swaziland and his four wives. As they were leaving, Margaret spied a member of another group exposing himself. She told John Coates, the president of the Olympic Committee, who went to have a look. He returned to tell Margaret that the man she saw was actually urinating against the table. Gough asked Margaret which man it was. When she told him it was one of the journalists he quipped, 'Wouldn't you know it, another press leak.'

Nineteen ninety-four and 1995 were full of more tours, together and apart. Their energy for and excitement about arriving in a different country never abated. No matter how tired Margaret was, her spirits soared when she walked down the streets, taking in all the new sights, sounds and smells.

Her body did not always keep up with her spirits.

Christmas Day 1995 she spent in hospital, having her left knee replaced. By May 1996 she was back on the road again with Gough, travelling to Italy. In September they led a tour to Argentina, Peru and Bolivia. At Christmas in 1996, however, she was in hospital again, having what was called 'a revision' of her hip replacement. By May 1997 they were off again, this time leading a tour to Spain and Portugal. Margaret never liked to dwell on her physical problems and hospital visits. Her response was always, 'You just have to bat on.'

A year later in May, always a lovely time to travel, Margaret and Gough were back in France. Margaret was leading a tour about artists' lives and their works. Afterwards, in June, they spent a week in Venice with Catherine and Kim Williams for their wedding. Kim had formerly been married to Kathy Lette, who was now married to barrister Geoffrey Robertson and living in London. Margaret and Gough were delighted that they were all friends, and to have Kim as an addition to their family.

Margaret couldn't wait for September to arrive as she was hoping to meet up with some long-lost Scottish relatives on a tour of England, Wales and Scotland. On the morning of her departure she had filled up the freezer with Gough's food and was all packed and ready for the taxi to arrive when she noticed a stray cord not plugged in next to the heater. Always thinking about Gough, she got up from her chair to remove it so there was no chance of him tripping over it. He had neurological problems which meant that his legs weren't working as well as they had. Both of them were now using canes to walk. In her effort to remove the cord, it became tangled around her leg. Attempting to disentangle herself, she stumbled, crashing to the floor. Knowing immediately that she had broken something because she couldn't get up, she dragged her long body slowly across to the cordless phone, pulled it down off the side table and dialled her doctor, followed by her daughter.

When Catherine burst into the room, she saw her mother having a quiet weep to herself. Margaret told her she had broken her pelvis. Catherine, normally the tough schoolgirl from the western suburbs, burst into floods of tears at the unfairness of it all. Her mother had been so looking forward to seeing her Scottish relatives. And here she was waiting to be hauled into yet another ambulance on her way to hospital.

Margaret was three weeks flat on her back waiting for the pelvis to mend. The worst part was being strapped to a frame and hoisted up to be bathed for the first week. She felt like a trapeze artist in a circus.

Stephen was already booked on this tour to accompany his mother, so he took over her role as guide. In his chats with the Wellings he discovered a little secret his mother had kept from the family. Earlier that year she had taken one-sixth of a share with the Wellings in a racehorse. Her father had been the vice-chairman of the Australian Jockey Club and she had always loved a small flutter on the horses. When the Wellings let it slip, all Stephen said was, 'I don't think Father knows about this.' He never told anyone and even though the horse never won a race, she had a lot of fun sharing her secret with the Wellings.

Nineteen ninety-nine was the year of the national referendum on whether Australia should become a republic with an Australian as the Head of State. Prime Minister Howard proposed a model that was very divisive, even among republicans. It split the 'yes' vote between those who wanted to elect the President and those who were prepared to let parliament decide. Gough was not in favour of a people's election where the President would have a competing mandate with the elected Prime Minister. He had suffered too much from a Governor-General who believed he had the right to sack an elected Prime Minister.

What amazed most Australians was the 'yes' campaign's television advertisement featuring Gough Whitlam and Malcolm Fraser, together urging Australians to vote 'yes'. Whitlam said, 'Malcolm, it's time.' Fraser replied, 'It is.'

Time had in fact been the great healer between them. Gough understood Malcolm's motives to be not personal but those of a politician. It was Kerr's betrayal and deception towards him that he could never forgive.

Margaret, however, was not so quick to forgive Fraser. 'I couldn't have put up with being in his company in the 1970s or '80s. But now I find him *almost* engaging.'

The thaw between Whitlam and Fraser had begun when they had appeared on stage together and shaken hands in support of the rally to protect the independence of the *Age* newspaper, in the cause of media diversity. They found themselves on the same side over conflicts with the conservatives regarding Indigenous land rights, saying 'sorry' to the Aborigines, and the rights of refugees and asylum-seekers.

By 2010 Fraser had resigned his membership of the Liberal Party. Gough's only media response was 'Malcolm has improved.'

On Mother's Day in 1999 Margaret returned home from a lunch and collapsed into a chair. She was feeling very strange. She told Gough the room was spinning around in circles. He immediately rang Catherine, who raced over in her car and took her mother to the emergency department of the Prince of Wales Hopsital, where her cardiologist, Dr Tony Freeman, practised. They admitted her, called him and after a few hours of testing, Dr Freeman made the decision to install a pacemaker.

It was the end of Margaret's career as a tour leader, but it didn't stop her travelling around Australia.

On 19 November 1999, Margaret turned eighty. She celebrated it in fine style at a lovely restaurant at Fox Studios. Only her friends and family were invited. No politicians, no ALP organisers. Her children wanted it to be totally her night. As the eldest child, Tony spoke in praise of his mother and Margaret replied with her signature self-deprecating humour.

Even though Gough was sitting right up on the front table, he did not speak. The children were afraid he would not have been able to keep himself from a one-hour recitation. All eyes that night were focused on Margaret. She moved among her guests, laughing and chatting, looking radiant. Not since her twenty-first birthday had she been celebrated in such a grand fashion.

New Year's Eve was always spent at Georgie and Snow Swift's Darling Point apartment overlooking the harbour and the bridge. Margaret and Gough had known them since they were in their twenties. Margaret always sat out on the balcony having cocktails and conversation with the other guests. Gough, not keen on either cocktails or conversation, sat inside reading a book. No one thought it strange. He was happy. He joined everyone for the 9 o'clock fireworks, after which he and Margaret went home in the taxi that Georgie had ordered for them.

The beginning of the new century was for them bittersweet. It was the year when the world came to Sydney to celebrate the

Olympics. It was also the year that Australia did not become a republic, as Gough and Margaret had hoped it would.

Prime Minister Howard and Mrs Howard set the tone for the new century. For the first time in her public life, Margaret allowed herself to speak out against the wife of a Prime Minister. She had liked all of the other wives, regardless of their politics, but now she had reached the august age of eighty she figured she had earned the right, when asked, to state her honest opinion.

It is insulting to the people of Canberra and Australia that she wouldn't live in the Lodge. That is where the Prime Minister lives. It is correct behaviour to do so. Kirribilli is for the weekends and for official guests. It was improper of them to claim it for their permanent home. Imagine the American President's wife refusing to live in the White House.

She was also critical of the virtual invisibility of Janette Howard in the role of the partner of the Prime Minister.

I think you have certain obligations to make the most of the position, to accept invitations, to support charitable causes, to let yourself be known to the people of Australia. People want to see you. What is she hiding? She doesn't even go to the old people's homes with Howard when he visits them. She is useless when it comes to giving back to the community. I fear she is a steely woman – never contributing anything but a smile. Not a grin – a grin indicates some sense of humour.

Margaret had always held very firm views on fulfilling your proper responsibilities and acting correctly. One incident that she found totally inexcusable was Janette Howard's failure to write her a personal note of acknowledgement to say she had received something she had asked Margaret to send her from the collection of gifts the Whitlams had received during their tenure. It was to be donated to the Lodge or Kirribilli House.

Margaret had chosen a handsome silver Mexican box that she packaged up and sent, together with a personal letter to Janette.

After several months, having received no response, Margaret rang Janette's secretary to check whether the package had, in fact, arrived. The secretary said she would check and ring her back. When she did, she assured Margaret that Mrs Howard had received it and would be writing to her.

Seven months passed with no response from Mrs Howard.

After ten months, a letter arrived addressed to Gough from the chairman of the Australian Fund of which the wife of the current Prime Minister is always the patron. Margaret was not impressed. Gough had always liked the fact that she was, above all else, 'her own person, with her own views and her own standards'. Not that he disagreed with her – he just didn't think Janette Howard was interesting enough to even comment on.

The year 2001 was a heart-rending year for both of them. For Margaret it meant another visit to emergency at the Prince of Wales Hospital and an operation to implant a new pacemaker. That heartache was easily fixed. Their son Nick's problems were highlighted by a vicious series of media attacks against him, focusing on his role as chairman of the National Roads and Motorists' Association (NRMA). This was followed by a very public Australian Securities and Investments Commission (ASIC) investigation.

Margaret and Gough knew that the name Whitlam still produced strong reactions from some members of the public and the media. They had both taught their children to fiercely defend their own reputations but to take total responsibility for their own actions. Gough and Margaret discussed the issues between themselves but never attempted to pass judgement or interfere in any of their children's lives.

Margaret was still capable of being shocked when total strangers took it upon themselves to pass judgement on Nick. One woman stopped her in the street and said, 'Mrs Whitlam, I've always admired you, which is more than I can say for your son.'

Margaret replied, 'Which son? I have three sons,' not wishing to enter into a conversation with this woman.

Not to be put off, the woman continued, 'Nick – he's been a very bad boy.'

Margaret said firmly, 'No, he's not. He's a good boy.'

'Well, I'm very angry with what he's doing to the NRMA,' the woman continued.

Margaret said, 'As far as I'm concerned, he's not a bad person at all' and walked off.

She told Nick about the conversation some time later, confessing that she didn't really understand all the issues regarding demutualisation or corporatisation and that it was probably better she didn't. He said he didn't want to worry her any more than was necessary.

Gough did not want to worry Margaret either, but he told Graham Freudenberg, 'This is the worst thing that has ever happened to us'.

'Worse than 1975?'

'Worse than 1975,' Gough confirmed.

Freudenberg knew he meant it because he had witnessed first-hand that beneath Gough's public persona was a deeply caring, deeply emotional family man. It was not a side of him many people ever glimpsed.

ASIC found against Nick and banned him from being a company director for five years. The media had even criticised Nick for going for a swim at his club in the middle of his hearings, implying he was not terribly involved. Margaret knew exactly why he'd gone for a swim. She had encouraged all of her children to swim in order to relieve stress or tension.

Nick appealed ASIC's decision and a year later the full bench of the Appeal Court fully acquitted him, dismissing the case, with costs against ASIC.

Gough said to Margaret, 'Now I can die happy.'

Judy Whitlam, Nick's wife, said that Nick's major reason for pursuing his exoneration was so as not to disgrace the Whitlam name. Nick had witnessed how his parents had coped with the events of 1975 and Judy said they followed their example. 'You don't whinge, you get on with your life. You never let your enemies beat you down.'

Nick wrote a book about this time in his life called *Still Standing*, which Margaret encouraged him to do in order to help 'sort things out'. Even though ASIC's case against him was eventually dismissed, great damage had been done to his career and his reputation. He and Judy decided to leave Sydney and buy a cottage in Scarborough on the south coast of New South Wales and a pub, which he ran with his daughter Alice and Chris, his son-in-law.

Following the example of his parents he didn't sit around sobbing, 'Woe is me.' He assessed the situation and got on with changes to improve the rest of his life. Margaret had always told her children, 'You can have regrets, but you don't harp on them. Occasionally you wish you'd done something differently, but you can't change what's past. You just have to find practical solutions to your problems.'

Gough demonstrated that age did not necessarily cement grudges but could in fact even produce empathy where once there was nothing but the desire for revenge. In 2002, with the death of former PM John Gorton, Gough became Australia's oldest living Prime Minister. Malcolm Fraser and his wife Tamie sat next to Gough and Margaret among the mourners at the front of the church at Gorton's funeral service. Tom Hughes QC, Gorton's former Attorney-General and Malcolm Turnbull's father-in-law, gave the eulogy. It was a twenty-minute attack on Malcolm Fraser, whom he accused of the 'political assassination of Gorton'. Fraser was trapped in the pew, his Easter Island statue face stony. When Hughes had finally finished his verbal annihilation, Gough reached across Tamie to tap Fraser gently on the shoulder, saying, 'Let not your heart be troubled, comrade.'

These were moments in their history when Margaret was pleased that other people were able to see Gough's innate kindness, as opposed to his cruel tongue.

The year 2002 generated another round of anniversaries. It was fifty years since Gough's election to parliament and thirty years since the election of his government. Gough gave a speech based on his life's work in Old Parliament House in which he emphasised that the central pillar of both his idealism and his pragmatic reforms was 'equality'. He had attempted to redefine the meaning of this word by applying it to contemporary Australia's society and economy. 'I maintained that, in modern communities, even the wealthiest family could not provide its family with the best education, the best medical treatment, the best environment, unaided by the community.' In other words, the national government must finance them or these standards would not be achieved or even aimed for. 'I specified that the goal of this concept of equality was not equality of incomes, but greater equality of the services which the community provides.'

He did not fail to mention the missed opportunities and the flawed judgements which had prevented his government from achieving its aims. What he could never fully realise was his own failure to take the time to communicate to the Australian people the need for his reforms and to take them with him on his journey, no matter how slowly it needed to proceed. His impatience with his own Caucus, his underestimation of the determination of the Liberals to end his government, whatever it took, meant that sometimes he crashed through but eventually he crashed.

Even though Margaret understood his need to indulge in these recollections and ruminations, she did not wish to visit the past, especially its hurts and betrayals. Nor did she wish to read about the personal failings of her husband, of which she was well aware. She knew that as long as they both lived there would be Whitlam-haters who would never miss an opportunity to denigrate him or her, and their legacy while in the Lodge.

Even though she was a romantic by temperament and sentimental about keeping photos and diaries of their life together, she was scathing of anything that smacked of hubris.

That year they also celebrated their sixtieth wedding anniversary. In a television interview to commemorate the occasion, Gough said, 'I've established all political records for matrimonial endurance. A couple of years ago we beat the Menzies' record and now we have established sixty years.'

Margaret gave a separate radio interview in which the interviewer gushed about how marvellous it was to have been married for sixty years, and finally asked the secret to the success of her long marriage. Margaret paused and replied, 'Inertia.'

* * *

This was also the year that Margaret decided it was time to stop driving her car. Her children had been nagging her to give up driving but she was reluctant to do so because her little old Honda allower her to go wherever and whenever she liked.

Even though she hadn't played golf for several years she liked the Woollahra club and had harboured a vague yearning to once again pick up her clubs. Having driven to the club and paid her annual fees, she started to back out of her parking spot when her foot slipped off the brake and onto the accelerator. She drove straight into the gardens. She stopped the car, grabbed her cane and went back into the clubhouse.

'I'm sorry. I'm afraid I've just cleaned up your flower-beds.'

No one seemed too perturbed but the accident was a signal to Margaret. A few days later she rang Alice, her grand-daughter, and gave her the car. Not that this stopped her from going out. Nothing, it seemed, would stop her attending concerts, theatre and opera, along with all her political and charitable functions.

She wanted to make the most of her life, to experience and enjoy it as much as she could. Even though she realised that her usefulness to others was declining with the demands of her age, she still liked to make whatever contribution she could to the community.

Barry Jones tells the story of how Margaret and Gough had attended a production of August Strindberg's play *The Dance of Death* starring Sir Ian McKellen as Edgar and Frances de la Tour as his tormented wife, Alice. A few weeks later Barry, as chairman of the Port Arthur historic site, arranged for them to be driven around the site in a people mover. Gough sat in the front with the driver and Margaret was in the back with Barry. Without looking behind him Gough boomed, 'Is Alice on board?'

'I'm here, Edgar,' Margaret responded, in a voice of doom. Incidents like this showed how they continued to play up to and amuse each other.

In February 2004, however, Margaret found herself in an ambulance on the way to the Prince of Wales emergency department. As she lay on the trolley-bed in the hospital, her cardiologist by her side, the room started to spin and she experienced a fading away, as if she was disappearing into a haze of nothingness. Suddenly there seemed to be ten people in the room. Her cardiologist was thumping her chest, shouting 'Cough, Margaret, cough!'

She had suffered major heart failure. The pacemaker was removed and a new bilateral cardioverter was inserted.

It had been a close call. Even she was prepared to admit it had been 'very scary'.

In August that same year she was back in hospital. This time it was the Royal Prince Alfred, where they attempted to relieve the agonising pain of a nerve pressing on broken bones in her spine, caused by the excessive coughing from a nasty bout of bronchitis.

When visitors arrived she would always point out the latest Jeffrey Smart painting that the industrial view from the hospital room afforded them. She was still capable of laughing at the indignities the treatments inevitably inflicted on her. She thought of herself as being unwillingly cast in a theatre-of-the-absurd play. Open and real as always, she said to visitors, 'I'm afraid this medication is making me fart. I'm sorry, but I can't help it. Just go out if it gets too much.'

Phone calls from Gough were incessant.

'Can you ring me back, darling? I've just got some visitors here.' And then, to the visitors, 'The old boy is hopeless in hospitals so he rings me all the time to see how I am and tell me about invitations to events and dinners to put in my diary. Funny old thing. He knows I like to have things to look forward to.'

Out of hospital in time for her eighty-fifth birthday, she celebrated at the Boathouse restaurant in Glebe with Gough, all their children and their partners. Tony once again spoke on their behalf. He began, 'Margaret, this is not a speech, it's an appreciation.'

Margaret looked at them all – her children – and thought how jolly they all were in their different ways. Of course she loved them, but she also liked them as individuals. They were all so very different.

A year later they gathered together again for lunch. This time it was to celebrate the eighty-fifth birthday of Gough's sister, Freda, at Lucio's in Paddington. Gough loved it when it was just their family and they could enjoy each other's company away from the stares of strangers.

That night when he and Margaret were settled down in their favourite armchairs in front of the telly Gough said, 'It went really well today, didn't it?' Margaret smiled back at him – her funny old boy. 'It was a great success, my darling.'

He nodded, paused and said quietly, 'Our kids have really all turned out well, haven't they?' Margaret agreed. She did allow herself a tiny smile of satisfaction. After all, she had practically brought them up alone. Gough would have acknowledged that if she had stated it – but tonight wasn't the night.

She knew how deeply emotional he was about his family and his children. No matter how often her kids sent her up for her sentimentality, she knew that it was Gough whose eyes would well with tears whenever his parents or his children were mentioned.

He had found the previous two years increasingly difficult, because of his increasing lack of mobility. Whenever they went out, he had to be in a wheelchair. At interval at the opera Margaret would take off on her cane to the bar for a champagne. She knew he would never be alone as people always came up to talk to him. He wasn't all that keen on being a public monument but most times he managed to smile and be pleasant. He knew they meant well.

Sometimes, totally fed up with the indignities and frustrations of his physical limitations, he would fly into uncontrollable rages. If they were with other people Margaret would apologise for him. People dismissed her apologies, assuring her there was no need to worry about it. They would say things like, 'We know how marvellous he has been in the past.' If it was at home, when it was just the two of them, Margaret would either ignore him or go into another room. If it continued, she would quietly and calmly tell him that his behaviour was not acceptable. He would calm down at her admonitions.

In the past if he had spoken to her like that (and there were occasions when he had) she would have burst into tears and not spoken to him for days. She didn't cry any more over his outbursts because she knew the cause was his old age and his frustrations at what was happening to him. She also knew that plenty of women her age had to deal with much worse.

The year 2005, the thirtieth anniversary of the dismissal, seemed to revive Gough's good spirits. Apart from speeches and interviews on the subject, his publisher invited him to write a new introduction to *The Truth of the Matter* that included supportive evidence that Kerr's actions were wrong. The media were eager to discuss and analyse the events of 1975, and so was he. The editorial in *The Australian* focused on the way Whitlam had been evicted from the Lodge and how it had made him a winner, a hero. Kerr was the loser. Living long enough to be vindicated and celebrated made the indignities of old age more bearable.

Margaret, as always, was far more interested in focusing on the present and looking forward to the future. Their first great-grandson, Stephen's first grandson, was born. He was named Oscar Cyrus, after the kings of Sweden and Persia. Margaret was 'tickled pink'. Oscar even looked just like Gough as a baby.

Margaret and Gough were continuing to receive invitations to visit towns and districts all over Australia, as well as numerous invitations to lunches and dinners in Sydney. They were reluctant to refuse 'good people', as they called them. Catherine decided it was time to step in and take over organising their life. Gough went to his office most days, but Catherine restricted Margaret to one event per day. She also organised a series of 'helpers' for her, one of whom was a personal exercise physiotherapist to keep her legs supple and her muscles strong.

As the youngest child Catherine saw the least of her mother while she was growing up, due to her father's political duties. Now the roles were reversed. She gave up her job to give her mother the strength and support she needed to look after herself and Gough. Even though Margaret really appreciated it and knew she relied on Catherine, that independent spirit still asserted itself. She had no wish to abandon her autonomy or not have a martini when she felt like one. Catherine says her parents used to 'get up each other's craw' like all couples who, having been together for a long time, knew each other's sore spots. 'Mum is naughty the way she does things that she knows will annoy Dad. I reprimand her about it.'

Judy Whitlam was touched by the way Margaret always wanted to look after Gough. He'd say, 'I'll do it' and she'd say, 'No, I'll do it' and neither of them was hugely mobile. She was touched by their vulnerability and dependence on each other, which she believed was firmly based on a very deep love for each other.

Margaret loved catching public transport. One day she and Georgie Swift decided they would have oysters for lunch at David Jones in Bondi Junction. Margaret insisted they catch the bus. She had forgotten that the bus didn't quite go all the way up to David Jones. When they stopped at the bus depot a couple of streets away, the bus driver saw the two of them looking a bit bewildered.

'Where are you going, Mrs Whitlam?'

'We were hoping to get off at David Jones,' said Margaret.

'No worries,' he said, putting the bus into gear and driving them up to the entrance.

When they thanked him effusively, he said, 'Nothing's too much for you, Mrs Whitlam. You and Mr Whitlam have given so much to our country.'

Margaret made every effort to keep up with her friends by making every social occasion special. Whenever she and Georgie were attending a movie at the Chauvel cinema in the Paddington Town Hall, they would organise a picnic lunch beforehand and invite their friends to join them at a table on the balcony attached to the first floor. Margaret always brought the best wine.

One of her favourite events was the Melbourne Cup Lunch at the renowned Susie Carleton's hotel, The Bellevue, in Paddington. As getting up and down from the table was difficult for her, a good-looking young male actor at their table was assigned to put on her bets. Margaret was delighted to have this handsome young man running around after her. After a visit to the loo, she returned to the table and announced to everyone, 'I have just glimpsed myself in the mirror and I look like Oscar Wilde.' (She was wearing a blouse with a big, floppy bow tied at her neck.)

Just at that moment, her young man bent down to give her some winnings. Patting him on his shiny blond locks she said, 'And you, my dear, are my Bosie.'

As the laughter at the table died down, she lifted her glass of wine and said, 'Isn't this fun?'

* * *

In April 2007, the Whitlams celebrated their sixty-fifth wedding anniversary with a packed auditorium at the ALP conference in Sydney. They were to be awarded the first joint national life membership of the ALP. Gough was in his wheelchair, Margaret beside him on her cane.

Upon their arrival, the roar of applause was followed by the familiar chants, 'We want Gough. We want Gough.' ALP leader Kevin Rudd, who had been one of the recipients of a free university education made possible by Gough, recalled Gough's advice to him as a fifteen-year-old member of the party who hoped to have a career in the diplomatic service.

'Go to university and study a language'.

Reminiscent of Franklin Roosevelt, Gough pulled himself up from his wheelchair and, with the support of the ALP National President John Faulkner, slowly moved towards the podium. A tsunami of applause swept over them. Wave after wave.

Gripping each side of the wooden podium he waited for the applause and shouting to die down. When he began to speak, he spoke of Margaret.

'Men and women of Australia's oldest and greatest party, I appreciate this honour all the more because of my co-recipient. Margaret has been the partner for my life and work for sixty-five years. If our generation had enjoyed the full benefits of the equality for women initiated by my government thirty-four years ago, no limits need be set on the positions and honours which might have come her way, as certainly as she receives this honour in her own right.'

No one was left in any doubt that his partnership with Margaret had made everything possible for him. Nor were they in any doubt that his admiration and belief in her talents was steadfast and that in another era, when all his policies regarding equal opportunity for women were taken for granted, women like Margaret would be able to achieve their full potential, as he had.

It was important for him to know that the party to which he had devoted his life recognised the contribution that Margaret had made, not just to him and his career, but to the nation. Theirs was an exceptional partnership.

One year later, they travelled together to Canberra to attend Kevin Rudd's Apology to Australia's Indigenous Peoples. It was the nation's final recognition of Aboriginal culture and an apology for what Australia had inflicted on them. This slow progression had been begun by Gough on the day he held the native soil in his hand and poured it into the hand of Vincent Lingiari.

On their return to Sydney, Catherine and her brothers gathered the family together to try to convince their parents that Margaret could no longer manage Gough's health problems. He needed permanent specialist care outside the home. Gough's mobility was very restricted. He could no longer lift himself up from his chair without assistance. Margaret's own strength was failing and she was physically incapable of helping him.

They both resisted the advice. A little later, when Gough contracted a serious infection in his lower leg and was admitted to St Vincent's hospital, they both knew that he would never return to the flat to live with Margaret. He spent several weeks of rehabilitation in nearby St Luke's hospital, after which he was moved to Lulworth House, the adjoining managed care centre, where he remained. Lulworth House, once the family home of Patrick White, was also the hospital in which Tony had been born. It was only a couple of streets from the first small flat where they had lived as a blissful, newly married couple. The same jacaranda trees still donned their purple gowns outside his windows.

Margaret was greatly relieved that she no longer bore the weight of responsibility for his well-being. But she missed that booming voice pronouncing 'J'arrive' when he came through the door every night. She missed him answering the phone and calling out, whichever child it was, 'Mum, it's the fave on the phone.' If they all arrived at the apartment at the same time for lunch or dinner, when he saw the first one he'd shout out, 'Mum, the fave is here.' She even missed him complaining about being forced to watch her favourite television programs, like *The Bill*. But above all else, she was a realist. And she knew this time in their lives had to be faced and that they had to make the most of it. True to form, she made a plan. He was still mentally alert enough to want to spend time in his office three days each week. Tuesdays she spent with him or had him transported to their flat for lunch. Fortunately he didn't lose his sense of humour and the first time he was wheeled into the living room for lunch after he had left home, he said to her, 'These are very nice premises I've got for you, Margaret.'

Weekends were spent visiting the family. They all took it in turns to take Margaret out in the evenings to the theatre, a concert or the opera. She had those friends who were still alive around for drinks, which she dispensed from a trolley with wheels, matched with cheese or nibbles that Catherine had set up for her. As Bette Davis famously quipped, 'Old age ain't no place for sissies.'

Neither of them were sissies. They took what joy they could from each other.

Gough was always reluctant to talk about his personal life, but never failed to heap praise on Margaret as a wife, a mother, a lover, a political companion and his best friend. 'She is very talented at getting along with people, that's why she was so good at leading those study tours. She wrote very good columns like Eleanor Roosevelt, even though she was never a political player like Eleanor. Of course, she always believed in freedom of choice and equality of pay for women.'

His only real criticism of her he blamed on her genetic inheritance. 'Her mother was bossy. She inherited that gene. So has Catherine.' By bossy, he no doubt meant that he didn't always get his own way. Whenever they talked about their marriage he said they told each other that 'neither of them could have done better'.

Ever the historical record-keeper, he was always eager to inform people that theirs was the longest Prime Ministerial marriage in Australian history. Their compatibility was based on broadly similar cultural interests for over six decades.

Regarding the hurtful rumours that the Liberals sought to spread about their marriage Gough said, 'There are some vicious bastards and bitches out there – but, apart from her bouts of illness, we have always slept in the same bed.' The fact that they no longer shared that pleasure was a great sadness to him. And to her.

Prior to his leaving the marital bed, a friend popped by one Saturday morning to drop off a book Margaret had lent her. The first thing Margaret said when she opened the door was, 'Come and look at my old boy.' The friend was led to the door of the bedroom, where Gough was blissfully asleep in his blue pyjamas.

Margaret whispered, 'Doesn't he look sweet. Like a big baby.'

After they'd had coffee, Gough was awake and they all shared a few laughs. 'Silly old thing, isn't he?' she said.

In early 2012 Margaret had a fall. This time it affected her ability to swallow. To be bedridden and unable to eat or drink without the aid of a tube was not a life Margaret wished to lead. She had always said, 'Life is not over until you put your cue in the rack.' Her cue was in the rack when Gough was called to her bedside. They spent her final hours together.

On 17 March, Gough issued a short statement regarding Margaret's death.

'We were married for almost seventy years. She encouraged and sustained me and our four children, their families and many other people in a life full of engagement with Australians from all walks of life. She was a remarkable person and the love of my life.'

The then Prime Minister, Julia Gillard, offered the family a state funeral but they refused, knowing that was not what Margaret would have wished.

The beautiful St James' Anglican Church behind the law courts in Sydney was overflowing with family, friends, colleagues, politicians past and present and former Prime Ministers and their wives: Malcolm and Tamie Fraser, Bob Hawke and Blanche d'Alpuget, Paul Keating and Annita van Iersel and Prime Minister Julia Gillard. The crowds outside flowed and swelled for several blocks. Media of every type jostled to get the best view or interview.

At 3.30 pm, with church bells pealing, the Whitlam family arrived. Gough was in a wheelchair, his head bent, unable to look up and witness the crowd.

The flowers inside the church were generous and exuberant, the music, carefully selected favourites of Margaret, was played by the Goldner String Quartet. Catherine and Tony spoke of their mother with passion and humour. The Reverend Father Edmund Campion read from 1 Corinthians 13, which begins: 'If I speak in the tongues of mortals and of angels, but do not have love, I am a noisy clanging symbol. And if I have prophetic powers, and understand all mysteries and all knowledge, and if I have all faith, so as to remove mountains, but do not have love, I am nothing.'

Throughout it all, Gough sat slumped in his wheelchair, head down, staring hard at his funeral program. It was as if he could not move or he might totally fall apart.

Margaret lives on vividly in the memory of those who loved her. Gough lives on too. Occasionally being taken into the office, or taken out by one of his children, he is always delighted to see them. Catherine organises friends and colleagues to visit him at Lulworth House to help him get through the days.

He has his books. He is well fed and cared for. He is loved. Even though his body is gradually fading, particularly his legs, his heart somehow keeps beating.

Without the love of his life, he is broken-hearted. And empty.

He still cannot speak about her without his eyes brimming with tears. Whenever he thinks of her, he says, he is reminded of the 1956 song from *My Fair Lady*, about growing so accustomed to your beloved that her face almost makes the day begin.

His love for her is undiminished. His loss of her, all-consuming.

Catherine has made Gough a special collage of photos of Margaret throughout their life together which he has placed close to him on his bedside table. When he wakes in the morning, Margaret's face is the first he sees. She still makes the day begin.

Epilogue

When these two young people caught each other's eye in the twilight on a hot summer's evening in 1939, they had no knowledge of where their strong attraction to each other would lead.

Their private and political partnership would change our lives and our nation. During their three years in the Lodge deep and lasting changes were made to our laws and our national attitudes governing education, health, Aborigines, women, refugees, migrants, the arts, the environment and divorce, just to name a few. Running through it all was the glue that held it together – a lifelong commitment to equality in all its forms.

Gough and Margaret spent the rest of their lives staying true to their values, their legacy and each other. They gave us pride in ourselves, our democracy and our own culture.

In an age of increasing cynicism, mistrust and disengagement regarding politics, the political process and our political leaders, we need to remind ourselves of Gough and Margaret and what they gave to our national life and the importance of our belief in Australian values.

What were once only the rights of the well-off and the entitled, Gough made available to every Australian. We now take those rights as our own, particularly the right to a national first-class public education and the right to a national first-class public health system. These two citadels of equality still define us as Australians and we are rightly proud of them. It is essential that we remember this time in our history and the leader who fought so hard to achieve his expansive and positive view of our nation.

And always, standing tall beside Gough – his life partner, the love of his life, his equal in all respects – was Margaret. She changed the way in which we viewed the role not just of women but of the Australian version of a 'first lady'.

Now, more than ever, we need our own heroes and heroines, especially the young who have embraced the Gallipoli and Anzac legend with such enthusiasm. They also need to know that there was a time when we did believe in politics and political leaders who made our nation a better place.

This is the story of Margaret and Gough Whitlam and their love. It is also the story of the strength of their love for our country and its people of all ages, races and religions.

They never lost their belief in equality and a fair go for all.

They never lost their belief in the political process as a means of achieving it.

They never lost their belief in the Australian people.

They never stopped believing in each other.

We must remember this. And pass it on.

Notes

Introduction

I was very fortunate to have permission to quote from and total access to all of Margaret Whitlam's personal diaries, journals, trip diaries, columns and other writings. I was also given access to Margaret and Gough's family, their personal friends and all their political contacts and colleagues. I have spent over 100 hours talking, dining and lunching and just 'hanging out' with Margaret since I first interviewed her for my book *The Matriarchs* in 1986 and wrote her biography in 2006. I have shared many meals, theatre performances and conversations with both Margaret and Gough during these years. This first-hand contact and friendship has provided the major source of my knowledge of them both.

I was also fortunate to have the two volumes of Jenny Hocking's excellent biography of Gough Whitlam – *A Moment in History* and *His Time* – as a wonderful resource, and I thank Jenny for her insights and dedication to her subject. Like me, she has obviously found the Whitlams fascinating.

Chapter 1

p. 13   'stopped being a believer', Jenny Hocking, *Gough Whitlam: A Moment in History*, The Miegunyah Press, Carlton, Victoria, 2009 p. 47.
p. 30   'take it on the chin', interview with Margaret Whitlam.
p. 32   'treat him like an equal', interview with Margaret Whitlam.
p. 33   'a law student who has unusual tastes', Hocking, *Gough Whitlam*, p. 69.
p. 34   'with good-looking sorts', interview with Margaret Whitlam.
p. 37   'he was a wonderful man but', interview with Margaret Whitlam.
p. 37   'she admitted to indulging', interview with Margaret Whitlam.

Chapter 2

p. 44   'I'm not mechanically minded', Hocking, *Gough Whitlam*, p. 73.
p. 45   'personal journal kept by Margaret', Margaret Whitlam gave me free access to her personal journals.
p. 52   'Dovey looks rather well in red', from Margaret Whitlam's private cache of collected letters.
p. 60   'In those days one used to think', private interview with Gough Whitlam.

Chapter 3

p. 79   'letters gave him the freedom to express his love and adoration', access to private letters.

Chapter 4

p. 82   'Missionaries taught Aborigines', Hocking, *Gough Whitlam*, p. 103.
p. 87   'As children [Tony] was the leader', private interview with Nicholas Whitlam.
p. 97   'Father was a terrible driver', private interview with Nicholas Whitlam.
p. 102 'The best friend that the Communists', Hocking, *Gough Whitlam*, p. 148.
p. 104 'He was at first amused', interview with Margaret Whitlam.
p. 105 'You really want to know? It's because the Labor Party cares', Susan Mitchell, *Margaret Whitlam: A Biography*, Sydney, Random House, 2006, p. 127.
p. 110 'Richard Glover, now a Sydney lawyer', private interview with Richard Glover.
p. 112 'He made us feel good', interview with Nicholas Whitlam.
p. 112 'They were neither Democratic, nor Labor, nor a party', Mitchell, *Margaret Whitlam*, p. 152.

Chapter 5

p. 119 'Tony observed how', private interview with Tony Whitlam.
p. 121 'had been erected by conservatives in Australia', Hocking, *Gough Whitlam*, p. 185.

p. 124   'Mr Whitlam would appear to have difficulty' *Canberra Times*, quoted in Mitchell, *Margaret Whitlam*, p. 143.

p. 124   'She always asked after my family', private interview with John Menadue.

p. 127   'My parents meant a great deal', ABC documentary *The Power and the Passion*.

p. 128   'She was a lot more sentimental' private interview with Tony Whitlam.

p. 128   'Nick said that his mother', private interview with Nick Whitlam.

p. 129   'Catherine remembers', private interview with Catherine Dovey.

p. 132   'ideologically intolerable', Hocking, *Gough Whitlam*, p. 206.

p. 132   'only the cranks', Hocking, *Gough Whitlam*, p. 207.

p. 134   'this truculent runt', David Marr, *Barwick: The Classic Biography of a Man in Power*, 2nd edn, Sydney, Allen & Unwin, Sydney, 1992, p. 157.

p. 136   'She openly admits', private interview with Kate Shea.

p. 143   'In February 1966, on television', Mitchell, *Margaret Whitlam*, p. 162.

p. 144   'We've got the numbers', Hocking, *Gough Whitlam*, p. 253.

p. 145   'a natural leader', private interview with Dame Leonie Kramer.

Chapter 6

p. 147   'support her husband', Mitchell, *Margaret Whitlam*, p. 189.

p. 147   'You must be joking', Mitchell, *Margaret Whitlam*, p. 189.

p. 147   'The first thing', Mitchell, *Margaret Whitlam*, p. 170.

p. 152   'In the diary of her trip', from Margaret's collection of personal trip diaries.

p. 153   'We wish to renovate' Hocking, *Gough Whitlam*, p. 333.

p. 155   'Mr Whitlam has passed the test', Ross McMullin, *The Light on the Hill: the Australian Labor Party, 1891–1991*, Melbourne, Oxford University Press, 1992, p. 326.

p. 156   'I know you will be sad', Mitchell, *Margaret Whitlam*, p. 178.

p. 156   'He particularly remembers', Mitchell, *Margaret Whitlam*, p. 123.

p. 157   'In an interview', Mitchell, *Margaret Whitlam*, p. 179.

p. 158   'Well, you don't ask a baby', Mitchell, *Margaret Whitlam*, p. 180.

p. 158   'In an interview with a male journalist', Mitchell, *Margaret Whitlam*, p. 181.

p. 161   'Gough reported back', Mitchell, *Margaret Whitlam*, p. 184.

p. 165   'Young and Menadue', Mitchell, *Margaret Whitlam*, p. 187.

p. 166   'The basic foundations', Hocking, *Gough Whitlam*, p. 395.

Chapter 7

p. 168   'It is a magnificent victory', Hocking, *Gough Whitlam: His Time*, p. 2.

p. 169   'It was wonderful to have that good feeling', private interview with Margaret Whitlam.

p. 170   'She told a press conference', Hocking, *Gough Whitlam: His Time*, p. 23.

p. 171   '"But Margaret," he said', interview with Margaret Whitlam.

p. 171   'I have always', Hocking, *Gough Whitlam: His Time*, p. 8.

p. 172   'No Australian understands', Hocking, *Gough Whitlam: His Time*, p. 9.

p. 173   'weekly column', Mitchell, *Margaret Whitlam*, p. 199.

p. 174   'Greer interview', Mitchell, *Margaret Whitlam*, p. 203.

p. 175 'Off-camera, off-microphone', Mitchell, *Margaret Whitlam*, p. 201.

p. 175 'You can't put on a show', Mitchell, *Margaret Whitlam*, p. 204.

p. 175 'openly described her own faults', Mitchell, *Margaret Whitlam*, p. 204.

p. 179 'There's nothing wrong with suburbia', Mitchell, *Margaret Whitlam*, p. 207.

p. 179 'like a tame poodle', Mitchell, *Margaret Whitlam*, p. 207.

p. 180 'a satellite interview', Mitchell, *Margaret Whitlam*, p. 208.

p. 185 'You can't imagine how relaxed', Margaret Whitlam's column, *Woman's Day*.

p. 186 'Leigh Bottrell, from London',

p. 187 'He is like an oyster', Mitchell, *Margaret Whitlam*, p. 216.

p. 187 'tremendous awareness', Hocking, *Gough Whitlam*, p. 80.

p. 188 'We have to attack', Hocking, *Gough Whitlam*, p. 83.

p. 194 'I don't care how many prima donnas', Hocking, *Gough Whitlam: His Time*.

p. 194 'They tell me, luv', http://www.whitlam.org.

p. 197 'the abiding virtues', Hocking, *Gough Whitlam*, p. 54.

Chapter 8

p. 202 'private journal', private journal of Margaret Whitlam recording the 1974 election trail.

p. 211 'terrible appointment', Hocking, *Gough Whitlam*, p. 138.

p. 212 'a total CIA front', Hocking, *Gough Whitlam*, p. 134.

p. 213 'vultures, praying mantises', Mitchell, *Margaret Whitlam*, p. 231.

p. 218 'Freudenberg was a witness', private interview with Graham Freudenberg.

p. 224 'And you should know', private interview with Elizabeth Reid.

p. 227 'It all depends', Mitchell, *Margaret Whitlam*, p. 258.

p. 228 'That was not a very clever', Mitchell, *Margaret Whitlam*, p. 259.

p. 229 'My old copper's instinct', Hocking, *Gough Whitlam*, p. 249.

Chapter 9

p. 231 '"Of course," replied Gough', Hocking, *Gough Whitlam*, p. 337.

p. 231 'that there are circumstances', Hocking, *Gough Whitlam*, p. 331.

p. 232 'Kerr and Gough were', Hocking, *Gough Whitlam*, p. 333.

p. 233 'When she picked up the phone', private interview with Margaret Whitlam.

p. 235 'John Menadue was eating', private interview with John Menadue.

p. 237 'Nick heard the news', private interview with Nick Whitlam.

p. 237 'grinning like a Cheshire cat', Hocking, *Gough Whitlam*, p. 345.

p. 238 'Well, I'm leaving Kirribilli House', interview with Margaret Whitlam.

Chapter 10

p. 247 'Butler saw Gough as', private interview with Richard Butler.

p. 256 'We do hope to go back', interview with Richard Butler.

p. 260 'It's his name', interview with Graham Freudenberg.

p. 260 'A former student', interview with Freda Whitlam.

p. 261 'The Bishop of Bathurst', interview with Catherine Dovey.

p. 265 'The man is dishonourable', interview with Margaret Whitlam.
p. 266 'As many thousands', Gough Whitlam, *The Truth of the Matter*, 3rd edition, Melbourne, MUP, 2005.
p. 267 'She had a big voice', interview with Margaret Whitlam.
p. 270 'I'll have to ask Margaret', interview with Margaret Whitlam.
p. 274 'I loved the way she treated', interview with Kathy Lette.
p. 276 'I can't believe', interview with Kathy Lette.
p. 277 'Margaret, be not concerned', interview with Margaret Whitlam.
p. 279 'Four former Liberal', Hocking, *Gough Whitlam*, p. 450.
p. 279 'There are many minders', Hocking, *Gough Whitlam*, p. 304.
p. 280 'Margaret called Strong', interview with James Strong.
p. 282 'When a friend asked', interview with Margaret Whitlam.
p. 284 'Broadcaster and columnist Phillip Adams', interview with Phillip Adams.

Chapter 11

p. 288 'when they were in Thailand', interview with John Wellings.
p. 290 'Freda says they were more', interview with Freda Whitlam.
p. 294 'I couldn't have put up', interview with Margaret Whitlam.
p. 296 'It is insulting', interview with Margaret Whitlam.
p. 299 'Nick's major reason', interview with Judy Whitlam.
p. 300 'Gough reached across', Hocking, *Gough Whitlam*, p. 469.
p. 309 'Kevin Rudd, who had been', conversation with Kevin Rudd.

Books

Clark, Manning, *A Short History of Australia*, Penguin Books, Ringwood, Victoria, 1995

Crisp, Leslie Findlay, *Ben Chifley: A Biography*, Longman, Melbourne, 1963

Daly, Fred, *From Curtin to Kerr*, rev. edn, Sun Books, Melbourne, 1984

Day, David, *Chifley: A Life*, HarperCollins, Sydney, 2001

Dunstan, Don, *Felicia: The Political Memoirs of Don Dunstan*, Macmillan, South Melbourne, 1981

Freudenberg, Graham, *A Certain Grandeur: Gough Whitlam in Politics*, Macmillan, South Melbourne, 1977

Hawke, Robert, *The Hawke Memoirs*, William Heinemann, Port Melbourne, 1994

Hocking, Jenny, *Gough Whitlam: A Moment in History*, The Miegunyah Press, Carlton, Victoria, 2009

Hocking, Jenny, *Gough Whitlam: His Time: The Biography, Volume II*, The Miegunyah Press, Carlton, Victoria, 2012

Jones, Barry, *A Thinking Reed*, Allen & Unwin, Sydney, 2006

Kelly, Paul, *November 1975: The Inside Story of Australia's Greatest Political Crisis*, Allen & Unwin, Sydney, 1985

Kelly, Paul, *The Unmaking of Gough*, Allen & Unwin, Sydney, 1994

Kerr, John, *Matters for Judgement: An Autobiography*, Macmillan, South Melbourne, 1978

McClelland, James, *Stirring the Possum: A Political Autobiography*, Penguin, Ringwood, Victoria, 1989

Marr, David, *Barwick: The Classic Biography of a Man in Power*, 2nd edn, Allen & Unwin, Sydney, 1992

Menadue, John, *Things You Learn Along the Way*, David Lovell Publishing, Melbourne, 1999

Mitchell, Susan, *The Matriarchs: Twelve Australian Women Talk about their Lives to Susan Mitchell*, Penguin, Ringwood, Victoria, 1987

Mitchell, Susan, *Margaret Whitlam: A Biography*, Random House, Milsons Point, NSW, 2006

Murphy, Denis, *Hayden: A Political Biography*, Angus & Robertson, Sydney, 1980

Oakes, Laurie, *Whitlam PM: A Biography*, Angus & Robertson, Sydney, 1973

Watson, Don, *Recollections of a Bleeding Heart: A Portrait of Paul Keating*, Knopf, Milsons Point, NSW, 2002

Whitlam, Gough, *The Whitlam Government 1972–1975*, Penguin Books, Melbourne, 1985

Whitlam, Gough, *Abiding Interests*, University of Queensland Press, Brisbane, 1997

Whitlam, Gough, *My Italian Notebook*, Allen & Unwin, Crows Nest, NSW, 2002

Whitlam, Gough, *The Truth of the Matter*, 3rd edn, Melbourne University Publishing, Melbourne, 2005

Whitlam, Margaret, *My Day*, Collins, Sydney, 1973

Whitlam, Nicholas, *Still Standing: A Memoir*, Lothian Books, Melbourne, 2004

Acknowledgements

I am so grateful to Margaret and Gough Whitlam for allowing me to share in their private lives.

After finishing the biography of Margaret, I realised that I had so much more material about them as a couple stretching over seventy years and that this was a wonderful story that should be told.

Jenny Hocking has written two outstanding volumes of biography of Gough Whitlam, dealing with his political life. Her books have helped me substantiate the knowledge I already had and backed up any key moments recreated within these pages.

Margaret had generously provided me with all her personal letters, diaries, journals and accounts of her many trips around the world, clippings, speeches, papers, photos and memorabilia, much of which I have been able to draw on in this story of their nearly seventy-year partnership. We also spent hundreds of hours talking, visiting films, opera, the theatre, having picnics and fish and chips by the sea and enjoying her famous sandwiches and cooking. I also drew on previous interviews with friends, many of whom, such as Georgie Swift, Clare Nichols, John Wellings and Margaret Olley, have since died. But their words remain.

Both Margaret and Gough gave of themselves by introducing me to their friends and family and entertaining us for lunches and dinners. This enabled me to paint an authentic portrait of their private life together with friends and family. Every member of the Whitlam clan had agreed to be interviewed and was honest, open and generous with their observations. Once again, I would like to thank Tony and Pip Whitlam, Nick and Judy Whitlam, Stephen Whitlam, Catherine Dovey and Freda Whitlam.

Nothing can replace these first-hand experiences for the biographer.

I conducted formal interviews with the following people, for which I thank them. Those politicians and staff members who knew them both well: Susan Ryan, Bill and Dallas Hayden, John Faulkner, Barry Jones, Richard Butler and John Menadue gave me wonderful insights and anecdotes.

Journalists Laurie Oakes, Phillip Adams, Alex Mitchell and Alan Ramsay told me wonderful gossip and anecdotes from the inside world which is often the most difficult to obtain. As previously mentioned, Jenny Hocking provided a wealth of information and material for me to draw on.

My literary agent, John Timlin, provided unending enthusiasm and encouragement. My accountant, John Masselos, kept me out of the shops. Gillian Harvie, despite a very heavy personal workload, generously typed the manuscript and helped me meet deadlines.

The following people from Hachette have all helped to make this book possible and I thank them all. Publishing Director, Fiona Hazard; Publisher, Vanessa Radnidge; Senior Editors, Karen Ward and Chris Kunz; Publishing and Production Manager, Anne Macpherson; Production Controller, Isabel Staas; Marketing and Publicity Director, Justin Ractcliffe; Publicity Manager, Jaki Arthur; copyeditor, Tricia Dearborn and designer, Christa Moffitt.

Index